SQUANTO

The Last Patuxet Indian
And the First American Native
to Befriend the Pilgrims of Plimouth Plantation,
Together With Diverse Anecdotes of his Times

A Biography
by

Charles Brashear

1481 Paymaster Court
Cool, CA 95614
Brashear@.sdsu.edu
www.CharlesBrashear.com

copyright, Charles Brashear, 2017

Rights reserved.

    Practically everythning the Pilgrims told us about Squanto was wrong, because it was deformed by their Puritan conscience. Though he was slightly older than William Bradford, the Pilgrims repeatedly referred to him as a boy, which led to the spate of children's books which we and aour children have been cursed with.

    Several men besides the Pilgrims knew, befriended, and wrote about Tisquantum, who came to be called Squanto, in his lifetime—James Rosier, Thomas Dermer, Capt. John Smith, and Sir Ferdinando Gorges, who led the effort from 1602 onward to colonize New England, especially Maine. From their accounts (along with those of the Pilgrim leaders, (William Bradford and Edward Winslow), I have pieced together the story of Squanto's life.

    I have quoted passages from these men's writings occasionally and in epigraphs, to lend the story a tone of a TV documentary. Admittedly, I have borrowed tints from other accounts of the times to fill in the outlines the documents give us, but by and large this is the story of Squanto's life and the forces that shaped his mind.

CONTENTS

Introduction.. . . . . -7-

1. A Batch of Peas. . . . . -11-

2. "Our Duty to Catch the Others". 23-

3. Beyond Monhegan Island, 1605. . . . . -31-

4. "Raise the Glass on High, Billy Bigh". . . . . -39-

5. Repatriation. . . . . -41-

6. The First Ship of the Season, 1606. . . . . -49-

7. Captured near Puerto Rico. . . . . -54-

8. The Jail in Seville, 1607. . . . . -58-

9. Draghan Di-Eshti. -63-

10. Escape in the Night. . . . . -70-

11. The Indian Show. -77-

12. The Strength of Gluskabe. . . . . -86-

13. "You Send Tisquantum Home?". . . . . -93-

14. "Next Season, with the First Ship". . . . . -101-

15. "Let Them Tie my Hands," 1611. . . . . -105-

16. "Like tars in the Winter Sky". . . . . -113-

17. "Home to Patuxet?". -122-

18. With Captain John Smith, 1614. . . . . -129-

19. "Are You a Yang-kaysh in Disguise?". . . . . . . -136-

20. Kidnaped Near Patuxet. . . . . -141-

21. The Slave Trade at Málaga. 147-

22. Brother Francisco. . . . . -154-

23. On the River Genil. -159-

24. Passage to Newfoundland, 1615. . . . . -164-

25. On Newfoundland, A Ready Listener. . . . . -168-

26. The Caplin Run on Newfoundland.. . . . . -174-

27. Awaiting the King's Pleasure. . . . . -179-

28. Welcome to Monhegan, 1619. . . . . -188-

29. Too many Ghosts. . . . . -201-

30. "No Bones for the Wolves". . . . . -209-

31. Another Kind of Rope. . . . . -217-

32. The Murderers.. . . . . -225-

33. "My Savage Entreated Hard for Me"............ -230-

34. "If he comes again, I Shall Have to Kill Him". . -238-

35. This Time, That Place; What Does it Matter?. . -244-

36. "There are Some English at Patuxet," 1621. . . -252-

37. Pow-Wow at Pokánoket. .... -262-

38. Ambassador........................ -273-

39. The Massasoit and the Peace of Patuxet. .... -283-

40. Squanto: "Friend of the Pilgrims". .... -296-

41. A Coat of Red Cotton. .... -308-

42. A Boy Lost and Found. .... -317-

43. "The Tongue of the English". .... -324-

44. "No Need to Fear Us". .... -337-

45. A Visit to Massachusetts Bay............. -343-

46. A Time of Thanksgiving, 1621............. -350-

47. The Snake-skin Message.. .... -365-

48. "To Serve his own Ends"................. -379-

49. Massasoit Demands the Head of Squanto. ... -391-

-v-

50. In These Troubled Times.................. -408-

51. "Pray for Poor Squanto", 1622.............. -418-

Epilog: Pilgrims Triumphant............... -431–447-

Introduction

In April 1621, when Squanto and Samoset walked into Plimouth Plantation and said "Hello, English," Squanto had already lived several years among the English. He had crossed the Atlantic at least four times, he had been to Spain twice, and to Newfoundland probably four times. He had visited with English Sea Captains almost every nook and cranny of the New England coast from Maine to Virginia. He had suffered kidnaping, imprisonment, and loss of his entire village to

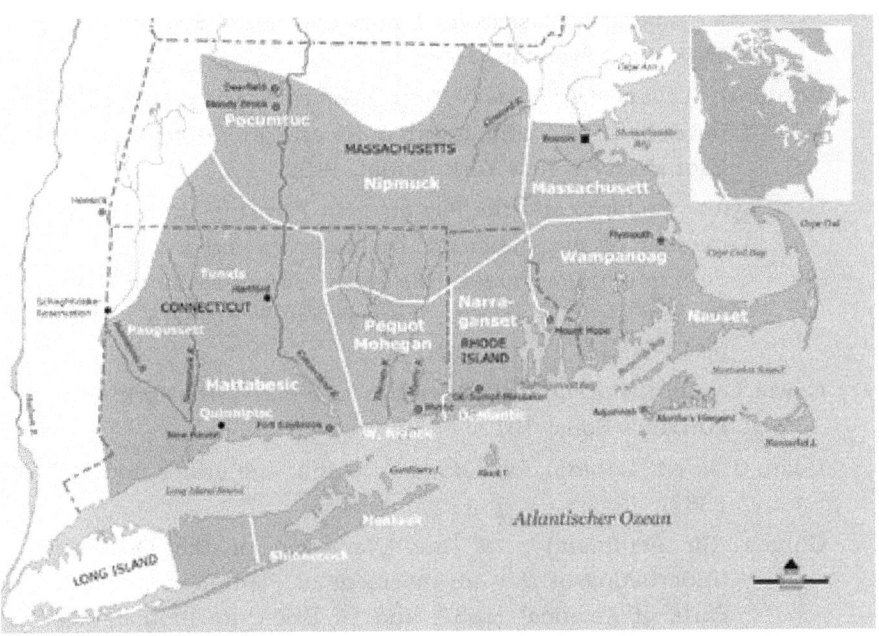

Territorial Subdivisions of New England Traibes, circa 1600

some mysterious plague. Little wonder that when he decided to stay with the Pilgrims and help them to survive, he was a psychological mess.

Some References

Adams, Charles Francis. *Three Episodes of Massachusetts History.* Boston and New York: Houghton, Mifflin and Co, 1892.

Arber, E. ed, *Travels and Works of Captain John Smith.* Edinburgh: J. Grant, 1910.

Baxter, James Phinney. *Sir Ferdinando Gorges and his Province of Maine.* (#131 Burt Franklin Research and Resource Works; #2 American Classics in History and Social Science) New York: Burt Franklin, 1890.

Bradford, William. *Of Plimouth Plantation*, 1620-1647, Originally published 1647; edition with notes and an intro by Samuel Eliot Morison, New York: Knopf, 1952.

Ceci, Lynn. "Squanto and the Pilgrims: On Planting Corn 'in the manner of the Indians.'" *The Invented Indian: Cultural Fictions and Government Policies*, ed. James A. Clifton. New Brunswick & London: Transaction Publishers, 1990, pp.71-90.

Cowie, Leonard. *The Pilgrim Fathers.* (Documentary) New York: G.P. Putnam's Sons, 1972.

Dean, J.W. ed. *Captain John Mason.* Boston: the Prince Society, 1887.

Gorges, Sir Ferdinando. "A Brief Narration of the Originall Undertaking of the Advancement of Plantation into the Parts of America" (1637) and "A Briefe Relation of the Discovery & Plantations of New England" (1672) repr. in

James Phinney Baxter, *Sir Ferdinando Gorges and His Province of Maine*.

Morison, Samuel E. "Squanto," in *Dictionary of American Biography*. New York: Charles Scribners Sons, 1935.

Mourt G. *A Relation or Journall of the Beginning and Proceedings of the English Plantation Setled at Plimouth in New England*. London, 1622. A recent edition: New York: Corinth Books, 1963, ed. D.B. Heath.

Purchas, Samuel. *Purchas His Pilgrimes*. London, 1625; reprint in 20 volumes: New York: AMS Publishing, 1965.

Preston, Richard Arthur. *Gorges of Plymouth Fort; a Life of Sir Ferdinando Gorges, Captain of Plymouth Fort, Governor of New England, and Lord of the Province of Maine*. Toronto: University of Toronto Press, 1953.

Rosier, James. "A True Relation of the Voyage of Captaine George Waymouth, 1605, In *Early English and French Voyages, Chiefly from Hakluyt, 1534-1608*, H.S. Burrage, ed. New York: Charles Scribner's Sons, 1932, pp.353-394.

Smith, John. "A Description of New England (1616)," *Massachusetts Historical Society Collections*, 6 (Series 3; 1836) 95-140; also in *Collected Works of Captain John Smith*.

Speck, Frank G. *Territorial Subdivisions and Boundaries of the Wampanoag, Massachusetts, and Nauset Indians*. New York: Museum of the American Indian (Heye Foundation), 1928.

Stoneman, John. "The Voyage of M. Henry Challons, intended for the North Plantation of Virginia, 1606...." *Purchas His Pilgrimes*. ed. Samuel Purchas, Originally published, London, 1625; reprint in 20 volumes: New York: AMS Publishing, 1965, V.19, pp.284-297.

Weeks, Alvin G. *Massasoit of the Wampanoags*. [Fall River, Mass.]: Privately Printed [The Plimpton Press], 1919.

Winslow, Edward. *Good News from New England: Or, a Relation of things remarkable in the Plantation*, London, 1623. Repr: *Purchas His Pilgrimes*, ed. Samuel Purchas, originally published, London, 1625; reprint in 20 vols: New York: AMS Publishing, 1965, V.19, pp.344-394.

1. A Batch of Peas

They sent one canoe with three men, one of which, when they came near unto us spoke in his language very loudly and very boldly; seeming as though he [Grand Chief Pow-da-we] would know why we were there, and by pointing with his oar toward the sea, we conjectured he meant we should be gone.

But when we showed them knives and their use, by cutting sticks, and gave them other trifles, [such] as combs and (looking) glasses], they came close to the ship, as if desirous to entertain our friendship.

— James Rosier, "A True Relation of the Voyage of Captaine George Waymouth, 1605"

Six men in two Passamaquoddy canoes approached the English ship cautiously in the mid-morning sun. The ship was bigger than a longhouse on the water, bigger than three longhouses. In one of the canoes, Tisquantum, a young man, though well-muscled, held his basket of berries chest high to show that he did not have any weapons. He called out "Strawberries! Strawberries! Straw-aw-berries!" Most of the tribes had learned a few words of English from the fishermen who visited the New England coastal waters regularly.

Suddenly, a shot boomed from the ship, causing the paddlers in both canoes to stop.

"See? They want to kill us!" cried one of the Indians. For protection, he put his hand to the magic lightning bars painted on his face. "My uncle told me their noise kills people."

But the others were less anxious to meet the "yang-kaysh," the English.

"I suspect we'll know soon enough," said the most cautious of the group. Bold, red lightning bars on his face made his eyes seem especially strong. "Maybe even sooner than we want to." I'll bet two pair of new moccasins that, long before we need to know anything, we will know too much for our own good," said the timid, shifty-eyed one. His face was painted white, to protect him from evil. "Their fire-sticks kill people."

"Let's go back, Tahanedo," muttered the one with lightning bars on his face, addressing their leader in the other canoe. "Pow-da-we told us to stay away from them. At least, let's go back to the shore and let them come to us."

Tisquantum sat down in the canoe, touched

the good luck symbol on his doeskin shirt, and reached for his paddle. Then he noticed that the gunsmoke was drifting off the front of the ship and toward the little rocky islands that ringed St. George's Bay. He tossed his shoulders to shrug off the threat and stood up. "That was not for us. See? It goes the other way. They are not trying to kill us."

Tahanedo, the sagamore of Pemaquid, sat calmly in the middle of the other canoe. He was dressed in a wildcat-skin cape which was both his emblem of office and his means of keeping warm. The other men wore only breech clouts, but their bodies were painted and heavily greased to insulate them against the chill wind.

Tisquantum wore doeskin leggings and a fringed shirt— traditional Wampanoag clothes— for he was a young captive from south of the Massachusetts tribe.

Touching the protective shell amulet that hung in his right ear-lobe, Tisquantum boldly encouraged his companions in their own language, Abenaki. "Come on! Pick up your paddles, my friends. Don't you want to see what the white men are like?"

"I think I'll go to the ocean-canoe with Assaquantem," announced Tahanedo, using the Passamaquoddy name they had given Tisquantum.

Tahanedo's forehead was painted red, and he wore a necklace of sea-shell totems and two eagle feathers in his scalp lock to denote his rank. The feathers stuck up in a big "V" toward the sky, indicating he had been successful in battle. His glance was firm and unwavering, his nose and nostrils noticeably large.

"They are dangerous," said Skettowaroes, a huge man whose courage was not questioned. He was body guard to Tahanedo. His big face was painted the same as Tahanedo's, but he wore no feathers or necklace. "It is best to keep unnecessary danger at a distance."

"They come from across the big water," said Tisquantum. "Don't you want to know how they live, what they eat, what their houses look like?"

"I think Assaquantem is right," said Tahanedo, adjusting his cape and touching a protective totem in his necklace. "The pale-faced men mean us no harm. I'd like to see them up close. Besides, they gave Pow-da-we a big-bladed knife; maybe they will give me a knife, too."

As the Indians neared the ship, they saw several of the sailors leaning over the rail. Tisquantum had heard that many of the English had hair on their faces, but he was not prepared for the variety in size and color of their beards. Some had golden hair on their chins; some red, some brown; still others, black hair. Some were neatly trimmed; some scraggly; and everything in between. Their baggy shirts were bleached white. Their skins were almost as pale. Those who were marine soldiers wore breast-plates of heavy leather, with sheets of metal riveted to them.

"Heya, Yang-kaysh," called Tisquantum. "Trade?" He held up the basket of berries again.

Two of the sailors lowered a rope ladder with wooden rungs and motioned for the Indians to come aboard. Tisquantum from one canoe and Tahanedo from the other climbed the ladder to the deck of the ship. Ed Welsh, the second mate, called three marine soldiers to the ready: "Trust in fate," he said, "but keep your lances in your hands. At least till we see what the beggars want."

"Peas? Peas?" asked Tisquantum. The Passamaquoddies who had been on other ships before thought stewed English peas were delicious.

Welsh smiled, to think the Indians were so simple. "I reckon we can cook up a batch of peas," he said. The English had been eating fresh salmon and cod in order to save their dried peas for a time when they had no fresh food. "Come aboard, and we'll stoke up the fire. Those look like nice enough berries." He held his nose close, in order to smell them above the usual, coastal scent of rotting fish and sea-weed. He held back his gray linsey cape to keep it from sweeping into the berry basket.

Tisquantum and Tahanedo did not understand the words, but they followed the motions and went with the mate to the galley, where the cook hung a pot of peas on the hook over the open fire. Welsh invited the Indians to sit at the mess table while the peas were cooking. He moved to a position where the odors of the cooking fire would drift toward him, so that it would disguise the smell of his guests without offending them.

Welsh was amused by the Indians' interest and wonder in the iron pot over the fire-pit, as well as the pewter dishes, utensils, cups, everything. Tahanedo tried his few words of French which the tribe had learned from the fishermen at Acadia and along the Quebec coast, but Welsh did not understand.

***

Before the food was cooked, one of the ship's longboats returned from the shore. James Rosier, the ship's officer of marines, who doubled as recorder of the voyage, stood in the prow of the longboat, his fowling piece cocked, loaded with pea gravel, and held at the ready. In addition to a thick leather body-shield, he wore a metal helmet and a bright red cape fastened to straps on his shoulder shields. His neatly trimmed and waxed beard gleamed red in the sunlight.

On the starboard side of the ship, he found two, large, birch-bark canoes floating in the mildly choppy water. Each could carry six or eight people. Two brightly painted natives sat in each canoe, waiting, watching, paddling only enough to keep themselves from drifting more than a few yards away from the ship.

Even before *The Archangel* dropped anchor in St. George's Bay, James Rosier had been collecting an Abenaki vocabulary in his journal. He had already learned a couple hundred words. "Welcome, friends," he called out in Abenaki. "Welcome to our big-water canoe."

The Indians gazed at him askance and did not respond.

Rosier climbed the rope ladder and discovered that two natives were already on board, sitting beside the fire in the galley, eating English peas. "Excellent," exclaimed Rosier, "but didn't you invite the others aboard?"

"Aye. We did, Sir," said Thomas Cam, the first mate, "but the savages are exceedingly wary and will not approach."

"Any signs of treachery?"

"None that I noticed."

The first several days, the Englishmen's

contact with the American natives had been ideal: without opposition, the Englishmen had erected a six-foot cross of discovery and possession on the rocky shore above the thin, sandy beach, as if the cross held some great power. They called the inlet St. George's Bay, in honor of the mythical saint of England.

They had traded, metal knives and bracelets for beaver and otter furs. Rosier was learning the language rapidly, for the Passamaquoddies, when they learned that he could repeat their words after writing them in his journal, came readily with more words than Rosier could easily understand.

Rosier talked with Tahanedo and Tisquantum, asking (with what words he had and what motions he could invent) more about their land and customs. They, too, were very curious about the foreigners.

"We come from England," Rosier told them, but they looked baffled. "England is a big island beyond Monhegan," he explained.

"Oh?" With difficulty and many repetitions, Tahanedo conveyed his astonishment and much more to Rosier. "An island? Beyond Monhegan? I have lived here all my life and know of no such island. Is it large?"

"Oh, quite large," said Rosier. "With thousands upon thousands of people."

"It would be good to be friends with so many," admitted Tahanedo, touching the protective totem in his necklace.

"Excellent! Excellent!" exclaimed Rosier. "We wish to be your friends. Won't your other men come up and eat some peas and make friends with us?"

"They are afraid of you," said Tahanedo simply, letting his wild-cat skin cape hang casually over a forearm.

"Pshaw! We are nothing to be afraid of," said Rosier, adjusting his leather body-shield and red cape to let some air in, for the armor got very hot. "We have only your best interests at heart. Come, Mr. Welsh, bring up a platter of peas. Offer our friends on the water a bite of our hospitality."

"Aye, Sir," said the second mate.

"And bring some bread," added Rosier.

When the platter of peas and the bread were offered, the natives in the canoes accepted them readily, but paddled rapidly to the forested shore to eat them.

***

Presently the ship's captain, George Waymouth, returned in the ship's other longboat, loaded with firewood. He was a thin man, with drawn features and hard, penetrating eyes that made others mistrust him. He wore thigh-shields, a breast-plate, a helmet of polished metal, and a wide, purple cape with gold piping. He held one edge of the cape in front of him, like a shield.

Captain Waymouth had sailed for the New England coast on Easter Sunday, March 31st, 1605, in the employ of Sir Ferdinando Gorges, Commandant of the Fort at Plimouth, England. His assignment was to search for a northwest passage to China, and, that failing, to catch fish to pay expenses of the voyage, trade with the natives for such beaver and buckskins as they had, and come away with as much knowledge as he could of their geography.

His crew had caught a great deal of Atlantic Salmon, which they smoked or dried, and almost enough cod to fill the barrels in which they salted the fish for transport to England. He and Rosier had made rough maps of the coast and inlets nearby. He was anxious to sail for England while the astrological signs were with them and the summer winds were fair.

When Waymouth climbed the rope-ladder, Mr. Rosier introduced him to the natives: "Here is Captain Tahanedo, sagamore of Pemaquid."

Hoping no one noticed his hesitation, Tahanedo took the skinny Waymouth by the hand, which was the Indian way of greeting. He shifted to get the wind in his own face, because the white man's odor was so strong.

"And this is his servant, Assaquantem," added Rosier.

"No. No Assaquantem," interjected the other native, smiling. "Name: Tisquantum."

"Assaquantem," insisted Tahanedo, pointing his big nose at the younger man's chest. "My slave," he added in Abenaki.

"Tisquantum," repeated the younger man. By making many signs of the sun passing and motioning toward the horizon, he communicated to the Englishmen that he came from a tribe several days' journey to the south, and he actually managed a rudimentary English sentence: "Tahanedo take Tisquantum," grabbing his own neck in pantomime and dragging himself away. Thus, he got the English to understand that he was a prisoner of war, who had been pressed into bondage as Tahanedo's servant.

"Tisquantum go Yangland?" asked the boy, from which Captain Waymouth surmised that Tisquantum was eager to travel with the English, possibly to escape his bondage.

"Tisquantum know rivers?" asked Waymouth, waving a wiry arm toward the coast.

"No," admitted Tisquantum. "Tahanedo

know rivers."

"Yes," said Tahanedo. "All my life, I have lived here. I have visited most of the rivers and islands along our coast."

"Well," said Waymouth, smiling to himself and Mr. Rosier, "would you fellows like to travel with us to England and tell us where the rivers lie, what towns lie upon them, how many warriors there are, and who are their ; leaders. Their sagamores?" He removed his metal helmet and accepted the wide-brimmed black hat with a white ostrich feather, which the cabin-boy offered.

Tisquantum nodded "yes" rapidly, but Tahanedo shook his head slowly in the negative.

2. "Our Duty to Catch the Others"

"... we determined, so soon as we could, to take some of them, lest (being suspicious we had discovered their plots) they should absent themselves from us."

— James Rosier, "A True Relation of the Voyage of Captain George Waymouth, 1605"

Shortly, Skettowaroes returned from the shore with the empty platter. Waymouth and Rosier, using Rosier's vocabulary, talked with him a while and found him "of ready capacity and wit." A tall, broad-faced man, he decided to stay aboard with the other two, because of his job as Tahanedo's body guard. Rosier thought it was because, "they were receiving exceedingly kind usage at our hands and were therefore much delighted in our company."

"What a fortunate accident this must be counted," exclaimed Captain Waymouth, beaming. "Why, they may even know the passage to China." He rocked on the balls of his feet in self-satisfaction. "But 'tis our duty to catch the others," he added in an even voice. "Be ready when they come to fetch these fellows, and we'll grab 'em."

All the mid-day, the ship's longboats plied back and forth, bringing good firewood, drinking water, as well as fresh-water fish and newly-killed venison to the ship, but the natives did not return.

Late in the afternoon, Waymouth sent Rosier to the shore in a longboat with seven men in leather armor. Rosier, cape flowing in the wind, stood in the bow, carrying a platter of peas. He had a box of merchandise at his feet, as was his routine when he went to trade with the natives. Before they landed, the native with lightning bars on his face withdrew into the woods ("being so suspiciously fearful of his own good," as Rosier wrote in his report). Two others met the Englishmen on the shore to receive the peas.

With great show, the Englishmen laid aside their oars and weapons, thinking the gesture would comfort the natives. They went up the beach to the Indians' fire and sat down with them.

Using his vocabulary list, Rosier talked with them and learned that the furtive, white-faced one was called Amoret, the smiling one with ochre spots that covered smallpox scars on his face was Maneddo. He introduced himself. The natives were most interested in eating the peas, though they were wary of the Englishman's power and magic.

"Your Captain Tahanedo and the other two have decided to sail with us to our island called England," Rosier announced.

The two natives had great difficulty understanding, but finally unraveled the curious ideas and the fractured Abenaki of the Englishman.

"You fellows"— he pointed to Amoret and Maneddo— "would be welcome to sail with us."

Again, the natives had difficulty understanding what the Englishman was saying. And when they understood, they balked, saying they had relatives that depended upon their ability to hunt through the summer. Amoret made motions to indicate the ocean waves, his unsteady stomach, and vomiting. Maneddo agreed with signs that he had no great love for oceans and voyages.

"We shall have to take them by force," Rosier told his men, keeping his voice neutral. "Get ready and, when I give the sign, seize them."

One of the sailors went up the beach to urinate behind a bush and, when he came back, positioned himself behind the two natives.

"Any idea how we can fetch old 'Lightning Bars'?" Rosier asked his men, but no one said anything. Swinging his cape back, Rosier opened the merchandise box. Thinking his broad gestures would banish the fear of 'Lightning Bars' in the woods and entice him to return, he presented a polished brass chain to spot-faced Maneddo. To white-faced Amoret, Rosier gave a cut-glass bauble on a strong leather thong.

Both of the natives hung these trinkets about their necks, apparently very pleased with themselves and their good fortune.

Rosier held up his largest bauble, such as he thought fitting for a super sagamore, and a piece of bread, but the third man did not come back.

Rosier closed the box, gave his men the signal, and said, "Take 'em. But be careful."

Three men grabbed at Maneddo and four at Amoret. The natives were so slick from the grease with which they insulated their naked bodies that they slipped free. One sailor clutched at the brass chain around Maneddo's neck and pulled him off balance. Rosier seized the long hair on Amoret, it being about the only hold Rosier could take, and ruined his footing. The other men were able to pick up his feet.

As soon as the men had the natives partly subdued, Rosier pushed aside their war axes and bows and arrows, not wanting to harm the Indians or give them a chance to harm his men.

One sailor had the white-faced native by the

throat strap and was choking him down. "Careful not to hurt him," Rosier cautioned. "He would be no good to us dead." The man guffawed and shoved the savage's head so hard Rosier thought Amoret's neck would pop, but the Indian only cried out in pain.

In a few moments, the men had tied the savages' ankles with short cords, brought for the purpose. Spot-faced Maneddo's hands were tied with the brass chain Rosier had given him. Panting with the effort, the Englishmen took the captives away to the longboat and to the ship, thanking the good spirits who were on their side.

Rosier and two others carried away what weapons the natives had. They towed the two birch-bark canoes containing the Indians' pottery, leather pouches, capes, paddles, and weapons, thinking the souvenirs might prove useful in some way no one had yet conceived.

"Excellent, Mr. Rosier," exclaimed the Captain. "Excellent! You did well. Your Virgo must be rising. I secluded the others in the Mates' compartment; otherwise this show of force must certainly have disquieted all of our guests."

He rocked on his heels and held the edge of his cape. "I think we are as well provisioned as we could hope for. Wood, water, a respectable cargo. And our stars in their good phases."

To his First Mate, Thomas Cam, he said: "Hoist anchor, Mr. Cam. Set sail, and pray for a fair wind to England."

***

On scant winds, *The Archangel* was slow in getting out of St. George's harbor. Many a sailor secretly held an amulet or silently prayed for fairies to puff up their cheeks and fill the sails. The sea was not especially choppy, but neither was it cooperative.

After about four hours, Waymouth finally found the current, and the ship picked up speed. With the course set and a fair wind in the sails, the crew was able to relax a bit.

"Maybe we ought to give our guests a breath, Sir," said Rosier. "They've been in that hold several hours and there's no porthole down there. We don't want them to suffocate before we find if they're useful or not."

"Quite right, Mr. Rosier. Bring the savages up."

Tahanedo and the four others were brought on deck, their hands still tied in front of them. When Tahanedo saw the sails bulging with wind, he touched his necklace and cried out, "They have captured us. They have taken us prisoners and will make us their slaves."

He seized a corner of his wildcat-skin cape to

hold it in place and turned, swinging it in every direction as if he could sweep away the annoyance; the thin, forested rim of land was diminishing behind them.

Tisquantum asked, "Waymut take Tahanedo?" and he pantomimed grabbing the sagamore by the neck.

"Oh, no, no," said Waymouth, waving "no" with his hands, using Rosier as his interpreter. "We are your friends. You are our guests."

"Where is our land? Where are you taking us?" cried Tahanedo, running up the stair-ladder to the poop deck. His wrists were still tied, but he used his hands as a clamp together.

Thomas Cam and the helmsman turned to face him and put their right hands on the handles of their weapons.

But Tahanedo only ran to the rail to look at the distant strip of land and the reasonably calm water. Coming back, he lifted one corner of his wildcat cape to show Waymouth the emblem of his rank. "Give us our canoes, and we will paddle to our home shores."

But Waymouth chose to ignore him, saying, through Rosier, "We are taking you to meet the head man of our town."

"Beyond Monhegan Island?" asked

Tahanedo.

"Yes, beyond Monhegan. It's a place called Plimouth."

"I have no business in Plimouth," said Tahanedo, meeting Waymouth's gaze.

"Oh, but you do," said Waymouth, looking away and wrapping his purple cloak around his shoulders. "The 'sagamore' of our town wants very much to meet and talk with the sagamore of Pemaquid. Our two towns will be friends. We will trade.... Nice things ... for useful things."

Ed Welsh stepped toward the bow of the ship, letting his gray cape flap in the wind freely. He inhaled deeply and exclaimed, "Take a whiff of that! The smell of the open sea!"

"We go England!" said Tisquantum, his voice a mixture of delight and dread.

3. Beyond Monhegan Island, 1605

> This accident must be acknowledged the means, under God, of putting on foot and giving life to all our plantations. God has indeed smiled upon our designs.
> — Sir Ferdinando Gorges,
> *Brief Narration of the Originall Undertaking of the Advancement of Plantation into the Parts of America.* (1637)

Homeward bound on the North Atlantic current and prevailing winds, the ship made good progress. Each day, the Indians were brought up on deck for air and exercise. One at a time, they were untied, so they could move their arms. They had to be taught to use the chamber pot, sling the refuse overboard, and rinse the pot with sea-water.

In rougher seas, Amoret and Maneddo, seeing the tilting horizon, regularly grabbed their stomachs with both hands and soon vomited. The sailors pulled up buckets of sea-water to slosh off the spume. Tisquantum was seasick the first few days, then found his sea-legs. Secretly, he attributed his adjustment to the shell amulet he wore in his right ear-lobe. Skettowaroes and Tahanedo, having had more experience with canoes in rough water, seemed immune to the discomfort.

Each sunny and warm day, James Rosier set up a table on the main deck, opened his journal, and interviewed the Indians, one at a time. He began trying to teach them a few words of English. Tahanedo was defiant and imposing: "I am a king in my own land! If you want to speak to me, you can learn my language." And he pulled his wildcat cloak in closer.

Maneddo followed his example and refused to learn, folding his arms before him. Amoret was too sea-sick to learn. Skettowaroes jumped into the task with gusto. "I am body-guard to my sagamore," he explained. "It is my duty to speak for him with other tribes."

Tisquantum was the best pupil. He seemed to delight in saying English words. He began bringing to Rosier questions about things that did not exist in either Wampanoag or Abenaki. He would pick up a rope and ask, "Wat?" As he got better at the language, he would ask—"What this?"

Rosier soon discovered that Tisquantum was not a good informant for Abenaki, because, as the young man said, "Tisquantum no Abenaki; Tisquantum Wampanoag." So he tried to dismiss the inquisitivefellow. But Tisquantum would not permit it. He came with question after question, and he often remembered the answers, not always with the right pronunciation.

Tisquantum was curious about everything on the ship, but most about the galley in that part of the forecastle nearest the main mast, where the cook, the carpenter, the cooper, and the sail-maker had their berths and shops.

The cook's pot hung over an open fire, built over a bed of stones and was flanked on both sides and the back by stone walls to keep the fire from spilling out during rough seas. There he cooked the peas and porridge, the hash made from dried meat, the soups made of sea-water and fresh fish.

The crew had adapted to a steady diet of hard-tack, but it soon constipated the Indians. Amoret was even feverish. Rosier and the cook prepared a physic of sassafras leaves, mullwort, and other herbs, which soon gave the Indians diarrhea.

Again, buckets of sea-water sloshed them clean, more or less. But without their protective coating of grease, the Indians were soon paralyzed with chill. They had to be dressed in sailor's shirts and pants.

"There's no end to it, and no middle ground," complained Rosier to Tisquantum. "Everything we do seems to upset you fellows in one way or another."

"Hands in rope much much," said Tisquantum, holding up his bound wrists.

"Well, I'm tired of being nursemaid!"

***

After a month's passage, they arrived at Plymouth Fort on the lands-end coast of England. On the 15th of July, 1605, Waymouth delivered his cargo of fish and the five American natives to Sir Ferdinando Gorges.

The Portugese family of Ferdinando Gorges had been in England for four generations and had gained wealth and position. Ferdinando had done creditable military service for Queen Elizabeth in her wars in France, for which he was knighted and made commander of the Fort at Plimouth, near Lands End. He carried a white, perfumed handkerchief at all times, his protection against offensive odors.

Sir Ferdinando was pleased with the quality of the salmon. He called his chef and had him slice bits of the smoked salmon and some of the dried cod and put them on thin slices of bread.

Stuffing his handkerchief into a waistcoat pocket, Gorges took up the little open-faced sandwiches with a forefinger and thumb and slid them into his mouth. "Delightful!" he said, with great conviction. "In London, this will pay for the voyage."

After reserving a share of the salmon for his own use, he sent the rest with Waymouth and *The Archangel* to London, for the benefit of his fellow investors, especially Sir John Popham, the Lord Chief Justice of England, and John Slaney, the Treasurer of The New England Company for Exploration and Trade.

He was even more happy with the five Indian captives, who were brought in from their locked room. He was so enthusiastic that he gave each man of the crew an extra crown as bonus.

"Welcome, Welcome, Captain Taneedo," he exclaimed, his eyes gleaming, as he put one foot forward to show a stockinged calf, waved his handkerchief, and made an elaborate, receding bow, the usual English method of greeting a person of quality.

He had taken to wearing pastel suits of shiny satin— pale green waistcoats and knee-length pants with mauve stockings, cummerbund, and collars; and white lace at the cuffs. He avoided pink and the colors of royalty, but used almost

By Charles Brashear 35

every other color.

Tahanedo took Gorges by the hand... and held on. He glanced to see that Rosier was there to translate. "Take Tahanedo to Pemaquid. Now." He had to hold his breath unobtrusively, so foul was the powder and perfume of the white man.

"But you've just arrived! I want to visit with you, learn about your home. You must stay the winter."

"I am a KING in my land," shouted Tahanedo, his wrists still tied. "Take me home!"

"Yes, yes. I understand," said Gorges. "Come and show me where you live." On a table, he rolled out the map which Waymouth and Rosier had drawn during the voyage.

Gorges dreamed of establishing a plantation or colony in Maine and fortifying it, in order to exploit the fishing off Maine and Newfoundland and prevent the French, Dutch, and Spanish from invading what he saw as his private fishing waters. He had put a good part of his personal fortune into the project and had helped in organizing the "New England Company for Exploration and Trade."

Tisquantum recognized the line of the coast. He pointed to a place off the edge of the map. "Pemaquid," he said. "Tahanedo house."

Tahanedo glanced at the map and did not contradict him. Using sticks, the Indians frequently drew maps on smooth sand for each other. He, too, recognized the contour of the coast.

"This fellow is not Abenaki," said Rosier, indicating Tisquantum. "He's from another tribe. We're not certain yet just which one."

"My slave," said Tahanedo. "Assaquantem." And he took Tisquantum by the neck to pantomime the capture.

"As-quan-tet. Tah-nay-doe," said Gorges. "I'll never learn to pronounce their names right." He waved his handkerchief, as if his mistakes were no great matter.

When Sir Ferdinando learned that the five Indians were from different families, he cried out, "Excellent! Excellent! That means they will have knowledge of many places and can make maps for us." Though his family had lived in England and had been openly Protestant for two generations, he made the sign of the cross.

Gorges turned, waving his handkerchief in all directions, indicating all his household and command at Plymouth Fort. "Use these savages kindly. Help them to learn good English and be content with civilization. Teach them to map and understand words on paper."

"This accident must be acknowledged the means of putting on foot and giving life to all our plantations. God has indeed smiled upon our designs."

4. "Raise the Glass on High, Billy Bigh"

Yea, raise the glass on high, on high, on high;
    tomorrow we may die.
    — Drinking Song.

Since Tisquantum's first language was Wampanoag, rather than Abenaki, he was of little interest to Sir Ferdinando. However, he had made so much progress in learning English, which he had a base in from his travels, and was so cooperative, that his wrists were often untied and he was allowed to walk freely in the presence of the guards. Two of the guards took a liking to Tisquantum and soon began taking him to the kitchen, rather than bringing the food to him.

"Yes, yes. That's fine," said Sir Ferdinando, waving his handkerchief. "Get him out of my hair for the time being."

In the kitchen, Tisquantum sat on a wooden bench beside a long table, where several of the guards and kitchen maids hunkered, leaning forward to catch all the entertainment they could. One of the maids brought a spoon and a bowl of rabbit and vegetable stew.

After a few bites, Tisquantum looked up and said, "Good! Good-good." Then dipping up a vegetable, of which there were plenty in the stew, he asked, "What this?"

"Why, that's a potato," said Oliver Gotochurch. "Don't you know anything?"

"Wampanoag no have po-tay-to. Eat corn, bean, squash."

"Corn?" said Sean Farquhar, astonished. "Corn, 'tis good only for making beer, or feeding to pigs. A person canna eat it!"

"Let's give him a beer," said Oliver. He drew a mug of beer and set it before Tisquantum. "Beer," said Oliver, pointing to the liquid. "Mug," he said, pointing. "Mug of beer." He made motions of drinking.

"Mug of beer," Tisquantum repeated, practicing the words. He picked up the mug and took a mouthful. It was worse than being sea-sick. He retched and coughed, spewing foam over those across the table from him.

"Tykes a bit of getting used to, it does," said Sean, laughing. "'Ere's how!" he picked up his own mug and drained it.

Tisquantum picked up his own mug and drank a few swallows rapidly. Those across from him withdrew quickly out of the line of fire. Again, his stomach rebelled. He gagged and coughed, again spewing foam on the table.

"I'm with you," said one of the maids, sitting down beside him. "I can only take it in sips. Like this." She demonstrated. "Otherwise, I do just what you did."

Tisquantum tried sipping the beer, with more success. The bitter liquid did not taste good to him, but this time it did not cause his stomach to revolt.

"Atta boy, Squantum," said Sean. "Ye 'll learn in no time, you will."

With a little practice, Tisquantum learned to drink the whole mug-full without retching, though it made him tipsy. It soon became great sport to the guards to take him to the kitchen and get him drunk.

Through all this, Tisquantum maintained good cheer. He quickly developed a taste for beer and beef, and he learned a fair amount of the commoners' language. The guards and sailors delighted in teaching him one of their favorite drinking songs: "Raise the Glass on High, Billy Bigh:"

Buck up, Billy, put your belly to the bar,
And we'll drink a wee pint for auld lang syne.

We're all of us fed, they've stopped the ole war;
So raise the glass on high, Billy Bigh, Billy Bigh,
> *We'll all of us live to a hundred and nine.*

Yea, raise the glass on high, on high, on high;
tomorrow we may die.

As the winter passed, Gorges began to see that Tisquantum might be of more use than he had originally thought. He was so cooperative that he was given the freedom of the fort and could wander within its halls as he pleased.

By spring, Tisquantum could hold an awkward conversation on the street, though Gorges seldom let any of the Indians out of his control, for fear they might try to escape, or, more likely, some competitor might kidnap them, or profit from them in some way no one had thought of yet.

John Slaney, the Company's treasurer, came to visit and deliver to Gorges some of the group's money for the coming year's supplies. He was quite taken by the enthusiasm of Tisquantum.

"That fellow is so inquisitive," noted Slaney. "He seems interested in everything. One could wish for a son at Oxford, who was such an apt pupil. You must let me take him with me to Cheapside, Sir Ferdinando. My wife and children will teach him another kind of English."

"No," said Gorges, narrowing his eyes to look closely at John Slaney. Gorges smiled tentatively. "Perhaps another time, John. I'm shaping up plans for him in New England this summer."

5. Repatriation

> "A friendly sagamore on the New England coast would be of more use to you than a literate enemy here."
>
> — Henry Challons, in Samuel Purchas, *Purchas His Pilgrimes*. London, 1625

By early March, three of Gorges' ships were tied up at the wharf in Plymouth harbor. The sailors were kept busy repairing sails, checking the rigging, laying in provisions for voyages to the New England coast. George Waymouth was not among his captains. "The fellow is so obnoxious," said Gorges, waving his handkerchief in dismissal.

"But he knows how to sail," said Henry Challons, another of Gorges' captains. Gorges had a soft spot of sympathy for Henry, because, like his own, Henry's family had come from the continent some generations back. And he had noticed Henry secretly making a tiny sign of the cross over his food.

"I know," said Gorges. "I've heard the arguments. He brings home the ship. And his cargoes are respectable. His crews cooperate. But

I simply detest the fellow. He hangs on Quality, like a leech from a swamp. Let him seek his preferment from someone more sympathetic to him."

"He is in London, waiting for your call," said Henry.

"Yes, I know. Let him stay there. If he's the last fish in the barrel, I'll send for him."

***

Tahanedo had refused to learn English, saying that his body-guard, Skettowaroes, could talk for him. Skettowaroes had learned a moderate amount of English, but spot-faced Maneddo had played dumb and refused to learn. Amoret had refused to eat, wasted away, and died of a fever in January.

"Tay-nay-doe is worse than recalcitrant," said Gorges, nibbling a pop-over pie made from dried fruit. "All he says is that he wants to go home."

"Then I suggest you let him," said Henry Challons. "A friendly sagamore on the New England coast would be of more use to you than a literate enemy here. And here, all you do is feed him and guard him."

Gorges stopped and looked again at Henry. This captain was in early middle age, robust and trim, and his thick, brown hair was well-managed. "You are quite right, Henry. I hadn't thought of it that way. Why don't you take Tisquantum as your interpreter and cultivate the fellow's favor? He hates us now with black passion. See if you can turn his attitudes around. Tell him we'll put him and his bodyguard on the first ship out this spring."

Henry and Tisquantum went to the cell where Tahanedo, Skettowaroes, and Maneddo were kept behind locked doors. Two guards came in with them, to make sure Skettowaroes did not attack and overpower Henry Challons.

"Sir Ferdinando Gorges has decided to send you home," announced Henry to Tahanedo, "home to Pemaquid."

After Tisquantum had translated, Tahanedo made no response. He did not even look at Henry, but continued to gaze through the window-bars at the activities in the inner courtyard and harbor of Plymouth Fort.

"I said, Sir Ferdinan— "

"And will he return my necklace, my power necklace?"

"Why, I don't know. I can ask him."

"I am tired of his empty promises," said Tahanedo. "I will believe it when it has happened. Let me stand a free man in Pemaquid, and I will believe him. Everything else he has told us was a lie. Why should we believe this latest bit of hot air?"

After Tisquantum had translated Tahanedo's response for Henry, he spoke to Tahanedo directly. "It is true, grandfather. I heard him myself. He plans to send you and Skettowaroes home on the first ship of the season. Maneddo and I will be put on a later ship."

Tahanedo turned from the window and lifted the edge of his wildcat skin cape as an emblem of his authority. "Listen, my Passamaquoddies. And do not translate this for the brown-haired one, Assaquantem. Lie to them every chance you get, just as they have lied to us. Make your lies clever, so they seem possible, but do not tell them anything of any importance. Pretend that you are cooperating, but let your words lead them to believe something that is false. That is my order to you, as your sagamore."

"What's he saying, Tisquantum?" asked Henry.

Tisquantum hesitated a moment, trying to figure out how he would respond to Henry, for he knew that Skettowaroes understood enough English to betray him if he made a wrong step. At last, he said, "He tell them how to act when they get home. They planning what they do when Sir

Ferdinando Gorges released them at Pemaquid."

"Then we can be friends there?" said Henry, taking Tahanedo by the hand in the Indian manner. "Each time we come to Pemaquid, we will bring you gifts and goods to trade. We will live in peace and harmony."

Tahanedo pulled his hand back and turned to the window. "I do not see any wind in the sails," he said.

"But there will be wind in them. When the right day comes, there will be wind in the sails."

"Ha," said Tahanedo scornfully. "I suppose he will fill the sails with the hot air of his lies. I have nothing more to say to you. None of my Passamaquoddies have anything more to say to you."

For several more days, Henry and Tisquantum tried to gain Tahanedo's trust, but Tahanedo remained antagonistic. Still, Henry recommended to Sir Ferdinando that he send Tahanedo home. "He's certainly of no use to you here".

"Quite right, Henry. Quite right. And I'll save on provisions and the expense of guards."

6. The First Ship of the Season, 1606

> First thing warrior do, make enemy afraid.
> Loud noise, fierce paint, make danger.
> hen enemy 'fraid, no fight good.
> Easy for warrior to shoot enemy.

Tahanedo and Skettowaroes were on the first ship of the 1606 season, not as prisoners, but as guests. Gorges instructed Captain Bartholomew Gosnold to deliver them at Pemaquid. "Cultivate their friendship as much as you can. When we plant our colony, we'll need friends there."

"And when will we plant that colony?" asked Henry Challons.

"I don't know, Henry. Right now, we need friends in the Royal Palace more than friends in New England."

"Then— I infer—He has not issued a charter?"

"No. He plays with things. He toys with our

projects. An enterprise of a thousand pounds is not as much consequence to him as what his cat eats at mid-day."

"Perhaps, if you introduced His Majesty to your savages."

"I doubt it would do any good, Henry. If Elizabeth had not left such a strong government, we would be adrift by now. Still, that's an idea. I'll write Sir John Popham; he sometimes has audiences with the King as part of his duties; perhaps he could arrange a hearing."

"Send Tisquantum. He makes a good impression on everyone."

"Perhaps, Henry, perhaps. Teach him how to act in the presence of Royalty, and we'll see what happens."

But, though they waited all summer, King James was not interested in seeing the American savages. "I know they are there," he said. "Why should I want to see them?"

***

With Tahanedo and Skettowaroes gone, Maneddo was also given freedom of the fort. But, since he was exceedingly ashamed of the smallpox scars on his face and knew little or no English, he did not use his freedom much. Finally, Tisquantum managed to get some rouge from Lady Gorges, and Maneddo painted his spots. After that, he felt more presentable and came out often.

To amuse themselves, Sir Ferdinando Gorges, his officers and sea captains decided to let Maneddo and Tisquantum perform a shooting demonstration in the courtyard with the bows and arrows that Rosier had confiscated at Pemaquid. Tisquantum was reluctant to participate. "Maneddo is warrior," he explained. "Tisquantum not warrior."

"Well, well," said Gorges. "Captain Challons can take your place. Let May-needo show us how a real warrior shoots in war. I'll wager two pairs of Paris shoes that a good English captain can match him point for point. You can stand there and tell him what we say and tell us what he says." The servants brought out a folding chair for Sir Ferdinando, who settled into it with a sigh and a wave of his embroidered handkerchief.

When Maneddo drew his first arrow, he looked toward Sir Ferdinando. "Don't do it," said Tisquantum, laying a hand on Maneddo's bow hand. "If you shoot Sir Ferdinando, they will surely kill us all."

"Let them start, as soon as my arrow flies," said Maneddo.

"Besides," Tisquantum went on, "He is sitting down and unarmed. There would be no honor in killing him. You would only tarnish your own reputation as a warrior."

Maneddo broke away and began running directly toward Gorges, screaming a war-cry. He outran Tisquantum. Henry Challons followed as rapidly as he could, trying to catch and restrain Maneddo.

With the arrow fully drawn, Maneddo ran to within a few feet of Gorges, who was squirming, screaming frantically, "Guards! Guards!"

"He is not a worthy victim," said Maneddo, lowering his aim and easing the tension on the bow-string. "See how he quails and cowers."

"What is he saying, Squantum?" asked Henry, who now had his arms around Maneddo, disabling and restraining him.

"He show: first thing warrior do, make enemy afraid. Loud noise, fierce paint, make danger. When enemy 'fraid, no fight good. Easy for warrior to shoot enemy."

"It certainly looks like he accomplished that first objective," said Henry very quietly.

***

In August, Tisquantum was a passenger and Maneddo a prisoner on the third ship of the season, commanded by Captain Henry Challons. Walking along the wharf where the ship was ready to set sail, Gorges put his hand across Henry's shoulder, like an indulgent father counseling a favorite son.

"Take care, Henry," said Gorges, pressing something into Henry's hand. "I wouldn't want anything to happen to you. Here's a good luck charm that I wish you would wear."

Henry glanced at the St. Christopher medal in his hands, then quickly closed his fingers over it before anyone else saw it.

"I won't be angry if you leave May-needo at Pee-milk-weed; the fellow is useless to us. But As-a-comet, I want you to bring back with you. With a bit of experience, he'll make a first rate guide and interpreter."

After a moment, he added, "As-a-comet may be the means of giving life to our plans. If so, God has, indeed, smiled upon our designs."

7. Captured near Puerto Rico

> "... having had a very great storm of wind and rain continuing fifty six hours and more before, the tenth day of November, about ten of the clock in the morning, suddenly we found ourselves in the midst of a fleet of eight sail of ships in a very thick fog of mist and rain, ..."
>
> — John Stoneman, "The Voyage of Master Henry Challons ... 1606".

The whole passage out was a flurry of feeble leads and failed tacks. Beyond Corso and Grand Canary Island, Captain Henry Challons would set a heading, only to find that a head wind prevailed.

"Why we go backward?" asked Tisquantum, who hung close to Henry, hoping to learn more about sailing.

"There must be a devil in the wind!" exclaimed Henry. He would set a tack, only to find that he was blown backward more than he moved forward.

"'Tis worse than a devil," muttered many in the crew. "'Tis the work of harpies!"

"Aye," said others. "Ye see their hands in the tangled rigging."

For three months— from August 6th to November 10th— gale winds and rains caught them and sent the ship southward, eastward, backward, westward. When Challons finally gained control of the ship again, he was off the coast of Puerto Rico in a dense fog, with tattered sails and damaged rigging. When the fog lifted, he discovered five Spanish warships on one side and three on the other.

A Spanish ship came onto them and fired a shot across the bow. There was nothing to do but yield. The Spaniards would find soon enough that the ship was unarmed, except for two six-pounders. And the holds were empty, except for trinkets they had brought to trade with the New England natives.

The Spaniards boarded the ship like hungry pirates, their cutlasses swinging. They wounded or beat several men. Capriciously, one sailor pierced Tisquantum through the upper arm.

Tisquantum was baffled by the pirate attitude. This was not the way a person was treated in England. He slipped under a hatch cover, crying, "King James! King James his ship! King James his ship!" as if claiming allegiance to King James would protect him.

Though unarmed, Henry Challons pushed the Spanish sailor back from Tisquantum with his shoulder, stammering, *"El... solo niño."*

"No tenemos lástima por Luteranos," cried the sailor, jerking his sword back and turning to attack Henry.

Before the sailor could get a footing for a thrust, Henry pushed him backward off the poop and onto the deck. Others who were still fighting, tumbled between the sailor and Henry.

Then the fighting was suddenly over. The English were all subdued. The Spanish captain climbed over the gunwale onto the deck.

Crouching to stay out of sight, Henry helped Tisquantum from under the hatch, saying, "Let's take a look at that cut."

The sword had gone through the fleshy back of his arm, and the wound was bleeding freely, but not spurting. "You're lucky, Squantum. The sword didn't hit any major veins. You'll be all right."

Henry tore the sleeve from Tisquantum's shirt, ripped it into strips, and bound the wound to limit the bleeding as much as possible. "You'll probably have a nasty scar," said Henry. "But I think you'll heal up in no time."

The Spanish captain swaggered along the deck, inspecting the English captives. Some were still being restrained by Spanish sailors. Others were lined up against one gunwale.

Henry Challons protested, holding up his St. Christopher medal. He tried to show his official documents, which identified them as a trading ship. The Spanish captain refused to look at the papers. "But I'm the Captain," exclaimed Henry. "Soy... Estoy... capitán!"

Tisquantum gazed at Henry in wonder, not understanding the words like "bleeding" and "heal," but perceiving the care. He had never heard of bandages, nor of a warrior taking care of another. He felt a warmth for Henry— and also a duty. He would now have to stick close to Henry and protect him as best he could. He owed Henry a great debt. He would have to be Henry's servant.

8. The Jail in Seville, 1607

> Each day brings a new sun.
> Each day, the goose learns again how to live.
> We do not know the future, or what it may bring.
> — Old Proverbs

Henry Challons tried to bargain their way to freedom. But the Spaniards were in no bargaining mood. The English were in Spanish territorial waters, committing wicked crimes that no one could imagine.

The Spanish captain confiscated the ship and took it to the harbor at Puerto Rico. There, the Spanish governor divided the English crew into five groups and put them on separate ships, to be taken to Spain: some were sold into slavery, some into service of the church, some were imprisoned. Maneddo was sold to a Moorish merchant from Algiers.

John Stoneman, the pilot, was in the first group to arrive in Seville, in December 1606, where authorities tried to bribe him to draw maps of the New England coast and join them. Henry Challons and Tisquantum were brought in together, early in January, 1607, and put in a prison in Seville.

The Spanish governor of Seville and the Archbishop called Challons and Stoneman before them.

"Here is bag of gold ... por los niños en su casa," said the governor. "You tell us about New England coast?"

"We make you barons," said the Archbishop. "You show us where harbors are ... you have ownership of much land."

Challons and Stoneman just looked at them amazed.

"You join us. Become espanish citizens."

"You become *generales grandes* and serve Spain."

"We make you rich, *muy rico*."

But no matter what they offered, Challons and Stoneman always refused.

As an added incentive, the two were given the freedom to move about the town, where they could make friends, borrow money, etc.

The common sailors and Tisquantum remained in prison. Periodically, the constable would arrest Challons anew, torture him for a while, and throw him in jail again. Then collect a new bail.

Like any educated man of his time, Henry Challons knew a few words of Spanish. He asked to see the English ambassador. The jailors only giggled. What a joke, to think a Luterano imagined he had rights.

Nevertheless, well-to-do and influential Dutch and French merchants living in Seville posted bond for Henry Challons, as they had for the ship's other officers. Henry Challons and John Stoneman managed to borrow enough money from their Dutch and French friends to buy food for the crew in jail.

Stoneman took an opportunity to free two of the crew, including his younger brother. The three then walked overland to Lisbon and caught an English bark bound for Plymouth, on the coast of Cornwall, where Stoneman wrote his report for Sir Ferdinando Gorges.

The Spanish governor was enraged; he threw Henry Challons back in jail and had him tortured with hot irons.

In the adjoining cell, Tisquantum passed the time learning Spanish words from the jailor, such as *"pan," "aqua," "puerto," "sabe," "dice,"* and the like.

"Jesus Christ, Assaquantem!" said Henry. "You're too damned cheerful. Don't you realize that it may take a sorcerer to get us out of this jail?"

"I say we not now in Passamaquoddy land. Bad luck name. You call me real name, okay? Wampanoag name, Tisquantum."

"Assaquantem, Squantum. What difference does it make? Without some wizard, we're likely to rot in this stinking hole. Look at this! I'm already rotting!" He held out his arms. The burns and gouges were swollen and red. Some oozed puss.

"Wampanoag medicine man put spider web on cuts. Stop bleed. Make well." He collected enough cobwebs from the window sill to plaster the worst of Henry's wounds.

Their good clothes, all of Henry's valuables, and even the good-luck shell amulet in Tisquantum's right ear lobe, had been taken from them, and they were clad in tattered rags. A small arm of golden sunlight came in at each of their windows, but they could not see clearly what debris and vermin were in the corners of their cells.

Each day, they grew a little thinner. "Better day come," said Tisquantum.

"How?" asked Henry. "What cause have we to expect improvement?"

"Each day bring new sun. Each day, goose learn again how to live. Not know future, or what it bring. Jailor, maybe decide turn us loose."

9. Draghan Di-Eshti

"Mashkando por los Gadyendos, leski shib es el Romeski zor." (When surrounded by outsiders, the only defense is the Gypsy's tongue).
— Old Gypsy Proverb

In mid-summer 1608, a year and a half after Squanto and Challons had been imprisoned, the Seville jail got a new keeper—an Andalusian Gypsy named Draghan Di-eshti. He was thick and stocky, with dark, flowing hair and a bushy mustache. He wore a bright red shirt with balloon sleeves and black leather boots up to his knees. When he turned, the sun flashed on his golden ear-ring, made of a Spanish doubloon.

As soon as he was left alone, he threw back his head and laughed at the ceiling. "Look at me!" he exclaimed to Henry and Tisquantum. "I should be there where you are! I robbed a *rom* in another clan, maybe even killed the fellow. But am I in jail?

"No! No, I am the jailor." He threw back his head and laughed again at the irony. "I am the jailor!"

"You see— why am I telling you this? Who are you to me, that I should give you my secrets? Well, no matter. You are victims, like myself. Like all *rom*! Like many, many *rom*, who have suffered much from Spanish bigotry. But, you see, the church and state are right now on a campaign to integrate Gypsies into Spanish society, so they are giving some of us regular jobs."

"*No comprendo,*" said Tisquantum. "I not understand."

"What's to understand?" cried Draghan. "This jail is better than a good luck charm. It's a perfect ruse: What Gypsy would think of seeking a fugitive like me in a jail?" And he laughed again at the irony.

When Draghan was made to understand that Tisquantum was an American native who had been captured and enslaved, kidnaped and transported, and was now captured and imprisoned again, his sympathies went out to him.

"Look at that!" said Draghan, drawing up a sleeve and holding his arm up next to Tisquantum's. "Your skin is almost walnut-colored, like mine. And your hair and eyes are black. We could be brothers! In fact, you look a lot like my brother, Yoro."

It also appealed to Draghan that Squantum,

as he called him, had been raised outside the Christian faith and spoke a sort of pidgin Spanish not unlike a Gypsy's first attempts at the language.

Draghan had been baptized in the Spanish Catholic Church, but that was only a conscious facade, a deception that was the Spanish Gypsy's defense during troubled times. "My grandparents survived the Spanish Inquisition by the old Gypsy trick of misleading the authorities," he said, laughing. *"Mashkando por los Gadyendos, leski shib es el Romeski zor."*

They both loved animals, but Draghan was amazed that Squantum believed that animals had spirit powers.

"You mean, not just souls, like horses have," asked Draghan, "but magic powers as well?"

That was too much for Tisquantum to understand.

"I've known a lot of cats who were witches," said Draghan, laughing, "and a lot of witches who were cats. Especially black cats. You always want to spit three times whenever you see a black cat. That will protect you against any spell the cat is throwing at that moment. It'll also protect you against priests and Christians," he added, laughing again at his own cleverness.

When Henry borrowed more money from a Dutch merchant, Draghan brought them generous portions of food— sausage and fresh bread— so that they regained some of their health and stamina. He liked to pull his chair up close to the bars of Squantum's door and ask questions like, "Tell me, Squantum. What does your God look like?"

Tisquantum had difficulty answering, because the Wampanoag do not conceive the Great Spirit to look like any man or animal. "He no look," said Tisquantum. "He no have body."

"No body!? Then how do you know where he is?"

"He there in spirit. In rock, in tree, in rain, in people. Grandfathers see him. Great Spirit and grandfathers, same thing."

"Really?" said Draghan, whose real religion was a form of ancestor worship, in spite of the Gypsy lip-service to Christianity. Six generations back, in 1440, his ancestor, Kuma, had been chief of the first band of Gypsies to enter Spain at Barcelona and, for several years, had maintained a *kumpania* at Sitges on the Mediterranean coast, a little south of Barcelona.

His great-grandfather, Tshurka, had been the first to submit to Catholic baptism and took the surname, Manos-del-Dio, (Hands of God). Tshurka's several sons, all as clever as Tshurka, were called Dio-di-eshti, (God's Family). Tshurka cleverly got the Church authorities to write the name into all their identification papers, though neither he nor any of his sons could read or write. In Draghan's young manhood, the worst part of the Inquisition having passed, the surname was shortened to Di-eshti.

Whenever Draghan thought of his great-grandfather, his eyes misted over, he became sentimental, and he often recited or sang "*Tshurkaki Dgili,*" "The Song of Tshurka", a long epic account of Tshurka's survival.

>Of thee I sing, Tshurka,
>Source of my tribe,
>Great-grandson of Kuma,
>Who brought the *Rom* to Barcelona so long, long ago.
>>Of many wanderings, I sing, Tshurka,
>Of your adventures in barrel-topped *vurdons*,
>Strung along the roads in colorful caravans.
>>Of your many clever moves, I sing, Tshurka,
>Of many times you fooled *Los Gadyos*
>And got them to do your wants.
>>Of your many generous *patshiva* I sing,
>When you honored the descendants of great men.
>>Of beauty in your daughters, I sing, Tshurka,
>>And their skill at *boojo.*

By Charles Brashear

> Of the great Flamenco dancers, I sing,
>> who were among your grand-daughters,
> I sing of the great singers who were relatives;
>> I sing of the bucket full of gold and coins
>> Which you left as heirlooms.
>> But most I sing of you, Tshurka,
>> Immortal ancestor of my tribe.
>> May we all live your hundred years
>> And gain a hundredth of your honor.

When he finished the song, Draghan was always silent for a few moments, and, when he tried to speak, his voice caught in his throat.

***

Draghan was delighted when he learned that Squantum liked beer and could sing "Raise the Glass on High, Billy Bigh." He began bringing beer and wine to the cell, so Squantum would sing for him. Draghan also took more than a sip of the wine and sang the wild, wailing *"Tshurkaki Dgili"*. He taught Squantum some of the words, including the magic in them, and got him to sing along.

> *By the shores at Sitges, Kuma*
>> *camped by big sea water,*
>>> *fifty vurdon led by Tshurka-Kuma,*
> *Tshurka-Kuma, grand patriarch of the tribe,*
> *great grandfather of patriarch of the tribe,*

long remembered in song.

"You and me, Squantum. You and me, we're alike. We're brothers. But you gotta have an ear-ring. An ear-ring makes a person human. As we *Rom* say, the dogs can't tell you from a tree and will piss on you, if you don't wear a golden ear-ring." He soon brought a thick gold coin to hang in Squantum's right ear lobe. Tisquantum brightened and smiled: he felt better-looking than he had since the Spanish had captured them. "This is your good luck," said Draghan. "With this gold, some day, somewhere, you'll buy your way out of trouble."

10. Escape in the Night

"Ashen Devlesa. Vaya con Díos."
(Go with God. Go with God.)
— Gypsy and Spanish farewell

Once, when Draghan was drinking more heavily than usual, Tisquantum noticed that Draghan had turned so the key on his belt was close to Tisquantum's hand. He lifted the key ring off the belt-hook and handed it to Henry Challons in the next cell. Henry took the keys and was silent.

Squantum began singing *"Tshurkaki Dgili"* and drank cup after cup with Draghan. Soon, Draghan passed out, though he had never passed out before.

Quickly, Henry let himself out of his cell, pulled Draghan in by the heels, and locked the door again. Then he opened Tisquantum's cell. Tisquantum was so drunk he could hardly walk by himself, and he only wanted to sing *"Tshurkaki Dgili"* or "Raise the Glass on High, Billy Bigh."

"Hush, Squantum," said Henry. "You'll raise the constable." Henry pulled Tisquantum's arm across his own shoulders, and they staggered out of the prison.

Draghan lifted his head and waved after them. *"Ashen Devlesa. Vaya con Dios."*

On the street, Tisquantum started singing "Raise the Glass on High, Billy Bigh."

"Shush, you'll give us away," scolded Henry, but Tisquantum would not stop. Henry began singing *"Tshurkaki Dgili,"* which he had learned part of in spite of himself. Tisquantum began singing along. Henry looked both ways in the street to see if a constable was coming, or if anyone was a threat. He only saw a few people, who clucked their tongues and exclaimed disgustedly, *"Gitános!"*

It was near midnight, not long after the evening meal; so Henry figured they had until about breakfast before Draghan would be discovered in the cell and give the alarm. They had to get out of town quickly. He steered Tisquantum in a direction he thought was toward the Guadalquivir River. That was probably where the constable would search for them first, but it was also the best place to hide.

Some time after midnight, they came across a Spaniard who had passed out on the street. "He must be on his way home from a bordello," said Henry. After glancing to see if there was anyone in the street, Henry ran his hands through the man's pockets and found several coins. Then he stripped the man and, because the clothes fit Tisquantum, but not Henry, soon had Tisquantum dressed as a well-to-do, Spanish citizen. Henry would have to continue as he was, as ragged as any Gypsy.

Tisquantum had stopped singing, but now only wanted to sleep. "Hold your head up, Squantum. We've got to be awake to get out of this mess." Henry kept looking back, for now they were also wanted for robbery. He tried to steer Tisquantum close to the houses, where the shadows were deeper.

At a fountain in a square, Henry splashed water in Tisquantum's face, which sobered him somewhat. "Where we are?" asked Tisquantum.

Henry looked around to see if anyone was watching. Two men and a horse were coming into the little plaza. Henry pulled Tisquantum into the darkness beside a wall. "Straighten up, will you?" said Henry. "Try to act normal. You're a Spanish Gypsy, and I'm your servant that can't speak the language. Can you pretend that?"

"*Si, si. Soy caballero Romani.*"

"Yeah, well, wish for the best of luck. I hope we can pull it off. No constable has shown up yet, but they can't be far behind us." He kept looking around, especially behind them.

Henry steered Tisquantum toward some lights he thought must be near the river. "It would be good if we could find a boat and get out of this town altogether. Now, come on. Be quiet, and stick as close to the shadows as you can."

Under a decrepit wharf, Henry found a leaky row-boat with one oar and a metal pan, apparently used for bailing water out of the boat. It would be risky to take it, but not as risky as staying in Seville. "God help us," muttered Henry.

In the darkness, they put out downstream, Henry paddling first on one side, then on the other, Tisquantum dipping water out of the leaky boat as fast as he could. They were soon beyond the lights of Seville and could see the banks of the river only as a darker dark. But Henry did not relax; he continued to paddle furiously.

About three o'clock, a sliver of a moon came up, and they could see a little better. "We make devil trail, like snake" said Tisquantum, pointing to their undulating wake in the moonlight.

"Keep dipping that water out, or we'll sink," said Henry, glancing backward.

Near morning, they found a cove at the edge of the river and decided to hide there during the day. With two leafy branches, Tisquantum herded small fish into the shallow water, where he could sweep them up on the bank. Henry split them with a sharp rock, and they ate them raw, having eaten nothing since supper the night before.

Hoping to slow the leaking of the boat, Henry pulled it up on the land and stuffed grass into the cracks, using a rock and a coin he had taken from the drunken Spaniard to tamp it in.

In the twilight, they put out again, Tisquantum using a branch as a paddle. That way, they traveled a bit faster, since they had to bail water less often and made a straighter wake.

At mid-morning the next day, they stopped at a village where Tisquantum pointed to bread and sausage, while holding out money and saying "*Pan. Carne.*"

Henry waited in the shabby boat, anxiously looking first in one direction, then another.

The store keeper hesitated, but decided a Gypsy's money was as good as any other. Besides, he over-charged him, and then also short-changed him.

"*Gitános estupidos,*" he said to his wife as Henry and Tisquantum were rowing downstream. "They're so easy to cheat, it's almost no fun. And they only know enough Spanish to point and grunt. You'd think they'd learn the language if they're going to live in this country."

In some days, Henry Challons and Tisquantum came to the mouth of the

Guadalquivir River and sighted a French ship. In the twilight, they finally got close to it. Henry banged his oar on the side, causing two watchmen to look over the gunwale.

"*Je suis Anglais,*" Henry said in his schoolboy French, "May we come aboard?"

"*Mon dieu,*" exclaimed one watchman, leaning over the gunwale with a torch in his hand. "What is Anglais doing in the dark?"

"*Et avec un Tsigan?!*" exclaimed the other.

"Call your captain, please," said Henry, saying a little silent prayer. "We want to book passage to wherever you're going."

"We sail for Marseilles tomorrow morning."

Tisquantum had not expected to lose his golden ear-ring so soon, but Draghan had said it was to buy his way out of trouble. With it and the coins Henry had taken, they bought passage to Marseilles.

There, Henry found an English resident who would lend money enough for him and Tisquantum to live on, while they waited for Henry's letters to go to England and letters of credit to come back.

After settling with the benefactor, the banker, and the landlord, they took passage on a ship bound for London.

On the passage out, Tisquantum did not

have his usual good cheer.

"What's the matter, Squantum?" asked Henry. "You were right: we never know what good fortunes the morrow may bring, or what jailor may allow us to escape. We can thank our lucky stars for that one."

"I wonder about Maneddo," said Tisquantum. "We find him and take him with us, okay?"

"He's probably as much at home as he'll ever be again," said Henry. "It's been two years. He's probably the father of two smiling, spot-faced Moorish children by now."

11. The Indian Show, 1609

> "Were I in England now (as I once was), and had but this fish painted, not a holiday fool there but would give a piece of silver [to gawk at it]: there would this monster make a man; any strange beast there makes a man! When they will not give a doit to relieve a lame beggar, they will lay out ten to see a dead Indian."
> — William Shakespeare,
> *The Tempest*, Act II, sc. 2 (1613).

When Tisquantum and Henry Challons walked down the gangplank in London, they met Captain George Waymouth. He was as skinny as ever, perhaps even skinnier. He looked like the one who had just spent two years in a Spanish jail.

"I've been waiting for you," said Waymouth to Henry Challons. "You are to go on to Plymouth Fort and report to Sir Ferdinando Gorges."

"So? Are you still working for him?"

"Aye. That I am. But I haven't had a berth in some time. Couple of years. He says the economics of exploration are bad, have been so for the past

---

By Charles Brashear 77

year, or more."

"How so?" asked Henry.

"Prices have fallen out of everything. That fort and trading post he and Sir John Popham established at Sagadahoc on the Maine coast in 1606 failed completely in 1607. 1608 has been no better."

"And Sir John Popham died, I've heard."

"Yes. I've been idle a great deal, since Gorges hasn't called on me to master a ship. I need a way to make some quick money. I'm to take charge of Squantum, and you're to go on to Plymouth."

"Take charge of Tisquantum?" asked Henry, baffled.

"Yes. We— I—am going to rent a suitable hall in town where most people of quality pass and set up an 'exhibit,' so to speak. We'll —ah—get a reading of the stars as to the right time. I'll get one of those birch-bark canoes I brought back from New England, some bows and arrows, and some of those other implements; we'll build an authentic Native house, and Squantum can sit there and tell people about his culture... and so on."

Waymouth hesitated, looking at his feet.

"We'll have to experiment a little to find the right admission. We'll start with half a crown. That ought to fetch a lot of folk." He took Tisquantum's arm and guided him away from the wharf. Henry looked after them, bewildered.

Waymouth set about collecting the souvenirs he had brought from New England in 1605. One of the birch-bark canoes and paddles were in the possession of John Slaney of London, one of the investors in Sir Ferdinando's schemes and the treasurer of their company. The war axes, bows and arrows, and even the leather carrying bags had been given as gifts to various people all over the country. Some of them were willing to lend the artifacts to Waymouth, on promise that he would return or replace them with new specimens.

"We not have wigwam," Tisquantum pointed out.

"That's no problem," Waymouth insisted. "We'll go out to the marshes, cut some reeds, and build one."

Tisquantum shook his head. "We not have woman to weave mats. Not woman to cut poles."

"You can do that, Squantum, can't you? Surely, you know how."

Tisquantum folded his arms, as if to close the matter. "Woman work. If man make house, witches come."

Nor would Tisquantum relent. So Waymouth found a Cockney family in Southwark who would work cheaply, ferried them in a long-boat down to a marshy area in Kent, and they cut enough good reeds to fabricate mats to build a wigwam.

Tisquantum still would not participate, for fear he would pull in unseen powers; so Waymouth had to give them instructions on how to weave the mats, cut the poles, set them in a rough circle, bend the poles into a dome, and tie on the mats. "Well," Waymouth conceded when it was finished, "No one in England will know it's not authentic."

Tisquantum was happy to get a new shirt and leggings made of Scottish deerskin. "Signs good," said Tisquantum. "Medicine good." He told the seamstress how to cut the leather and helped her do the sewing with thongs and sinew. The fringes on the sleeves and yoke weren't quite long enough, but they would do. And Waymouth found some paints and pigments which had been intended for the now-defunct New England trade. "Here, Squantum," he said, "you can properly decorate your buckskins."

Tisquantum painted some Wampanoag good luck symbols on his clothes and felt more like a real person than he had in many months. But the feeling made him homesick, and he went into a depression that Waymouth could hardly get him out of.

"Patuxet... home village... Tisquantum never

see again, Yes?"

"Oh, surely you will," Waymouth tried to reassure him. "You're young; I'm sure you'll go home one of these days."

"You take Tisquantum... to Patuxet?"

"Well, I don't know. I'll promise you this: the next time I see Sir Ferdinando Gorges, I'll ask when and if we can take you home. In the meantime, here, have a beer; it'll cheer you up."

"In Patuxet... man drink water," said Tisquantum, his eyes fixed on something distant. "You have water?"

"No, no," said Waymouth. "The water here is bad. Dirty. Nasty. Don't drink the water in London. Or any other big city, for that matter. The hags and hellions have thrown so much filth in the streets and along the roads that the water is polluted with fevers. You have to get way out in the country to find drinkable water nowadays.

"That's why sensible Englishmen drink only beer, or stout, or sometimes wine or whiskey. You have to use alcohol to clean the water. Otherwise, you get sick. Besides, water doesn't taste as good as beer."

"Beer taste good," admitted Tisquantum.

"Right," said Waymouth. "And a pint is magic to a man's mood. Here's to Patuxet... the return to Patuxet."

Buck up, Squantum, put your belly to the bar,

And we'll drink a wee pint for auld lang syne...

After a great deal of encouraging, Waymouth got Squantum to sing a verse of "Raise the Glass on High, Billy Bigh." Damn, he thought, I'll have to teach him another song or two; I'm getting tired of that one.

Waymouth hired men to bring dirt into the hall, and they covered the floor with loose grass and straw. He arranged the canoe and paddles so they looked like they were at the edge of a lake or bay. He even brought in the remnants of a campfire and reconstructed it, with orange paper to represent flames, along with a couple of wooden food trays and clay cooking pots.

Waymouth tried to get Squantum to wear a headband full of dyed duck feathers, but Tisquantum refused because he had not earned the right to wear feathers or totems. Waymouth argued with him, but could not convince him that this was only pretense, a show.

Finally, he had to content himself with

hanging the head-dress on the wall near the entrance to the hall, above the extra war axes and a bow with two arrows, which he crossed on the wall under the head-dress, like a coat of arms.

At last, all was ready.

Tisquantum accepted the necklace of colored beads which Waymouth produced, but would not submit to black rings painted around his eyes and a face streaked with red and black pigments. He had not had his dream-vision, nor had he been caught by any totemic animal or power. He was not entitled to wear paint on his face.

Tisquantum sat cross-legged on the dirt in front of the wigwam, holding a bow and arrow. Outside the door, a man stood in the street, ringing a bell and crying out: "Come one, come all. See the real authentic savage from New England. Half a crown, and you'll see a real native of the New World."

The first patrons filed in to find a man, misty-eyed and silent.

Sitting on English soil in front of a fake wigwam, Tisquantum was nevertheless so strongly reminded of his Wampanoag home and all he had lost, that he could not keep back the tears.

The people paid their half-crown and stood behind the little rope, staring at the weeping savage, slumped over his fire. Women drew back, mumbling "He looks fierce," and clung to their husbands' sleeves. Children cried when they saw the man with a painted bow and one arrow; they clenched their mothers' skirts or climbed to the protection of their fathers' arms. Young men displayed their bravado for their fellows: "You don't look like much to me, Mr. Savage. I'll bet I can take you at arm wrestling. Want to try it?"

Tisquantum closed his eyes, but they did not go away.

How could Captain Waymouth do this? He was fond of clapping Tisquantum on the shoulder like a friend. They sat at table and ate food together, a sacrament of brotherhood. Waymouth taught Tisquantum things he needed to know. Those were not the acts of a wizard. "I thought he loved me as a friend," reflected Tisquantum. "How could he do this to me?"

There was no end to the English demands; they had no sensitivity to the personal needs of those they exploited. World-weary, life-weary, he simply refused to talk. He gazed long hours at the fire that wasn't burning.

12. The Strength of Gluskabe

"I prefer not to." —Herman Melville,
Bartleby, the Scrivener

With a start, Tisquantum realized that Captain Waymouth had kept him away from other Englishmen. There was no one else Tisquantum could turn to. Without a rope, Waymouth had taken him away from his old friend, Henry Challons, who had gone back to Plymouth Fort to write a report for Sir Ferdinando Gorges.

He and Challons had rowed a boat and eaten sausage together. They had sailed to London together. Tisquantum had developed a feeling of trust and love for Henry Challons. Now, he feared he might never see Henry again. That made him sad, for Henry had helped him get out of ail.

Draghan had once said to him: "A prison isn't always made of stone walls and bars on the doors. When a big man carries a big stick, you have to do what he wants, or get beaten to death."

Captain Waymouth had not allowed him to

make other friends among the English. It was a kind of control. He did not have to carry a big stick; but it was still power.

The English had all the big sticks in their hands, all the lances and muskets. They had the food in their hands, too: they could choose how much a man ate, and what he ate, even if he would eat or starve. That, too, was a big stick.

They extended or withdrew their friendship and camaraderie like weapons, too. What was a poor Tisquantum to do, with no family or clan, no food of his own and no magic to get any, with no hands that would pick up the weapons that lay on the dirt in front of him?

He looked at the bow and arrow beside his fake fire. It was a Passamaquoddy bow of witch hazel, with a double sinew string knotted through a hole at each end; the straight, ash arrow had a bone point, suitable for hunting small animals like woodchucks or large birds like turkeys.

At close range, with good luck, he could drive one arrow into one Englishman, even if he wasn't a warrior; and then, what would he do? They would draw their swords, or point their muskets and he would be dead.

Survive. He had to survive. Above all else, he had to survive, as his people had survived. Hunger had come to the people. Cold repeatedly attacked them. The All-Destroyer was always lurking in the north, waiting to catch them when they were sad. And always the people fought back by surviving.

The All-Destroyer had all the big sticks but one. He said to the people, "Die! Die!"

And the people said, "We prefer not to."

***

"Come on, Squantum," said George Waymouth. "You've got to talk. This thing won't work its spell for us if you don't talk."

"I prefer not to," said Tisquantum. He felt weary and hopeless. His whole body hung heavy against the earth. Even his fingernails felt heavy. He closed his eyes; Gluskabe, the All-Maker, jumped into his mind, ready to destroy him.

He tried to open his eyes, then stopped resisting. He let the dream remain. What did it matter? He was not even afraid. If Gluskabe wanted to obliterate him, he had no power to stop it.

In addition to being the creator of all things, Gluskabe was also a great warrior. He had defeated the race of giants, the tribe of magicians, all the sorcerers, wicked spirits, goblins, fiends of the night, cannibals, and witches.

Gluskabe puffed up like a grouse and said to his sister, "There is none I cannot conquer."

His sister only laughed and said, "Are you sure, Mr. Puff? There is yet one who is unconquered, and even you cannot overcome him."

"Oh, really?" said Gluskabe. "Who is this mighty one? Bring him on, that I might prove him inferior to me."

"You don't want to do that," said his sister. "I'd strongly advise you to have nothing to do with Wasis. That is what he is called: Wasis."

"Bring him on!" shouted Gluskabe, his eyes sparking fire.

Wasis was only a baby, who sat on the floor, sucking a lump of maple sugar and crooning a little song, "Goo, goo," to himself.

Now, Gluskabe did not have a wife and children; so he knew nothing of how to manage a child. With perfect confidence, he commanded the baby, "Come to me."

Wasis smiled at Gluskabe, and said "Goo, Goo," but he did not move.

Gluskabe imitated the call of the most beautiful bird he could think of, the most beautiful song in the forest. "Come to me," said the song.

Wasis hardly looked up, as he continued sucking his lump of maple sugar.

Gluskabe imitated the look of a beautiful landscape, a golden sun rising over a placid sea and luxurious trees, where deer and mountain goats gamboled. "Come to me," said the magic of the forest.

Still, Wasis gave him no attention.

A thing like this had never happened to Gluskabe before, and this— this— Wasis infuriated him. His eyes widened, his breath came in gulps, and he cried out in anger: "You little beast! Don't you know who I am? I said 'Come to me,' and I meant 'Come to me.'" He bulged out his muscles so that the earth rumbled. He flashed lightning from his eyes and repeated, "I demand you come to me at once."

Wasis burst into a howl and tears, which drowned out even Gluskabe's thundering, but he would not budge in spite of any threat.

Gluskabe puffed up as big as the sky and called on all the magic in the universe. He recited the formulas of power and the incantations of success, even the spells that could raise the dead, but still Wasis sat on the floor, whimpering, sucking his maple sugar, and looking a little bored.

At last, in despair, Gluskabe rushed from the wigwam, out the door and beyond the sky, leaving the earth forever, while Wasis sang to himself his little song, "Goo, goo."

And to this day, the people say that when a

baby croons to himself, "Goo, Goo," he is remembering the time he conquered the All-Maker Gluskabe.

Tisquantum emerged from the dream, feeling a new strength, a strength he had never had.

Tisquantum slowly became aware of his surroundings.

The hall in London where he sat was not well lit. The air of the city was full of soot from two million coal fires and the fog that came every night, holding the dirty air down like a blanket. The room was full of people, coughing and breathing through perfumed handkerchiefs. Many of them had the lung-sickness. It was no place to survive. It was no place to find help.

"Make them think it is to their advantage to help you," Draghan said again in Tisquantum's mind. "Make them think it is their idea to do what you desire."

"How?" said Tisquantum aloud.

"How?" echoed a man in a gray waistcoat. "Is that a greeting? Is that the way you say 'hello'?"

The man in the gray waistcoat was leaning forward, his puffy, pink face near Tisquantum's. His side-whiskers hung like pieces of meat on a stick over an open fire. "How?" said the man.

"'How?'" echoed Tisquantum.

"Hey, hey! Listen, everyone! The savage is conversing," yelled the man in the gray waistcoat. He leaned again into Tisquantum's face. "How?"

Tisquantum ignored him. Behind the man, a woman was carrying a baby. Tisquantum stood up and reached for the baby. Reluctantly, the woman allowed him to take the baby in his arms, but the baby began at once to scream and cry. He squirmed and looked for his mother. Tisquantum handed the baby back.

"See?" he said to the man in the gray waistcoat. "Baby, wizard. Baby, strongest person in world."

"Did you hear that?" yelled the man. "Did you all hear that? The savage is a philosopher. He says a baby is the strongest thing on earth. What a curious idea!"

When Captain George Waymouth returned, Tisquantum announced: "I have big dream. Tisquantum find totem. Find power-animal."

"That's nice," said Waymouth, pulling his cloak in tightly.

"Tisquantum have strength of baby."

13. "You Send Tisquantum Home?"

> "Work is work, my friend. It makes no difference which servant does it. If you get hungry enough, you too will learn to plant corn."
> —John Slaney

When John Slaney heard of Waymouth's "Indian Show," he put a stop to it at once. He retrieved his birch-bark canoe and other artifacts and took possession of Tisquantum. When Waymouth objected, Slaney merely commented that Tisquantum belonged to Sir Ferdinando Gorges and the estate of Sir John Popham, and, as treasurer of their "New England Company for Exploration and Trade," he, Slaney, was responsible for protecting their interests. An "Indian Show" was hardly in their best interests.

So Tisquantum moved to John Slaney's household in the Cheapside district of London, where Tisquantum took an interest in the horses in Slaney's stable. Slaney allowed his children and his hostler to teach Tisquantum about horses—how to care for the children's ponies, how to lead them with a rope, how to harness them, how to drive them in harness, even how to ride in a saddle.

Tisquantum was shocked to find a man working in the kitchen garden. "Woman work," he said.

Slaney just laughed and said, "Work is work, my friend. It makes no difference which servant does it. If you get hungry enough, you too will learn to plant corn."

Tisquantum was startled by Slaney's habit of speaking in proverbs; it reminded him of Draghan. So Tisquantum went against his tribal traditions and watched as the gardener put kitchen scraps in the hills where he planted vegetables. "Tis food fer the plant, it is," explained the gardener. "If ye don't manure, yer plants will come to naught, come to naught."

Tisquantum nodded his understanding of the magic, for the Wampanoag understood that good soil is necessary for plant growth. That was why they moved their fields to new grounds every four years.

Evenings, after supper, Slaney often invited a number of friends in, to talk with Tisquantum. Over a glass of good Madeira, Tisquantum asked for and got explanations of things he did not understand, and the guests were very curious about American native customs and practices.

"Long ago and far away," Tisquantum told Slaney's guests one night, "Gluskabe, the All-Maker. He live on earth. No other spirits. Just him.

"One day, he walk by sea. Water make air moist. Wind make dirt foam on water. Sun shine on foam and make a baby. Poof! Up stand a young man. 'Hello, Mother's-Brother,' he say to Gluskabe. 'Hello, Uncle.'"

Many of the men in the audience smiled at the savage's naïve notion of reproduction and peeked at the low-cut bodices of the women.

"'Hello, Great-Nephew,' say Gluskabe.

"Great-Nephew, he stay with Gluskabe. Become big helper. They do everything together. They make deer. They make bear. They make all we see.

"One day, Gluskabe and Great-Nephew stand by plant they make. Beautiful green plant. Big leaves. Dew from sky fall onto leaf and run down to stem. Little tiny pinch of dirt down there, between leaf and stem. At high noon, sun warm dirt and dew in crotch of plant, and up come a beautiful woman. Like Great-Nephew, she born of earth, air, sun, water.

"'I am Love,' she say. 'I am Strength-Giver. I

am All-Nourisher. I give love and strength to all men and animals. They all love me.'"

Women in the audience fanned themselves quickly and glanced at their men, as if to say "I told you so."

"Gluskabe and Great-Nephew, they thank Great Mystery Above for send them beautiful woman. Great-Nephew, he marry Strength-Giver, and they have babies. Gluskabe, he teach babies how to live. Gluskabe teach humans all they need to know. Then Gluskabe go away. He live far to North, because he not needed. He come back when he needed.

"First-Mother and Great-Nephew, they make many babies. Many, many people. Live all over earth. They hunt deer. They hunt turkey. They live by hunting. Then, too many people; not enough deer. People go hungry. People get thin. Some starve. First-Mother, she weep, because these her children, and world not have enough strength to give them.

"'We hungry,' say children. 'Feed us.' But First-Mother not got something to give them. So she weep. Weep, weep, weep.

"She say, 'Be patient. I make food. Then your little bellies be full.'

"Great-Nephew, he say to First-Mother, 'How I make you smile? How I make you happy?'

"First-Mother say, 'Only one thing. Only one thing stop tears.'

"'What?' say Great-Nephew. 'What? I do.'

"'You kill me,' say First-Mother. 'You must kill me.'

"'No, No,' say Great-Nephew. 'I not kill you. I not can kill you.'

"'You have to,' say First-Mother. 'You have to kill me, or I go on weeping and grieving forever.'

"Great-Nephew, he go away. He go to end of earth, all the way up north. He say, 'Uncle, Great Mother's-Brother, what I do?"

"Gluskabe, he say, 'You do what she want. You must kill her.'

"So now Great-Nephew, he weep. He not want kill wife.

"First-Mother, she tell them how. 'Tomorrow. High Noon. You kill me,' she say. 'Then, two of our sons take my hair in hands. Drag body over empty patch of earth. Drag me back and forth, until all my flesh ripped off my body. Then bury my bones in middle of field. After that, you must leave this place for growing season.'"

"Great-Nephew weep. Their sons weep. All the people weep.

"First-Mother smile and say. 'Wait seven months. Come back. You find my flesh in field. My flesh, I give out of love. It nourish you, give you strength forever and ever.'

"Great-Nephew do what she say. Their sons do what she say. They kill her and drag flesh off her bones. Bury bones. Go away, weeping."

Women in the audience put their dainty hands to the soft flesh of their breasts, imagining their flesh being torn from their bodices.

"After seven moons, they come back. All the children, all the children's children. They find earth covered with plants. Tall green plants, tassels at the top. Between leaf and stalk is fruit of plant: corn, First-Mother's flesh come back. Her Spirit say to them, 'Save some to plant later'; so they save some. Then they eat First-Mother's flesh. Very sweet. Very good. Strength. Love. We eat First-Mother's strength and love, when we eat corn.

"Where bones buried is another plant. Big leaves, green. Tobacco.

First-Mother's spirit say to them, 'Burn this up. Smoke it. It is sacred. It is my breath. It clear your minds. It help your prayers. It gladden your hearts.'

"And People happy to be nourished.

"'Remember,' say spirit of First-Mother, 'Take good care of corn, because it is First-Mother's flesh. It is her goodness turned to food. Take good care tobacco, because it is her breath, because it is her love turned into smoke. When you smoke or eat, you know that First-Mother gives her life so that you can live. Yet, First-Mother is not dead. She live in smoke. She live in corn. She live in undying love. She live in strength. She live in nourishing.'"

A moment after Tisquantum had finished the tale, the guests broke into spontaneous applause and added exclamations like "That was wonderful!" "How touching!" "How interesting!" and the like.

There was no little rope separating him from the guests, but they sounded just like one of Waymouth's crowds.

Tisquantum stared into his wine glass. The sadness collected there in the bottom of the glass would not let his mind go.

"You send Tisquantum home?" he asked Slaney. "You send Tisquantum to Patuxet. Tisquantum lonesome for Wampanoag relatives. Almost seven years, not see mother and father. Tisquantum want to be where ancestors are."

"Why, yes," said Slaney. "I see no reason why we shouldn't send you home. I'll write to Sir Ferdinando Gorges and see what he says. A man's heart is happiest near his own hearth."

In the bottom of the wine glass, Tisquantum

could almost see an encampment of many dusky people dancing around a fire, people who traveled and belonged together, ate together, sang songs together. People who knew their grandfathers and where the grandfathers had come from. Sad beyond the events of the moment, he broke into what he could remember of the wild and wailing *"Tshurkaki Dgili."*

After a few verses, he translated for his English friends, knowing they could not distinguish Romani from Wampanoag:

> *By the shores at Sitges, Kuma*
> *camped by shining, big-sea water,*
> *ifty vurdon led by Tshurka-Kuma,*
> *Tshurka-Kuma great patriarch of the tribe,*
> *great grandfather of patriarch of the tribe,*
> *long remembered in song.*

14. "Next Season, with the First Ship

"I meet your ships when they come to Patuxet. Each summer, when trading season comes, I stand on shore and heart leap up when I see ship. I go with your captains. I be your voice in trade."

In the summer of 1611, Tisquantum was allowed to return to Plymouth Fort near Lands End and the custody of Sir Ferdinando Gorges. It had been almost five years since Tisquantum had sailed from that port with Captain Henry Challons, bound for the New England coast, but ended up in the Seville jail.

"You've become quite a traveler since I saw you last, Assaquamet," said Sir Ferdinando, touching his moist mouth with his perfumed handkerchief. "Spain, Marseilles, London."

"Not see much," said Tisquantum, who added, "My name is Tisquantum. Not Assaquantem. Assaquantem is Passamaquoddy name." He fingered a stone is his pocket, a good luck stone he had picked up near John Slaney's stable.

"Well, Tisquantum, Assaquamet, Squantum, Squanto; I guess I'll always get them mixed up. Your English has improved considerably since you've been in London."

"You will send me home? To Patuxet?" asked Tisquantum, caressing the stone. "Where is Henry Challons? He take me home, no? My heart is heavy with the home-sickness. Eight summers pass since I last saw my parents and relatives. I want to take a squaw, and plant corn, and live among people I know."

"But I can't let you quit on me now. You're too valuable a man. You know the language too well. We want you to be our interpreter with all the Natives on the New England coast."

Tisquantum hesitated. He had been a prisoner for many years: first among the Passamaquoddy, then with Sir Ferdinando, then on the Spanish ship and in the Seville jail; even in Marseilles where there were no bars on the doors, he was not free to go wherever he wanted. His liberty in London had certainly been limited.

And, now, he was again within the confines of Plymouth Fort and under the control of Sir Ferdinando. What was he to do? He was tired of the English and their exploitations of him. He wanted to get away from being handled with a rope, even imaginary ropes like that of Sir

Ferdinando Gorges.

But how could he get back to Patuxet? He remembered Tahanedo got back to Pemaquid by telling the English things that misled them. And Draghan's advice was, "Tell them what they want to know. If they think it's to their benefit, they'll do what you want them to. Fool 'em."

He saw that he would have to be the voice of the English in America, but he did not need to be their voice in England.

"Of course, Sir Ferdinando," Tisquantum said, "I still be your guide and talk for you. I meet your ships when they come to Patuxet. Each summer, when trading season comes, I stand on shore and heart leap up when I see ship. I go with your captains. I be your voice in trade. I give up hunt for meat. You pay me in trade goods, I buy meat from others who hunt."

"Well, that might work. Ummm…"

"Then I spend winters with my people. You don't have to feed me."

"Yes. You're right. That is a certain expense."

"I look out from shore with happy face when your ship arrive. I get to speak English again. Eat peas and porridge. Wear good English shirt and trousers." He pinched up a fold of his peasant shirt between his thumb and forefinger.

"Yes, yes. I think you're right. That would work out. I'll send you home."

"Good. I thank Sir Ferdinando." He attempted a receding bow, the way he had seen Englishmen do.

"But it will have to be next season," Gorges went on. "The winds have already changed this year, and you just can't sail that way. Ships are blown off course, or have to turn back. You know about that, I suppose."

Tisquantum smiled, nodding. He had no desire to be captured again by Spaniards after a storm.

"Next season, with the first ship, I'll send you out. When the trading is done for the season, I'll tell the Captain to leave you on the New England coast."

"Near Patuxet?"

"Yes. Yes, this will work out best for everybody."

15. "Let Them Tie my Hands," 1611

"Their greed blinds them, just as your anger blinds you. They will believe the greatest of fabrications, if they think their avarice will be satisfied. It blinds their hearts."

When the ships came in fom the New England coast that fall, Sir Ferdinando Gorges had five new captive American native s. One of his Captains, Edward Harlow, had been "making fish" off Cape Cod preparatory to setting sail for England, when he put in at Nauset Harbor. Harlow discovered there a *pow-wow*. He and his men overpowered five men and took them away.

"Quite a catch, I'd say," boasted Captain Edward Harlow. "This fellow," he gestured to a tall, strong man, "is Epanow, sachem of Capawack Island, what we call Martha's Vineyard. We had quite a time, getting him tied. The only other one of note is this man— I'd say he is in his fifties— Cawnacamón. He is chief of Manomet, a village on the mainland, west side of Cape Cod Bay."

Gorges put Epanow in locked quarters, then

called Tisquantum. "Here's a visitor from your part of the world," said Sir Ferdinando, waving his handkerchief. "His name is Apenow, Epanuff, or something; I can't understand him. I'll just lock the door while you two get acquainted."

Epanow was tall, even by English standards, and strong and thick through the shoulders, almost a small giant. In captivity, he had not been able to wear the face-paint that was his war-totem, nor did he now have the feathers in his hair that designated his rank. They had dressed him in Irish trousers and a great-coat.

He eyed with suspicion the dusky stranger in peasant's clothing. His hands were still tied behind his back, for the English bound the natives any time they had to move them from one room to another. He muttered a little magic formula that cursed his enemies and protected himself.

When the English guards were gone, Tisquantum touched the small stone he carried in his pocket for good luck and said in Wampanoag, "I am Tisquantum, from Patuxet. I have been a prisoner of the Yang-kaysh about six years."

Epanow's face brightened, for he understood. Tisquantum's Wampanoag was a dialect of his own language. "Untie me," he demanded.

As soon as Tisquantum did so, Epanow

dashed to the door and jerked at the handle.

"It's no use, Grandfather," said Tisquantum, using the term of respect for an elder or leader. "They have fastened the door. It will not open. And they will have guards outside with muskets and lances. Even if you could get passed the door and the guards, you would be in a land where you cannot speak the language. You would be unable to protect yourself against cold and hunger or witches and demons. That is as much a prison as this."

"Whose side are you on, anyway?" asked Epanow. "This is no way to treat the Head Man of Capawack Island."

Tisquantum smiled, impressed by the man's pride and strength. How could he make a chief understand what was in his best interest? "Look at it this way, Grandfather: The English are very powerful. It makes no difference to them how important or brave you are on your home grounds. To them, you are just another prisoner. They treated Tahanedo of Pemaquid the same way."

"I heard about him," admitted Epanow. "I heard they took him home after one winter."

"Yes, and they were sending me home, later that year, but the wind blew us away." He briefly related the capture by Spaniards, the time spent in the Seville jail, the time in Marseilles and London.

"Sir Ferdinando has promised to send me home with the first ship next spring."

"The skunks lie, as well as stink!" said Epanow. "They steal people away from their homes. They take wood, water, deer, and turkeys from the woods, as it pleases them. They kill people if the idea happens to enter their heads. They are not to be trusted."

Tisquantum rubbed the stone in his pocket for courage. "But when they have the muskets in their hands, you have no choice but to play their game," said Tisquantum, suddenly surprised at how much what he said sounded like a Romani proverb, even in Wampanoag.

"No! No!" shouted Epanow. "It's not to be tolerated! How dare they treat a man this way!"

"Your anger blinds you, my friend. Look at it this way: You are thirty-five days journey away from your home— that is, if you get a good wind and a good ship. You do not know how to sail on the ocean; you do not even know which way to start. You are in a strange land, among people who do not care if you starve or live. Your anger will only put bile into your own stomach. It will eat at your heart. It will eat at your mind. Your anger harms only yourself."

"I am Epanow, sachem of Capawack Island. Even the Narragansetts quake when I am angry."

Tisquantum rubbed his stone, smiled at the man's stubbornness, saying, "I do not doubt that. When I have crossed the ocean, I will inform them of your anger and watch them quail."

"You are awfully fresh, aren't you? And such a young man, not over thirty-one or -two summers. Don't you realize that I am Epanow, sachem of Capawack Island? And I deserve a better respect!"

"On Capawack, I will bend my knee to you," said Tisquantum, making a slight English bow. "Here in this prison at Plymouth Fort, I am more powerful than you. I speak their language. I understand some of their wants. You may have to depend upon me before you get out of here."

Epanow did not respond. He went to the narrow window and looked at it. It was too small for a man as big and strong as he to squeeze through.

"Besides," added Tisquantum, as if reading his thoughts, "there is likely to be a man outside, a man with a musket. Even if you could get through this crack they call a window, you could not get far."

Epanow was silent. He clenched and unclenched his big fists with his fury.

"You have a choice, Grandfather. If you want the English to tie your hands with a rope when they take us to their table to eat, they will do so. If you wish it, you can walk with your hands swinging free."

"How?" demanded Epanow.

"By pretending to serve their wants."

"Pretend?! Pretend?! I am a sachem. I do not pretend!"

"Your resistance does not serve their wants, that is true. But then, neither does it serve yours."

Epanow just stared a moment at Tisquantum, as he realized that the young man was right. He nodded an acknowledgment, ever so slightly.

"Let me become your counselor, grandfather," Tisquantum went on, holding tight to the stone in his pocket. "Let me become your advisor. The English are greedy. They will do anything to satisfy their greed."

Epanow stood, waiting.

"Tahanedo made them believe that their greed would be best served if he were at Pemaquid, rather than at Plymouth. And they took him home. I do not know how he fared after he got back to Pemaquid, but he told us who were his fellow captives that we should mislead the English at every turn.

"We were to give them directions that seemed sensible, but led to the wrong destination.

We were to lead them to supplies that turned out to be meager. With smiles on our faces and seeming friendship, we were to lead them on a chase that ended with no goose."

"Impossible!" said Epanow. "They will not believe such lies."

"Oh, but they do," insisted Tisquantum, holding out his empty hands, as if to show he concealed nothing. "Their greed blinds them, just as your anger blinds you. They will believe the greatest of fabrications, if they think their avarice will be satisfied. It blinds their hearts."

Epanow scoffed, but said, "Go on."

"If you want to get back to Capawack, Grandfather, you must make them believe that they will benefit more from the trip than you will. Make them believe that you will not benefit at all. You must make them think they will get rich by taking you there. You must learn enough of their language to understand what they think riches are and then slyly suggest that you know where such treasure lies. You must use their greed to manipulate them."

"Then I will be no better than a lying Englishman."

"When they hold the stick, you have to take the trail they point to."

"Aaugh, say no more," scoffed Epanow. "You

have become an Englishman. You have traded your Wampanoag soul for a tiny little English spirit. Do not talk to me. I have nothing more to say to you."

"I am sorry to hear that, Grandfather. Perhaps, someday, you will hear the truth in what I say. Let their own gullibility and greed do your work for you. Tell them what they want to hear."

Epanow held his wrists together in front of him. "Let them tie my hands when they take me to eat."

16. "Like Stars in the Winter Sky"

"As in all humanaffairs, there is nothing more certain than the uncertainty thereof..."
— Sir Ferdinando Gorges, *"The Discovery and Plantation of New England"* (1672)

When Captain Nicholas Hobson returned at the end of the 1612 season, he reported to Gorges that he had left Tisquantum on Newfoundland. "The winds prevented us from going westward toward Pemaquid or Cape Cod, but we thought Tisquantum might catch a ride we hadn't expected. He seemed to be familiar with the island and even spoke the local language. Captain Guy assured me he would take good care of your native."

"Best you could do?" asked Gorges.

"Aye, Sir. A fierce wind forced us east almost to the Bahamas. We were lucky to touch Newfoundland on the way back."

When Epanow heard the news, he began to change his mind about Tisquantum's advice. The fellow's guile had worked for him; perhaps it would also work for Epanow.

That winter, three of the Wampanoags died of pneumonia. Epanow, and Cawnacamón were still healthy, but Epanow decided he would have to do something soon, or he might also die of the English air. He began talking more with Sir Ferdinando Gorges and one of his Captains, Edward Harlow, who had originally kidnaped Epanow and the other four.

He was learning their language and trying to figure out what they valued most. It was not food, nor clothing, nor a house to live in; it was the gold coins they collected. For bags of gold, they would lie, and cheat each other, and perhaps even kill. But where the gold coins came from and how they came into being baffled Epanow.

Epanow noticed that common sailors and guards also coveted the coins. He observed that a sailor, when given a coin, would bite it, putting a dent in it with his teeth. This seemed to satisfy him, to prove to him and others that the coin was genuine. But still Epanow could not understand how the coins got into the little leather bags in the first place.

Then, he saw Sir Ferdinando pour out on a black velvet cloth a mixture of gold nuggets and coins. He noticed the nuggets had teeth marks in them also. "How?" he asked. "Shining rocks ...

coins ... same bag?"

"Yes," said Sir Ferdinando, laughing. "The coins are made from the nuggets. We melt the gold and pour it in a mold to make the coins."

"Same?" said Epanow, trying to look surprised. Then he tried a daring move: he asked the guard for the knife at his belt (Sir Ferdinando nodded his consent, waving his handkerchief), and Epanow pressed the knife through the nugget on the table.

"Jeezus! Did you see that?!" exclaimed Sir Ferdinando to the others who were watching, including Harlow. "The fellow is sure strong!"

"Same," pronounced Epanow, tossing the pieces back onto the velvet cloth and laying down the knife. "Rock ... no use. Many rock ... no use ... on Capawack."

Sir Ferdinando and Harlow suddenly leaned forward and gazed at Epanow. Sir Ferdinando picked up one piece of the nugget Epanow had sliced, held it out in his hand, and, when he spoke, his voice was different, more husky, "Rock ... like this?"

Epanow was taken by surprise. Tisquantum had not told him that you can see their hunger in their eyes and hear it in their voices.

"Many rocks ... like this? On Capawack?" asked Harlow, also in a dusky voice.

"Yes," said Epanow. "Many rock ... like this ... no use." He shifted his feet and looked toward the door. "When ... we eat? I hungry."

"Guard, go out and get Chief Epanow some roast beef," said Sir Ferdinando. "And some bread."

"Bring beer," added Epanow.

The guard looked at Sir Ferdinando, who nodded. "Yes, sir. Shall I take my knife?"

"Yes. We'll be all right."

"Where ... rocks of no use?" asked Harlow. His voice sounded wet to Epanow.

"Where on Capawack?" asked Sir Ferdinando, his voice also wet.

"In hole ... by ..." He paused, searching for a word in his limited vocabulary. "By ... where water run."

"By a stream," prompted Harlow.

"In hole ... in stream," said Epanow. "Big hole," he added, immediately afraid he was overdoing the story.

"Big hole?" grunted Sir Ferdinando.

"How big hole?" asked Harlow.

Epanow looked around for something to compare. "Two ... this room ..."

"Twice the size of this room. Yes. Go on,"

said Harlow.

"Many rock ... in water," said Epanow.

"How many rocks ... in water?" asked Sir Ferdinando.

"Many ... many," said Epanow, pausing to find a comparison. "Like stars in winter sky."

Sir Ferdinando and Captain Edward Harlow both sighed and slumped back in their seats.

The guard brought the roast beef and bread, so Epanow began eating, as if he had no interest at all in the conversation.

"Uhh, Chief," said Sir Ferdinando, leaning forward and touching his moist lips with his handkerchief. "Can you show us where these holes in stream are?"

Epanow shook his head, "No," his mouth full of beef and bread. When he swallowed, he explained. "Holes on Capawack. Epanow here." He took another big bite of the beef and bread. "Beer?" he asked, looking at the guard.

"He means ..." said Harlow, glancing at Sir Ferdinando, who nodded. "He means ... we take you to Capawack ... you show us holes."

Epanow swallowed. "Why? Rock ... no use.... Too soft."

"Not too soft for us," said Sir Ferdinando, his voice catching on a bubble. "We trade," he went on, after clearing his throat. "We take you to Capawack in Spring. You show us holes where no-use rocks. Yes?"

"All right," said Epanow, biting into the beef again, as if food were all that mattered in the world.

"Yes," said Harlow, rocking on his heels. "I can be ready to sail on the March wind. My rigging is more than half-worn, and some of the sail-cloth also has to be replaced. But I'll speed up the work to make the ship shape, and we can surely lay in enough supplies by then."

"Yes," said Sir Ferdinando, "Yes. Fifty-fifty, Ed?"

Harlow only nodded.

"You take Cawnacamón?" asked Epanow. "He my friend."

"Yes," said Sir Ferdinando. "Yes, we can take Cawnacamón, too. Does he know of soft rock in his territory, too?"

Epanow shrugged to indicate he knew nothing of Cawnacamón's area. He went on chewing his beef. "No beer?" he asked the guard.

Afterwards, in the room where he slept, Epanow allowed himself to smile inwardly. And he appreciated the advice Tisquantum had given.

The fellow had been right, except he didn't

tell Epanow that you could smell the swampy stench of English greed. But he was right about the main thing: their greed would lead them to believe the wildest of fabrications— useless rocks, like stars in the winter sky, indeed!

***

Captain Edward Harlow sailed on the first fair wind of March, 1614, with Epanow and Cawnacamón aboard. The passage out went without major problem. To please Epanow, Harlow agreed to put Cawnacamón ashore at Nauset Harbor. "Get word to my people," Epanow told him in their own language. "Tell them to be ready to make war on this ship."

Cawnacamón nodded. "I hope we will meet again, brother."

"We will," said Epanow. "I feel certain we will. Fare you well, and choose a fast runner."

Harlow had some trouble getting around Monomoy Point and through Nantucket Sound because of strong head winds, but finally he came to the harbor on the north side of Martha's Vineyard. As soon as the ship was well within the harbor, natives in canoes began paddling close, behind them, on both sides, everywhere. Some of the natives were armed with bows and arrows, but not all of them by any means.

However, they did not offer any baskets of

food for trade.

"God be damned!" exclaimed Harlow. "There must be a hundred of 'em. Keep a close watch on the chief, you hear. And get out the muskets; we may need them."

Harlow had dressed Epanow in a large, loose coat with three buckles and baggy, flowing sleeves, thinking he would be easy to grab if anything happened. Suddenly, the chief lifted both his arms. The sailor on either side of him obediently grabbed a sleeve. Epanow slammed his arms together across his chest; the two sailors smashed face—on and crumpled to the deck.

In a moment, Epanow had unbuckled the great-coat, shucked it off, and was jumping over the rail of the ship, yelling to his tribesmen in the water, "Kill the white-faces!"

The natives who had not seemed to be armed picked up their bows from the bottoms of canoes. A shower of arrows suddenly fluttered at all sides of the ship; most of the sailors looking over the rail were hit at least once.

Harlow later reported to Gorges that several of them were killed before they had time enough to charge their muskets, though he did not give a number. So many were wounded that he had barely enough sailors to man the sails, and he was forced to withdraw, defeated.

The natives paddled rapidly out of musket range. Epanow was still swimming alongside a canoe, his powerful arms lashing up a wake. Finally, he grabbed the edge of a canoe, gave a robust frog kick, shot up out of the water, turned, and landed on his back in the middle of the canoe. Looking up, he cried out, "Like stars in the winter sky!" and burst into a huge laugh.

His tribesmen looked at each other, baffled, wondering what was so funny.

17. "Home to Patuxet?"

"Because of you, we will take Captain Hunt by the arm in friendship. Tell him he is welcome at Lower Nauset. And if he comes again, he will find friends in my town."

— Ohquamehud, of Lower Nauset

Late in 1613, Tisquantum returned to England from Newfoundland, having been unable to find a ship bound for the New England coast. He met Captain John Smith, who was then working for Sir Ferdinando Gorges. Smith was rather famous for his writings on Virginia and his map of Chesapeake Bay and the Virginia Tidelands, which included an engraved portrait of himself with his medium beard, neatly trimmed.

Gorges saw Smith as a skillful sailor and effective administrator, but a repulsive braggart. He was sending Smith out the next season with two ships to make a map of the New England coast. In his spare time, he was to find the gold mines of New England, catch whales and codfish, trade for what furs he could, and bring back as much knowledge as he could of the New England natives from Penobscot to Cape Cod.

"Tisquantum go with Captain Smith, please? Home to Patuxet?" In the brightly colored shirts he tended to prefer, he looked like an English Gypsy in the prime of his life. He touched the small bead of corn pollen he had sewn into the edge of his collar.

Smith knew a few hundred words of Virginian Algonquin, from his time in the Jamestown colony. With that knowledge and hand signs, he thought he could make himself understood all along the New England coast. Besides, he knew from reports that the natives in all these parts knew a few words of broken English, Dutch, and French, which they had learned from explorers, traders, pirates, and fishermen. His ego-confidence was large enough to make him believe he could do the job alone.

"As-a-comet does know that coast," Gorges pointed out, waving his handkerchief vaguely in the direction of New England. "He has lived there, traveled it, speaks a number of the languages. He would be valuable as a guide."

Smith was an outspoken man and a strong critic of ineptitude, but for once, he let himself be schooled by Sir Ferdinando Gorges, not just because Gorges was paying the bills. Smith knew and respected Gorges as a forceful soldier in Queen Elizabeth's French wars and a capable administrator of Plymouth Fort near Lands End. He rather liked Gorges, in spite of the slack jaw and over-eating.

"Aye," he conceded. "Your Squanto will be a great help. I can't be playing nursemaid to all of the crew all of the time. When some of the men go ashore without me, they'll need an interpreter. And when we have filled our holds and completed our survey, we can leave him there at his home. That's the idea, eh?"

"Yes, that's the idea. He'll be our contact man, guide, and future interpreter in New England." Gorges dabbed at his moist lips.

"Welcome to my crew, Squanto," said Smith, taking the American Native by the hand. "Think ye can pull a rope, hoist a sail?"

"All the way home to Patuxet," said Squantum, smiling.

***

On the third of March, 1614, John Smith sailed from Plymouth Harbor with two of Sir Ferdinando Gorges' ships. Captain Smith commanded the larger ship, while Thomas Hunt was master of the smaller. Hunt was a small, squint-eyed man, with more interest in personal gain than in benefits to the company or mankind, but he was a capable seaman.

Gorges appointed John Smith Commander-in-chief of the voyage, an office for which Smith gave himself the title, "Admiral of New England." Such self-aggrandizing gestures often made Smith the target of other men's jealousies.

To catch the most favorable winds, "Admiral" Smith took the southern route across the Atlantic, from Grand Canary Island to the West Indies, believing that his numbers were sufficient defense against the many pirates of many nations that hunted in those waters. They turned north on good winds and struck land at Cape Cod, as Captain Bartholomew Gosnold had named it for the good fishing he discovered there in 1602. In 1607, Gosnold was commander of the three ships that landed the settlers at Jamestown.

Smith was not a total stranger to these waters. In 1609, when he left the Jamestown colony because of a gunpowder burn, and because he had openly criticized the incompetent gentlemen in charge, he sailed up the New England coast to the Penobscot river, then across to Newfoundland, and on to England. His rough charts were part of what convinced Sir Ferdinando Gorges to sponsor the present voyage of exploration, discovery, map-making, fishing, and trade.

Smith stopped south of Nauset harbor to

take on water and wood and to shoot a deer or two, so the men could have fresh meat after the long voyage. In his red peasant shirt, Tisquantum led Captain Thomas Hunt and a group of armored men on a shore party. They were soon met by a small army of Nauset Indians led by Ohquamehud, sachem of Lower Nauset.

Tisquantum hailed them in Wampanoag. "Aha. *Towam!* I am Tisquantum of Patuxet."

Ohquamehud was startled by the dusky stranger in a red shirt and white trousers speaking a language he understood. He touched the protective talisman in his necklace and looked closer at the foreigner.

"Why are you with these accursed yang-kaysh?" asked Ohquamehud, suspiciously. "They take away our people, and we never see them again."

"They took me away," admitted Tisquantum, "but now I am returning to Patuxet. They are taking me home."

"Patuxet? Are you from Patuxet?"

"Yes, I was born there, but I have not been there for nine years. These English friends are returning me to my home."

"I see," said Ohquamehud. "They put Cawnacamón of Manomet ashore near Nauset earlier this year. He told us the yang-kaysh were taking Epanow back to Capawack Island. Were you captured at the same time as Epanow and Cawnacamón?"

"No. I was taken from Pemaquid, far to the north. I saw Epanow and Cawnacamón in England."

"Then are you the one who helped Cawnacamón and Epanow?"

"Probably," said Tisquantum. "I gave them advice about how to deal with Englishmen." He gestured toward Thomas Hunt and the hunters.

Ohquamehud noticed them, as if for the first time. "Are these the same men who stole five men from the pow-wow in my town three years ago?"

"No. That was Captain Edward Harlow. They told me he was bringing Epanow back to Capawack."

Ohquamehud nodded, then turned to Thomas Hunt. "Three men from Lower Nauset are still missing. You are bringing back my tribesmen?"

After Tisquantum had translated, Hunt temporized, pretending to know nothing of the kidnaping, nor the men's death. "I had nothing to do with that," he said to Ohquamehud through Tisquantum. "I don't know where they are."

"I saw Epanow in England," Tisquantum told Ohquamehud. "I am glad that he has returned to his home."

"Cawnacamón told us of your advice and friendship," said Ohquamehud, nodding. "Because of you, we will take Captain Hunt by the arm in friendship. Tell him he is welcome at Lower Nauset. And if he comes again, he will find friends in my town."

"That's mighty nice of him," said Hunt, squinting. He gave Chief Ohquamehud a great-coat of gray worsted wool and a butcher knife with a long, curved blade, which melted the last sliver of the chief's resistance.

18. With Captain John Smith, 1614

"Know that we are ready to strike when we are provoked. If you turn your arrows toward us, we will be forced to turn our muskets toward you."

— Captain John Smith

Back on the ship, Squanto, as he called himself now, because Smith called him nothing else, wanted to be put ashore, so he could walk home to Patuxet.

"No, no, no," said Smith, taking him by the upper arm. "We'll come around to your coast bye and bye. And in the meantime, you are to guide my smaller boats and help us with trade. That was the agreement you made with Sir Ferdinando, wasn't it?"

"Yes," said Squanto, freeing his arm and touching the bead of pollen in his collar, "that was the agreement."

***

In mid-April, they put in at the harbor on the north side of Monhegan Island and found a ship belonging to Sir Francis Popham, a grandson of Sir John Popham who had tried to plant a colony in Maine. He had worked the Indian trade so hard that the natives had no more furs to trade. Still, the captains exchanged courtesies, drinking cider on each other's deck.

There on Monhegan Island, Squanto met tall, lean Samoset again. Samoset, the sagamore of Monhegan, greeted the Englishmen warmly, as usual, taking them by the hand and inviting them to his fire and food. He was always glad to pass on news of other ships that had passed his way—the Dutch fishermen, the French warships that were protecting the new French colonies at Acadia and the Quebec colony of New France, and the few English ships that came that way. And he was always glad to learn a few more words of English, or drink a pint of beer. "Samoset like beer," he declared.

He envied Tisquantum his travels and his control of the English language. Squanto had no status in Algonquin society, was not even a member of a ruling clan, yet Samoset was eager to eat and drink with him, so they could talk of foreign shores.

Samoset was curious about every aspect of European life. He wanted to know what clothes each nationality wore, what foods they ate, what songs they sang. When Squantum taught him to sing a verse of "Raise the Glass on High, Billy Bigh," they became firm friends. And he taught him the beginning of Tshurkaki-dgili: "By the shore at Sitges, Kuma camped by shining, big-sea water..."

"I want to go home to Patuxet," Tisquantum said, almost weeping in his beer. "Nine summers. I have been gone nine summers. My father must think I am dead."

"Soon," consoled Samoset. "When the English have loaded their ships, they will let you go home. Home to Patuxet."

Though it was nearing the end of the salmon season, Smith's men caught good quantities of Atlantic salmon in the Penobscot estuary and smoked or dried them. When the salmon diminished, Smith moved to the banks off Sagadahoc, where his men caught so many cod they could not dry them fast enough, and they ran out of salt to pack them in barrels. They had to stop fishing a few days to let the processing catch up.

In busy times and slack times alike, Smith sent scouting parties out in the small boats with navigational instruments to take sightings for making maps. Smith's mates, as well as Captain Thomas Hunt and his mates, all became surveyors and assistants in John Smith's explorations.

Squanto guided them, helping them talk with the natives, and spread cheerfulness and good will. Smith collated their several findings, verified some of them, and began assembling the most accurate map of the New England coast that had been made up to that time. Map-making and discovery were more important to Smith than cod-fishing, for, like Sir Ferdinando Gorges, he dreamed of founding a colony of Englishmen on the New England coast.

At Sagadahoc, Smith and Squanto found the abandoned buildings of the Popham colony, but no trace of any settlers. Squanto spoke with the Passamaquoddies in the area and learned that Tahanedo and Skettowaroes were still alive— and still powerful. Squanto had no great desire to meet them, for fear Tahanedo would try to regain his mastery over him.

"Squanto not like to be slave," he told John Smith. Nor were Tahanedo and Skettowaroes anxious to meet the English, perhaps for fear they might be kidnaped again.

Everywhere they went, Smith and Squanto made friends with the Indians. Smith, dressed in his ruff collar and shiny breast-plate, gave the leaders presents, like knives and hatchets, and traded them bracelets, necklaces, and loose beads for furs. He was always careful to leave the Indians satisfied with the trade, even when he thought they were exacting a bit too high a price for their furs.

He wanted the good will of the American natives more than he wanted their goods, and he was always careful to let them know that Squanto was a free man, whom Captain Smith was taking back to his home at Patuxet.

As they worked their way down the coast toward Cape Ann and Massachusetts Bay, Smith continued collecting sightings and soundings to add to his map.

He did not find the mines or mountains of gold that legend had put on the New England coast. Nor did he find any whales, being either too late or too early in the season; so he made no oil for lamps on English tables. But he was making friends, and he was making a map, and his holds were nearly full of salted or dried quality fish. He felt his voyage was already successful. He became anxious to report his success to his employer at Plymouth Fort.

***

At Massachusetts Bay, they went ashore to get water and wood and to trade with the natives, if they found any.

At a freshwater spring, a group of about fifty Indians approached. They carried bows and stone-tipped arrows, suitable for killing large animals, like deer.

"Who are they, Squanto?" asked Smith.

"From the Massachusetts tribe," said Squanto, touching the bead of pollen in his collar.

"Are they friendly?"

"They often attack my people," said Squanto, looking away from Smith. "I think they are bad people."

"Be sure your muskets are charged," yelled Smith to his men. "And keep your fuses lit."

The Massachusetts leader gave a signal and a war cry. The Indians lifted their bows and let fly their arrows. With that, the little war was on.

The Englishmen's helmets, breastplates, and arm- and leg-armor served them well, for they were nearly immune to the Indians' arrows. Only one man received a wound on a shoulder, and that slight.

With their muskets, the English killed about fourteen Massachusetts warriors who came close enough to shoot an arrow. The main body of warriors soon retreated. Smith captured a few Indians to take a message back to the Massachusetts leaders.

Squanto did not dare go with the messengers, because he feared for his safety, and no bead of pollen nor lucky stone would help.

"Tell your sagamores," Smith said through Squanto, "that the English will always strive to be your friends and maintain the peace between our two peoples. But know that we are ready to strike when we are provoked. If you turn your arrows toward us, we will be forced to turn our muskets toward you. Go, now, and when you come again, let us be at peace."

19. "Are You a Yang-kaysh in Disguise?"

"It is hard to believe; yet you speak the language of Patuxet."
— a Wampanoag Leader

Smith's holds were now filled to capacity with fish, though Thomas Hunt's ship still had some vacant space. After consultation, they decided that Smith would take on wood and water, then sail for England. Hunt would finish "making fish" in Cape Cod Bay to fill his holds and would follow.

At Cohasset, some miles south of Massachusetts Bay, about forty or fifty Wampanoags attacked the water and wood gathering party. The musketeers fired on them, killing a few before Squanto could get Smith to stop his men.

"Stop! Stop! They are friends, *towam*," he told Smith. "These are Wampanoags, people of my own tribe. Cohasset is a Wampanoag town. I will go out and get them to leave our men alone."

"Good. Do what you can," said Smith, for he truly wanted to leave the coast with the good will of the Indians.

So Squanto walked out toward the Wampanoags, yelling "*towam*" at the top of his voice.

Baffled to see an Indian in English clothes—a baggy red shirt and knee-length linen pants—and surprised to hear their own language, the warriors of Cohasset lowered their arrows.

"The English are not here to hurt you," yelled Tisquantum. "They are ready to go home. They want only to get wood and water, and then they will sail their ship back across the ocean."

"How? Who are you? How did you come to be with the yang-kaysh?" The war-leader was so astonished at Tisquantum's presence that he could hardly understand what the man was saying. "Are you a yang-kaysh in disguise?"

"No, but I have lived in England with the English. I am Tisquantum. I was taken from my home at Patuxet when I was a young man. I lived among the Passamaquoddies for a time, then among the English on their big island which is far beyond Monhegan. I am on my way home to Patuxet. At last, I am on my way home."

"It is hard to believe; yet you speak the

language of Patuxet."

Tisquantum began to warm to the task of negotiation. "Yes, I speak the language of Patuxet, and I speak the language of the Yang-kaysh. I can help you. Come, sit with the yang-kaysh and talk peace. Captain Smith will give you a metal butcher knife, and bronze hatchets, and copper bracelets for yourselves and your wives.

They wish to be at peace with you, so they can trade you more of these things and other useful implements for your otter and beaver furs. They will give you shirts and stroud blankets for deer skins. The people of their homeland want these things and will pay you for them in trade."

"It is hard to believe; yet I hear you speaking the language of Patuxet."

Tisquantum pulled off his red shirt, so that his bronze skin showed. "See? I am just like you. I can help you, and you can help me. Come, sit with the yang-kaysh and eat and smoke. They will give you some of their stewed peas and sliced mallard. They will buy your tobacco from you. They will clasp your arms in friendship, if you will let them."

"It is hard to believe; yet you know the language of Patuxet."

At the peace party that followed, the Cohasset warriors were so startled by being able to communicate with the yang-kaysh that they forgot to mention that some of their warriors had been killed at the beginning of this encounter. Captain Smith brought it up.

"We are heartily sorry that some of your men were killed. We would like to give special presents to the families of the slain men." To one family, he gave a coat of blue cotton and a pair of leather shoes; to another, a hat and a pair of breeches; to another, a cast iron pot and a linen shirt; to all, he gave small knives, glass beads, and finely ground rouge.

The families were so proud of their new wealth that their grief for their losses was diminished, forgotten for the moment.

"We will only collect firewood and water," said Smith. "Then we will be gone."

Tisquantum would stay with the Cohassets.

"Are you sure?" said Smith. "I can take you on to Patuxet."

But the Cohasset people were so anxious to hear all of Tisquantum's story, so proud to be host to a world traveler, so ready to gain status in the eyes of all Wampanoag villages, that they insisted Tisquantum be their guest. They would send runners to Patuxet and all the other towns to tell them that Tisquantum was on his way home to Patuxet.

The idea of a triumphal journey filled with honors and celebrations in every town appealed to Squanto. He would be the envy of the northern part of the Wampanoag Confederation. He was now in a clan by himself. Though he was unknown to most of the Wampanoag Nation, yet he was already their primary ambassador. "I am home now," he told Smith. "I will walk to Patuxet."

The next day offered a good wind, so Captain John Smith set sail for England, leaving Hunt and his ship to "make fish" in Cape Cod bay.

20. Kidnaped Near Patuxet

> "... it happened there had been one Hunt (a worthless fellow of our Nation) set out by certain merchants for love of gain; who (not content with the commodity he had by the fish, and peaceable trade he found among the savages) after he had made his dispatch, and was ready to set sail, (more savage than they) seized upon the poor innocent creatures, that in confidence of his honesty had put themselves into his hands. And stowing them under hatches, to the number of twenty four, carried them into the Straights [of Gibraltar], where he sought to sell them for slaves, and sold as many as he could get money for."— Sir Ferdinando Gorges, *"The Discovery and Plantation of New England"* (1672)

When the Cohasset runners brought the news to Patuxet, about twenty of his own tribesmen came to meet Tisquantum and escort him home to Patuxet. The people of Patuxet sent him a new doe-skin shirt, painted with protective symbols of good fortune. Even though he still had only his white linen trousers, he felt quite handsome and quite at home in the new shirt.

Tisquantum and his friends were about halfway home, when Captain Thomas Hunt hailed them from the beach where his men were gathering wood and water. "Squanto! Squanto! I never thought I'd see you again. And so many friends you have with you!"

Tisquantum saw no reason to distrust Thomas Hunt. He was willing to speak for his Patuxet friends, so that they could receive presents of knives and beads from Hunt.

"I am ready to go home now," said Hunt, glancing rapidly over Squanto's twenty companions. "I caught plenty of fish in Cape Cod bay, and I traded for corn with the people at Nauset and Cummaquid; so we have sufficient grain and table fare. As soon as we fetch aboard enough wood and water, we'll set our sails and pray for fair winds."

"You will have pleasant trip," said Squanto. "So early in season. Good weather."

"Aye, we expect it to be pleasant," said Hunt, squinting and looking Squanto and the Patuxets up and down. "Would you like to come with us?"

"No, no. I am almost home now. I will be here when Captain Smith come again next year. Maybe I take a wife, become papa."

"An old world-traveler like you will never settle down to family life," said Hunt, laughing a tight little squeal.

"Maybe," admitted Squanto, smiling, reaching for the protective bead of pollen, which wasn't there. He faltered, then went on, "To stand on ground that not moving make feet itch."

"Spoken like a sailor!" exclaimed Hunt. "Come aboard and we'll drink a pint of beer."

Tisquantum hesitated, glancing at his twenty friends from Patuxet.

Hunt smiled so broadly that his eyes squinted almost shut. "Your friends are welcome on board, too. Perhaps they would like to see what an English ship looks like. We'll take them on a tour. Give them some good English food."

Squantum discussed the invitation with his friends for a few minutes. Many of them were curious to see what a ship was like. Some were afraid that some unexpected danger would spring up. All anticipated receiving small presents of beads and powdered rouge, and getting a taste of yang-kaysh food.

Captain Hunt had his men unload the longboat of the fire wood and casks of water, so all twenty of the Wampanoags could be transported at once by half a dozen oarsmen. The other sailors waited on shore.

When the boat was in shouting distance, Captain Hunt hailed his mate on deck. "Shift the livestock to a smaller pen."

"Aye," answered the mate. "'Tis already done. I saw what you're doing."

"Excellent," answered Hunt. As they neared the rope ladder, he became nervous, shifting rapidly from one foot to the other, looking over his shoulder as if someone were following him. He was the first to climb the rope ladder at the side of the ship. "Tell your men to follow me, Squanto," said Hunt.

The twenty Wampanoags climbed the ladder, one by one. On the deck was a large group of sailors, carrying belaying pins. A hatch gaped open, so Squanto could see an almost empty hold, like a big room just below the main deck. It was supposed to be filled with barrels of cured fish.

Each of the Wampanoags greeted the sailors with some pidgin phrase, like "Hello, Yang-kaysh," or offered his name. They were directed down a ladder to the open hold, where Captain Hunt and six of his sailors stood waiting. Hunt was dancing back and forth with his nervousness.

When all the Wampanoag men were below the deck, Hunt climbed the steep ladder back to the main deck. His men followed, and others shoved the hatch cover into the closed position.

The Wampanoag men below deck tried to look at one another in the dim light from the few, small port holes. "What is going on?" Squanto yelled. "What have— Why have you closed the hatch, Captain Hunt?"

After a few minutes, the hatch cover opened a bit, and seven Nauset men from Cummaquid were dropped into the hold. They quickly told how Hunt had traded copper and beads for corn with Ohquamehud of Lower Nauset, so they at Cummaquid thought the English were friends and honest. But Hunt and his men had lured seven men from Cummaquid on board the ship, then shut a hatch over them. Three of them were brothers.

Some of the Wampanoags saw what was happening— and understood. Some of the Indians leaped up and grabbed the edge of the hatch, but a sailor was ready to crack the knuckles of each with a belaying pin.

"Well done!" exclaimed Hunt. "Fetch the rest of the wood and water, Mr. Smith. We've made our cargo. We can sail at once."

"Captain Hunt! Captain Hunt!" yelled Squanto, feeling naked with no talisman to protect himself. "What you doing? Are you not friend to Wampanoag?"

"I'm friend to no one but myself."

"What you do? Where you taking us?"

Hunt squinted and laughed, calm for the

first time in an hour. "There's an excellent slave market in Málaga. You'll each bring about twenty pounds. You'll make me rich."

"What will Sir Ferdinando say? You follow Gorges, do you not?"

"Gorges, Porges, Smorges. He can go to hell with all his handkerchiefs, for all I care. With this start and his ship, I figure I'll go into pirating. I'd make a pretty good pirate, don't you think?"

21. The Slave Trade at Málaga

"Pity poor Squanto. Save poor Squanto from slavery,"

"Pity poor Squanto. Save poor Squanto from slavery," he cried out to the crowd in every language he could think of. There was so much noise, so many voices, that he despaired of being heard, and they had taken his new shirt; he had nothing to protect himself. His hands were tied behind his back. The mate and a few of the sailors led several of the almost-naked American Natives with a rope wrapped around each man's shoulders and arms.

Dozens of men from several Mediterranean nations milled about the plaza of Málaga. The Englishmen had sold several of the Nausets and Wampanoags to Spanish and Moroccan bidders for twenty pounds each. Squanto's turn on the auction block was coming up. *"Je ne suis pas Français, je suis Anglais. No quiero hacerlo."* He even cried out in Romani, *"Te yertil o Dei, tai te aves yertimé tut mandar."*

The mate grabbed Squanto's rope from the

sailor's hands and jerked it, so that Squanto fell on the cobblestone street. "Shet yer trap, y' heathen, 'r I'll break yer legs, I will."

"No hurt Squanto. Please, no hit Squanto. Squanto talk for you. Squanto be your voice." He was trying to get up, which was difficult without the use of his hands and arms. The sun in the plaza was unmerciful. The heat from the stone pavement burned his cheek and chest.

"Shet up," repeated the mate, jerking him again. "I got no use fer yer voice. I got no patience fer yer mumbling in this heat."

"Where Captain Smith? Where Sir Ferdinando Gorges? I be Gorges' voice. I help Smith trade. I talk for—"

"I sed shet up, y' idiot." The mate slapped at him with a gloved hand and kicked him in the side. The men in the crowd nearby hardly watched.

"Sir Ferdinando Gor—"

The sweating mate jerked Squanto's rope again. "Sir Ferdinando Gorges be damned. I don't care a fig fer Sir Ferdinando Gorges. He's as much a pirate and slaver as the rest of us, he is. He jist goes about it different. He'll steal and rob y' blind, with a smile on his face and a kerchief in his hand, he will. He's jist like the rest of us."

Suddenly, a thick, brown-sleeved arm crossed the mate's wrists and took the rope from the mate's hands before he knew what was happening. There were four of them: men in brown woolen robes, with rosaries and crucifixes on their chests. The big one in front was the leader.

The hood of his brown robe was thrown back so that the sun shone on his shaved head and face. They all carried sturdy hiking staffs, which looked a lot like weapons. One of the monks held his staff horizontally to prevent the other sailors from going to aid the mate; another held his staff against the crowd, but no one was trying to interfere.

"You no have slaves to sell," the lead monk said to the mate, in English. "Go back you to the ship. Sail you from Málaga on the wind first, or I call the Constable. He take you in the ropes to the dungeon."

"Here now, ye can't do this, y' can't."

"I can. I do," said the lead monk. "Thou art an abomination before God. Get thee from my sight!" Much of the English the monk knew was in the form of set phrases and sentences of condemnation from the church, but he also knew a few formulas of consolation.

"These'r Captain Hunt's slaves, they are."

"Thees are men. Men in the just eyes of God. It is our duty their souls to save."

The mate glanced around. He could see that

the crowd was moving to support the monks. Being considered "Luterano," he and his men did not have a chance. The crowd might even turn belligerent. The constable might show up and take them to jail for no reason. It was not a good idea for an Englishman to be in a Spanish jail. "C'mon, men," he said, wiping the sweat from his forehead. "They've stolen our slaves. But they're still slaves. Slaves of the Popish church, they are."

Disgruntled, the Englishmen withdrew, some of them walking backward to watch for attacks from the crowd.

Squanto was finally getting to his feet. It had all happened so rapidly that he hardly understood. "Who are you?" he asked. "What happen?"

"*Mon Dieu!*" said the monk, "Speak you the English?"

"*Sí, un poco,*" said Squanto.

The big monk loosened the rope from around Squanto's arms and shoulders and untied his hands. "I call myself Brother Francisco."

"My name is Squanto. Tisquantum. I," he said, patting his own chest, then gesturing toward the others, "We, from town of Patuxet in Wampanoag nation. Across ocean. Right across ocean. These English kidnap us. These English, bad people."

"Sí. Bad English," agreed Brother Francisco.

He seemed cool, in spite of the bald sun in an open sky.

The other monks untied the other American Natives. The monks could speak no Wampanoag. The Wampanoags could speak no Spanish. They smiled at each other and trusted in the other's good will.

"These are holy men of this place," Tisquantum called out in Wampanoag. "They will be kind to us. Do not resist them, for they are friends." The other Indians repeated *"towam"* and pointed from their own chests to the monks.

The monks looked to Brother Francisco for an explanation, and Brother Francisco to Squanto.

"Towam significa 'amigo'," said Squanto.

"Ahh! *Towam, sí,*" said the monks, nodding.

"I tell them you help us. Be friend," Squanto explained to Brother Francisco.

"O, *sí, sí.*"

Some twenty of the American Natives had already been sold. "Others?" asked Squanto. "Those sold? Help them too?"

"*Lo siento mucho,*" said Brother Francisco, tilting his big head like a shamed child. "They are gone, taken away. God comfort them in their sorrows."

Squanto looked down, holding back his

tears. "They were friends of mine," he said. "Men from my own home. Men of my clan. Can we do nothing?"

"It sorrows me," said Brother Francisco, looking only at the coiled rope in his hands. "Is impossible to find them now. They are gone already. We came as soon as we heard what Captain Hunt doing. We save who we can."

"May God comfort them in their sorrows," said Squanto, flexing his shoulders and arms to get the stiffness from the ropes out of them.

"We take his slaves. As many as possible. A free man casts a good shadow."

Squanto turned and looked at Brother Francisco intently, trying to see him for the first time. Was this holy man a Gypsy in disguise?

The monks led the Indians away from the torrid plaza and toward the cool, peaceful monastery. "What a stroke of good fortune," each was thinking in his own way— "a chance to Christianize a savage from the New World. And what luck, that one of them can communicate. They would soon know enough of the natives' language, or the Americans would know enough Spanish, to speed their salvation a thousandfold. This accident must be acknowledged the means of putting on foot and giving life to all our conversions. God has indeed smiled upon our designs."

22. Brother Francisco

> He did not dare refuse to honor a holy man's request. Where were all those who had resisted the inquisitions of the church?
> –Captain of a Meditarranean Packet

After Squanto retold the story of his imprisonment in Seville, he asked Brother Francisco if he had ever heard of Draghan Di-eshti.

No, he hadn't, but Brother Francisco was sympathetic and volunteered to help Squanto find out what had happened to his Gypsy friend. He wrote to a childhood comrade who had become a priest in Seville. He also gave Tisquantum a necklace with a wooden crucifix on it. "For your protection," said Brother Francisco.

Tisquantum smiled, feeling comfortable again. He had not even noticed that he was uncomfortable. "I thank you," he said sincerely. "I thank Brother Francisco. I thank the Franciscan brotherhood." He touched the crucifix, not feeling

By Charles Brashear 153

the protection it was supposed to afford, but accepting on faith that it was there.

In the spring, the friend in Seville responded that he had discovered that some of Draghan's tribe lived semi-permanently north of Seville on the river Genil, a branch of the Guadalquivir River.

The Spanish Government had forbidden the Gypsies to travel; so they had set up a village in caves in the high bank of the Genil, where at least some of them were at all times. Brother Francisco and Squanto decided they would journey to Seville and the river Genil. So Squanto was soon dressed again like a Gypsy in Spanish clothing.

At the Málaga wharf, they discovered a ship, a coastal trading packet bound for Cadíz. The master of the little ship had a regular business, bartering and delivering leather, furniture, and produce at most of the towns along the windy Spanish coast, through the Straits of Gibraltar, and around to Cadíz, even along the Atlantic coast of Morocco and back to Tangier. Brother Francisco was not hesitant about begging passage.

The master eyed the brown cassock, the crucifix, and nodded his head. Then he looked at Squanto. "¿El gitáno tambien?"

"No es un gitáno," said Brother Francisco. "Es un gentilhomme del mundo nuevo. Del mundo nuevo del norte."

The master narrowed his eyes and hesitated, as if he were about to snort "gentilhomme indeed!" but he noticed the stranger was also wearing a crucifix. He did not dare refuse to honor a holy man's request. Where were all those who had resisted the inquisitions of the church? "*Vamanos mañana,*" was all he said. The spring was mild; there was nothing to be gained by delay.

"*Vayamanos con Díos,*" said Brother Francisco, making the sign of the cross.

The Brotherhood of St. Francis at Cadíz lent them a two-wheeled cart and a shaggy burro, provided they would deliver a sack of grain to each of the parish churches along the road to San Sebastian Meadows on the River Guadalquivir, south of Seville. The route took them through low-lying agricultural country of small, white-washed pueblos.

Occasional patches of irrigation turned desert rocks into vegetable gardens, vineyards, and orchards of oranges, almonds, and olives. These fruits and vegetables were the produce which the master of the trading packet sold at towns along the mountainous south coast of Spain.

At San Sebastian Meadows, they found a leaky row-boat, which Squanto repaired by stuffing grass in the cracks and pounding it in with a rock and a coin. They made fair progress with their makeshift paddles. Along the way, they found still-water bayous where Squanto could herd small fish into the shallow water with branches and sweep them up onto the sandy bank. They split them with sharp rocks and roasted them on willow spits over an open fire.

It reminded him of Henry Challons. No one in England knew anything about Henry, not even Sir Ferdinando Gorges. Perhaps he had died in obscurity. In English life: a man might rise like a comet to prominence, wealth, influence; and as quickly fade into loneliness and poverty, where he might die without friends or causes.

Englishmen were interested in a person only so long as that person could feed the Englishmen's greed. They did not know how to nurture a friendship. Henry Challons had been a real friend to Squanto; perhaps that was why he failed in English society.

In Seville, Brother Francisco's friend joined them for a walk up the valley to *el Rio Genil* and the Gypsy settlement.

Tisquantum kissed the crucifix on his necklace as he had seen the Franciscan priests do, and he tried to make the sign of the cross, but could not remember which side to start on. If you did such powerful magic wrong, there was no telling what evil might come of the mistake.

23. On the River Genil

"Te aves yertil tut o Dei, tai te yertimé mandar,"
(May God forgive him, as I forgive him.)
— Gypsy Proverb

Women in bright dresses bent over their big iron cooking pots, stirring the frying vegetables and meat. Young men trained horses in the fields, amid the crack of whips. Children played in the meadow, practicing picking each other's pockets. The men in high leather boots and bright neckerchiefs, *diklos,* eyed the strangers with suspicion. Outsiders, *gadyos,* were not welcome, especially the beggars in black and brown robes.

No one knew anything about Draghan Dieshti.

At every campfire, the heads shook negatively, the eyes turned away.

Squanto stood back and looked at the camp. He heard horses galloping in the fresh meadows. He smelled paprika cooking, and the camp smoke lay close to the ground. He saw children in bright dress standing in the mouths of caves. The sight of the lean-to's covering the beds on the ground was hardly different in their permanence from the temporary coverings.

The high-wheeled, barrel-topped *vurdons* were decorated in olive green and red, with little garlands of fresh flowers tied in unexpected places. Except those *vurdon* built into the mouths of caves, they looked almost ready to roll, though grass had grown in their tracks. It seemed he had been to this village before, or heard it described in song. He began singing in Romani, softly at first:

"By the shore at Sitges, Kuma
camped by shining, big-sea water..."

The women stopped stirring their vegetables. The children, sensing something, paused to listen. The men unfolded their high leather boots from under their haunches and began getting to their feet. "*Tshurkaki-dgili,*" whispered one. Then he said, louder, "He's singing 'The Song of Tshurka.'"

An older man, still muscular and sturdy but tending toward paunchiness, came out to challenge Squanto. "I am Yoro Di-eshti. That song belongs to my family," he said. "Where did you learn it?"

After the translation and Squanto's explanation, everyone had to talk at once. The translations got hopelessly entangled, but no matter: here was a person whom Draghan had valued highly enough to teach "The Song of Tshurka." All else was minor detail.

When Squanto asked again about Draghan, he got a different answer. Yoro Di-eshti was Draghan's brother. "I am sorry," he said, taking Squanto's arm and meeting his gaze squarely. "Our brother Draghan is dead."

Then practically the whole camp crowded behind Yoro and Squanto, as Yoro led him to the churchyard and showed him a wooden cross which had not yet rotted.

Draghan had cheated another gypsy in life, an act that made him forever unclean, *marimé*, and he may even have caused the death of one of the tribe. He had run away from his family and sought refuge among the *gadyos*, to escape the revenge on his life that the tribe demanded. No one knew where he was, until he was executed in Seville for helping prisoners escape.

He had not been a good man, but he was dead now. All transgression was forgotten in death. The living could not afford to be at war with the dead. One had to live at peace with ghosts.

"*Te aves yertil tut o Dei, tai te yertimé*

mandar," said Squanto.

"Exactly," said Yoro. "May God forgive him, as I forgive him. May there be no enmity between his spirit and ours." He burst into tears, which he did not bother to hide. And he sang a wailing, emotional song about constant death and fickle life.

Then everyone went back to the Gypsy camp for a spontaneous ceremonial, *patshiva,* to honor the ancestors of Draghan and Yoro. For three days, they ate huge amounts of food, drank quantities of wine and brandy, sang hundreds of songs, and danced dozens of dances, the men in their bright, satin shirts, the women in floral print dresses.

Yoro poured wine on the ground, so Draghan's spirit could enjoy himself, too. Everyone was laughing and singing, and doing all they could to assure that the dead were having a good time.

Yoro gave presents to everyone, even the beggars in black and brown robes, but especially to Draghan's friend Squanto. He gave Squanto a red shirt, a pair of leather boots, and three gold coins, whispering, "Keep these for yourself. Tie them in the corner of this kerchief. Do not let the beggars in brown and black take them from you. These are for you."

"Here is a golden ear-ring for you, Squanto," said Yoro loudly, reaching up to hang it in his right ear. "It makes a man human. As we Rom say, 'When a man wears a golden ear-ring, the dogs can distinguish him from a tree and won't piss on him.' May you live a hundred years and die with the ring in your ear."

Squanto choked with emotion. He embraced Yoro, patting him on the back and holding onto his upper arm. He burst into tears of thankfulness, sorrow, happiness, and regret.

24. Passage to Newfoundland, 1605

"A free man casts a good shadow."
— Gypsy Proverb

In late summer, *The Diligence*, a two-masted merchant-man from Bristol, rocked gently at the Málaga wharf, as longshoremen rolled cask after cask of wine up the gang-plank and stowed them in the hold. Heavy sherries and light sherries, dry Spanish reds and syrupy sweet reds—The Brotherhood of St. Francis at Málaga was shipping it all to Newfoundland, in exchange for dried or salted Atlantic salmon or Icelandic cod. It was a regular and frequent route of trade.

Squanto and Brother Francisco discovered that, with patience and repetition, they could understand the mate who was supervising the loading. "Aye, we're outboun' fer Newfunlun'."

"Captain John Guy?" asked Squanto, who had spent the winter of 1611 with John Guy's colony on Newfoundland.

"Nay, th' good Guy's gone. Retorned to England, 'e is. 'E tuk ship as we was syelin in July. They'll 'ave a new capn, they 'ill."

"You take Squanto to Newfoundland?" Squanto suggested.

"Now, why would Oi do uh thang lak thet?"

"Squanto find friends on Newfoundland. Find ship. Sail to Patuxet."

"Not bloody loikely. Too meny stor-r-rms, this toime o'year-r. We'll syel nort o' th' Azore Oislands, then roight nor-w'st. Thet wy we sty free o' pirates and cotch th' edge o' th' stor-r-rms. But nobody syels west from Newfunlun, nobody."

"You take Squanto to Newfoundland?"

"Hey, lad. This 'ere ain't no charity."

"The Brotherhood has no money," said Brother Francisco, "but we collect wine as tithe. We put two casks of wine on deck for your private use."

"Squanto can pull rope. Lift sail."

"So y' thank yer a syelor, do ye?"

"Squanto sail with Captain John Smith. Squanto watch what sailors pull. Squanto can pull rope when mate yell 'heave.'"

"Maik thet three casks," said the mate to Brother Francisco, "and we won't sy a thang t' th' capn, eh?"

By Charles Brashear 163

"It is a personal contract," said Brother Francisco.

"'Eave 'o, Myte."

"Done," said Squanto, in the manner of an Englishman closing a deal.

Squanto and Brother Francisco walked back to the monastery through the plaza of Málaga. Fewer people strolled there now in late summer, 1615, and almost none from other nations.

The abandoned and ruined castle of the Moors, the Castillo, stood on a hill, like a smaller Alhambra in the landscape. It might have been interesting to go there and see the ruins, but he had not gone in the year he had been at Málaga, and now it was too late. Squanto had to collect his boots and the hidden kerchief with three gold coins tied in the corner, and prepare to sail on the morrow.

The other Wampanoags were now speaking Andalusian Spanish with some ease. They were well fed, well clothed, and treated with kindness. They fitted into the life of the monastery. They would be strangers again in an English environment. That made Squanto feel less guilty about leaving them with the monks.

"You take other Wampanoags back home?"

"Oh, *sí, sí,*" said Brother Francisco, nodding rapidly. "Their instruction progresses rapidly.

When they have accepted God and professed Christianity, we will send them as assistants and interpreters with the missionaries to New Spain."

"Where New Spain?"

"Across the ocean, where you came from. Right across the ocean."

The assurance made Tisquantum feel better. He was not abandoning his tribesmen. They would be in good hands.

In his ignorance, he did not consider, as the monks in their ignorance never imagined, that these Wampanoag Indians would find the Caribbean and Aztec languages and customs of New Spain as unknown and as baffling as did the Spanish explorers and missionaries.

For his own part, Tisquantum was happy to be leaving tomorrow. He was happy to be escaping the slave markets of Málaga. The summer sun nurtures all life, so a strong man hardly needs a protection.

"A free man casts a good shadow."

25. On Newfoundland, A Ready Listener

> "... Tisquantum, after years of danger and hardship, had been so fortunate as to get on board an English ship then in the port of Málaga, and at last to find his way to Newfoundland, not many days' journey from his native home. He was in a proper mood to descant warmly on the beauties of the New England coast, and in Dermer, who had also listened to the glowing descriptions of the same shores by the enthusiastic [Captain John] Smith, he found a ready listener."
>
> — James Phinney Baxter, *Sir Ferdinando Gorges and his Province of Maine.*

February is a nice time on Newfoundland. The mountain-splitting cold of winter has passed, but the tempests of March and April have not yet come. The sun frequently shines a few hours in a clear sky; the birds and animals come out of their winter inactivity to start the business of living another year; the snow melts, warmed by the northeasterly Atlantic stream; and one could almost think there was something spring-like in the air, except that almost every night brings another solid freeze.

In the winter just passed on Newfoundland, Squanto had met and become friends with a young Englishman named ThomasDermer.

On warm days, Squanto and Dermer both found themselves looking for something to do. The frozen earth was still too hard to work up the garden plot. The edge ice in Cupid's Inlet prevented them from launching even the smallest boat, so they carried a skiff across the neck and set it into the larger Conception Bay, where the water was more turbulent and less icy. They paddled about, fishing, looking for fire wood, exploring.

Dermer taught Squanto the basics of sailing a small boat and found his friend an apt pupil. "You're doing well," said Dermer. "Good training and knowledge are the best guarantees of good luck."

"Really?" asked Squanto. "Wampanoag want something to touch or hold."

"Well, a good man doesn't need that sort of crutch. A capable man doesn't need a piece of papist superstition, like you're wearing."

Tisquantum took off his crucifix and put it in his pocket, recognizing that Dermer disliked it. He soon lost it and hardly noticed.

Thomas Dermer asked Captain John Mason if he could take a long-boat and explore the coasts of Newfoundland, to take sightings and soundings for a better map than they had.

Mason consented. "We might as well make use of all that energy you've got. Aye, and I do need better data about the shoreline. And a catalog of the resources of the plantation."

"Can I take Squanto along?" asked Dermer, trying to make the request sound incidental or off-handed.

"What for? He can't speak the language of the natives here. And he can't operate a sextant or an astrolabe."

"But he's good to talk to," replied Dermer. "Besides, he feels all cooped up here in the cabins. We're both getting cabin-fever."

"All right," conceded Mason. "If you can find enough men who want to get out of the cabins and will row for you, you can take a shallop and explore two weeks along the south and west coasts of the island. But lay low and head for the cover of a headland if you see a Frenchman, especially on the west side on the way to New France. One never knows when they may take a notion they're at war with England, or when one of 'em is gonna decide he's a pirate and get frisky or belligerent."

In an open, gaff-rigged pinnace with eight oarsmen, Dermer and Squanto coasted the warm south and west sides of the island. When the wind was right, they hoisted the sail. Squanto quickly learned to tack and come to. Each night, they camped on the shore, sleeping beside a fire under a makeshift lean-to or the upturned shallop, drawn up on land and propped up on its oars, a technique Squanto taught the English. "Wampanoag use canoe as house. Learn that from brother turtle."

It was hardly a disadvantage that Squanto could not speak the Micmac language of the natives, for the English encountered few inhabitants, and the natives were very hard to make contact with. Dermer measured the angles and distances between points, sounded the depth of the bays and inlets, and made notes on what grasses and bushes grew along the coast.

The sassafras shrubs reminded Squanto of his homeland. "Same plant grow at Patuxet," he said, "only bigger. Like tree."

"The size of a tree, you mean?" asked Dermer, not bothering to disguise his interest.

"Yes. Sometimes, whole forest of sassafras."

"Well, that would certainly be a lot better than this," admitted Dermer, throwing away the branches and twigs he held.

"Why better?" asked Squanto.

"Why, the harvest would be better. The take would be richer."

"Better for you? or better for the Sassafras tree?" asked Squanto, grinning.

Sassafras was considered a valuable natural resource, because the English treasured it as a medicine. Both the pulverized bark and a tea made of its leaves were said to relieve fever, indigestion, ague, palsy, and tremors. Each ship's captain who went out to New England was told, if he couldn't bring back a hold full of gold, furs, or fish, at least bring back a shipload of sassafras.

They also found small stands of scrubby oak on the warm headlands, and stunted fir and cedar forests along the inlets and up the streambeds. All of these trees, Squanto said, "grow bigger in Wampanoag country."

"I expect they will also grow bigger here, if we went a ways inland," said Dermer, shading his eyes to discern what was in the distance. They could not see very far inland— no lofty mountains nor rounded highlands; and there were no very large streams to indicate a broad watershed. But Captain Mason wanted to think these things were there, so Dermer exaggerated his report, but only a little. In a season of thaw, he reasoned, there would surely be stronger streams than they found along the coasts in February. In time, the trees would get their growth.

They found a few small deer and snowshoe

rabbits, pawing in the snow-covered fields to get at the moss and grass. Dermer shot some with his musket and kept the party in meat. Bread and vegetables were in very short supply.

"Wampanoag store corn and squash for winter," said Squanto.

"I don't know if corn or squash would grow here on the west side," said Dermer, scratching the rocky earth with a boot heel. "It looks like the season is pretty short."

"Soon be time to plant corn and squash at home," said Squanto.

"You really want to go home, don't you?"

"Yes. Squanto home-sick. Away from home ten, eleven years now." He held up the fingers of both hands. "Wonder if mother lives. Who did sisters marry? Who is Squanto uncle to? Squanto supposed to take care of his nephews."

"Well, if things work out the way I want them to," said Dermer, grasping his friend's upper arm, "I'll take you back to New England, as soon as I can." He did not tell Squanto yet, but he was formulating a plan that would serve both their wants.

26. The Caplin Run on Newfoundland

> "June has Caplin, a fish much resembling smelt in form and eating, in such abundance dry on shore as to load carts."
>
> —Captain John Mason, governor of the Newfoundland colony

Thomas Dermer had sailed as third mate on Captain John Smith's voyage of 1614 and gained a lot of valuable experience. Smith's ship met contrary winds, and they were blown further south than they intended. A French warship captured Smith and his party.

Captain Smith was imprisoned aboard the French man-o-war, leaving Thomas Dermer to man the captured English ship and its skeleton crew. Under cover of darkness and lax French guards, Dermer managed to escape on a downwind and brought the ship back to Sir Ferdinando Gorges at Plymouth Fort.

Thus, though he had no command, Dermer

came to be called Captain Thomas Dermer, because he had demonstrated his ability to master a ship, navigate it under difficult circumstances, and bring it home to a safe haven. His easy efficiency could make his less competent supervisors look good to their land-loving employers.

Captain John Mason, the governor of the little settlement at Conception Bay, valued Thomas Dermer highly, for the young man could be trusted to do business correctly. He spoke good, clear, London English, and he wrote with clarity and specificity. He understood what enterprise was about.

Mason was in partnership with Sir Ferdinando Gorges, who had financed the Newfoundland colony. Together, he and Gorges planned to secure patents from King James for colonies in New England; Mason was going to call his settlement New Hampshire, after his home province in England, while Gorges would call his Maine, after the mainland of America. Mason and Gorges often used Dermer as a courier, a go-between who could get the job done, and done right.

By mid-April, Dermer and Squanto were back at Cupid's Inlet on Conception Bay, where the settlers were breaking the ground and getting ready to seed their gardens, as they had done since 1610 when Captain John Guy supervised the first colony there for Gorges, Popham, Slaney, and Company.

In late April, the caplin run began. Thousands, even millions of the little fish beached themselves to spawn. The Newfoundlanders raked up cart-loads of the fish that lay dead on the beach and worked them into their garden soil.

The process reminded Squanto of how John Slaney's gardener had spread the stable muck and kitchen scraps on the garden to make the plants grow. He mentioned the practice to Captain John Mason.

"Yes," said Mason, laughing at Squanto's naivete. "Tis the manner of this place."

"Master Slaney use barn sweepings in London," said Squanto.

"Aye, that's a good way, too. But, as you see, we have few cattle here and no horses. We've got no muck to mix in; so we are forced to be content with rotting fish."

"Corn grow better with fish in ground?" he asked, a bit amazed. The Wampanoags did not follow any such practice.

"Aye, a plant has to eat, just like a human or an animal. I've heard that the fishermen of New France haul home their stinking fish-heads and guts, so they'll have some rot to spread on their gardens."

It was clear to Squanto that Mason found the practice distasteful. "We can count ourselves fortunate that the caplin run in such great numbers, just at the time the frost has ended and we can seed our plots with fresh fish. The fish-rot is food for the plant. If you don't plant fish with your corn, here, the crop will come to naught, and the land will be starved after a few years."

Squanto understood that. "Wampanoags move to new fields," he explained. "After four years, let old fields rest, so they come new again." But he made a mental note of the English custom.

"We may have to do that here, too," admitted Mason. "Though, as you have seen, there aren't many new fields to move to. If it weren't for the great fishing, our Newfoundland colony would hardly be a profitable venture."

Nevertheless, Captain John Mason wrote glowing accounts of the Newfoundland colony's promise: "June has Caplin, a fish much resembling smelt in form and eating, in such abundance dry on shore as to load carts." He claimed great success in using the excess fish as fertilizer: "For one acre thereof be inclosed with the Creatures therein ... would exceed one thousand acres of the best Pasture with the stock thereon which we have in England."

"Why is he not tell truth?" a troubled Squanto asked Dermer.

"To get people to come here," said Dermer, barely noticing his friend's distress. "Captain Mason describes what he hopes will be true when many people have settled here to live."

"He lies," said Squanto, wondering at the procedure. "He know he lies."

"He stretches the truth," admitted Dermer. "Unless he paint a paradise, no one will travel to it."

Squanto thought about that. Unless you paint a paradise, no one will take you home to it. He could no longer make the English believe there were mountains of gold in New England, nor nuggets as numerous as the sparkling waves in the streams, but he had to find something to feed their greed. Something in the manner of the English. "Many fish swarm in streams at Patuxet; thick in water like stars in sky."

27. Awaiting the King's Pleasure

"... by this savage, Captain Dermer understood so much of the state of his country, as drew his affection wholly to follow his hopes that way, to which purpose he writes [in 1619], that if I pleased to send a commission to meet him in New England, he would endeavor to come from Newfoundland to receive it, and to observe such other instruction as I pleased to give him..."

— Sir Ferdinando Gorges, *A Description of New England*, Chap XIV.

All year, 1616, the captains of fishing vessels brought news of a widespread civil war among the natives of North America. The Hurons and Ottawas, stirred, urged on, and armed by Samuel de Champlain, the French adventurer who founded the colony at Quebec in New France, had gone to war against the Iroquoian tribes, from the Seneca on the west, to their allies, the Narragansetts, on the east.

The Abenaki of Penobscot were allies of the Hurons and Ottawas. They had advanced a great way down the Atlantic coast toward the Narragansett nation, but their Emperor, Bashabes, was killed in battle. No leader of equal charisma had yet emerged, yet there was no end of the war in sight.

Late in the summer of 1616, reports of widespread sickness among the natives began coming to the English. They heard reports of whole villages falling ill to some pox and thousands of people dying. What war could not accomplish, plague soon would.

In September, 1616, Thomas Dermer wrote a letter to Sir Ferdinando Gorges at Plymouth Fort. He described his adventures and friendship with Squanto and reminded Sir Ferdinando that Tisquantum was one of his, Gorges's, savages from prior years, who might be "recovered" and put to good use. Dermer had caught some of Squanto's enthusiasm for the New England coast and relayed his ardent descriptions of the richness of the forests, the fertility of the land.

Dermer had little means of his own, but he proposed that he could invest his own labor, beyond his own board and supplies, in mounting an expedition to the new world in partnership with Gorges. As soon as the Indian civil war had diminished would be the best time to plant a colony, reasoned Dermer, for the natives would be so decimated that the English would encounter less resistance.

Squanto seemed anxious and willing to be a guide and ally. Dermer confessed that he thought Squanto had formed an emotional attachment to him, Dermer, and consequently could be trusted as a servant and fellow-traveler.

Sir Ferdinando Gorges was impressed and sent his authorization for Dermer to bring Squanto back to England.

So it happened, in the fall of 1616, that Thomas Dermer was sent to London with Squanto as his companion. He carried one of Mason's sensational accounts of Newfoundland to John Slaney, the treasurer of the company. Squanto was glad of the chance to visit his old friend and benefactor in London. "Master Slaney, good man," he said. "Teach Squanto to ride horse."

Slaney had copies of "A Description of New England," by Captain John Smith, which had just been published in 1616. Smith had used his time in captivity on the French warship to write it. In England, following his release in Normandy, he added his "Map of New England."

Slaney wanted to verify the details of Smith's map with Squanto if he could. Smith was an accomplished navigator, but nevertheless such a flamboyant, excessive proponent of his own interests and glory, that Slaney felt one had to sift his data to separate the truth from Smith's fictions.

Squanto understood maps, as did most of the American natives; they often drew diagrams in the sand for each other, or for the seamen they came in contact with. Still, much of Smith's chart made no sense to Squanto, for it was beyond his range of experience.

He recognized Cape Cod (called Cape James on the map, in honor of the King), and he recognized the inlet and stream which Smith had called New Plymouth on the map, for that was Patuxet, his home. His eyes misted over. "Squanto want to go home. Home to Patuxet. You let Squanto go home?"

"Of course, we will," said Slaney, putting a comforting arm across Squanto's shoulder. "As soon as the sun shines on the right opportunity. But remember, 'Every shadow is someone's sunshine.' So try not to miss what is good for you while you are waiting."

Slaney also wanted to confirm Smith's descriptions of the plants and animals of the New England coast. Yes, admitted Tisquantum, they had deer, beaver, rabbits. Turkeys, ducks, geese, partridges, pheasants. Whales, cod, mackerel, perch, shad. Fir, pine, cedar, sassafras, birch. Pumpkins, squash, beans, strawberries, corn. And much more. Also it was warm there.

Except for the time he was in Spain, Squanto did not think he had been really warm or dry since he left home. "You send Squanto home? Home to Patuxet?"

"That's what we're planning," said John Slaney. "As soon as we secure our patents from the King, we plan to send Captain Thomas Dermer to find a suitable site to plant a colony. We want you to go along and help him."

"Good! Squanto like Thomas Dermer. He speak truth. He teach Squanto to catch wind on sail boat."

"Aye," said Slaney. "We, too, think he is a good man and honest. Hard qualities to find nowadays. Any man who peddles honesty casts a good shadow."

"Free man cast good shadow," Squanto corrected. "Squanto want to be free. Free, at home, in Patuxet."

Squanto spent the following winter in John Slaney's household in London. Slaney's children had a pony, which they could harness to a cart and drive up and down Cheapside streets. Squanto enjoyed the children, enjoyed riding with them, enjoyed helping the hostler to care for the horses in Slaney's stable.

He liked living with Slaney. Slaney was always ready to talk with Squanto, to tell him about England, as well as suck up information about New England. Slaney no longer invited large numbers of people into his house to gawk at the stranger and ask the same, silly questions from their ignorant curiosity.

Especially, he did not invite their competitors. Slaney and Gorges agreed that other adventurers could use the information they would get from a talkative Squanto, the same as anyone could; so why give your competitors a leg up, when your own schemes were not yet mounted?

By spring, Squanto's homesickness had abated. Slaney mentioned it. "You don't seem as anxious to go home now, as you were formerly."

"Yes," admitted Squanto. "I have learn to like Master Slaney's house. It is home to Squanto. But I still want to go home to Patuxet."

"I thought as much," said Slaney, smiling. "But you can't have both. You have to decide. One arse cannot sit on two horses."

Squanto grinned. He rather liked John Slaney's pithy sayings. That one was also one of Draghan's sayings.

***

In the early summer of 1617, Thomas Dermer came and got Squanto. They moved to Plymouth Fort with Sir Ferdinando Gorges, awaiting the opportunity to sail. The time was never better, Gorges thought, for the natives were so decimated by war and plague that they could hardly make a resistance. Still, the Royal patents did not come.

To make use of a good man, Gorges sent Thomas Dermer out to Newfoundland as a passenger on a supply ship. Dermer would carry important messages to Captain John Mason. Dermer requested that Squanto accompany him.

"Master Slaney tells me he is good with horses," said Gorges, dabbing his mouth with his handkerchief. "He can go along to help care for the teams of draft animals we're sending out for Mason's use."

"If we catch a ship, can we go on to New England?" asked Dermer, trying not to look too enthusiastic. "I'd really like to get out there and see for myself what others describe."

"Aye, if you catch a ship. I can send your commission out to Monhegan, when the King grants us our patents."

But no ship passed that way, against the storms. Captain Mason employed Dermer and Squanto to explore more of the coasts of

Newfoundland and extend their map. They coasted both the east and west sides of the island, taking sightings and soundings. They even visited the French colony on the mainland. Squanto thought of walking home to Patuxet from there.

"It's a long way," said Dermer, fearing he was about to lose a valuable friend and guide. "A trip among strangers who are at war. It would be too dangerous."

"Danger is a thin wall to desire," said Squanto, smiling. It was one of Master Slaney's sayings.

"True," agreed Dermer, taking Squanto by the upper arm. "But I would hate to lose you, my friend. I've come to depend on having you with me."

Squanto was touched. He trusted Dermer, perhaps even loved him; and now he felt that Dermer loved him, too. They were like brothers. Besides, there was no ship, and it was too far to walk alone. In the end, they returned to Plymouth Fort on the Lands End coast of England.

In his disappointment, Squanto fell into a deep depression. Gorges and Dermer tried to cheer him up, with little success. They gave him beer and sang "Raise the Glass on High, Billy Bigh," but Squanto only cried in his beer.

"Will Tisquantum ever go home to Patuxet?"

he whined. "I want to go home."

The patent letters authorizing colonization, which Gorges and his company expected from King James, were delayed, and delayed, and delayed. Whimsical and childish, James drifted whichever way his counselors puffed, but he refused to make up his mind. Gorges and Slaney sent him a rare parrot from Florida, thinking it would sway his mind to favor them, but it only absorbed his attention in feeding bits of fruit to the bird.

A decision for the adventurers was of no consequence to him; it would hardly change his life. He already had a colony in Virginia, which was more trouble and expense than it was worth; why would he want a second one in New England?

28. Welcome to Monhegan, 1619

> "Upon arriving in Monhegan harbor, Rowcroft had discovered a French fishing barque. Declaring them to be in violation of the royal patent to "The Second Colony," the Company of Northern Virginia, he immediately seized the barque and took the crew prisoners." — Thomas Dermer's report to Sir Ferdinando Gorges, in "A Brief Narration of the Originall Undertaking of the Advancement of Plantation into the Parts of America" (1637).

Squanto shifted from one foot to the other at the ship's rail, looked away, then as quickly looked back. He wanted to shout as the ship came to and headed into the bay, for he recognized Monhegan Island. He could see the wide beach, the stand of fir and pine trees, and the smoke rising from the wigwams of Samoset's village. He bit his lip and touched the lucky charm in his earlobe to hold in his emotions and looked again, unable to believe his eyes. A chill March wind filled the sails, but his heart beat so rapidly, he felt a glow all over.

As soon as the ship dropped anchor, Squanto and Thomas Dermer were in the longboat and anxious to go ashore. Dermer grasped Squanto's upper arm and gave it a squeeze, to let him know that he shared his excitement and happiness at finally arriving in New England. Squanto smiled at his friend to acknowledge the intimate gesture, then looked back toward the beach. A number of Indians were already gathering to welcome the visitors. Even after all these years and at such a distance, he recognized Samoset's tall, straight form.

"Row faster, my friends," said Squanto to the sailors. "Don't you want to get there as soon as possible?"

"We'll get there soon enough," muttered one sailor.

"Probably sooner than we need to," said another.

"Heave to," said a third. "I want to see the natives up close."

As soon as the longboat was in knee-deep water, Squanto leaped over the side and splashed ashore. He embraced Samoset, saying in the Passamaquoddy dialect, "Greetings, grandfather; my heart is glad to see you again."

"Welcome, friend. Welcome to Monhegan," said Samoset in English, embracing Squanto. He added in Passamaquoddy: "This is the fourth time that you have crossed the ocean."

"Yes," admitted Squanto. "I have been away from home for fourteen years, but all I want is to stand in my Patuxet again."

"Patuxet? But you have been to so many interesting places," said Samoset. "Take me with you next time!"

"Oh, grandfather, you don't know how weary one gets. I have visited a great many places in England, and I have been to Newfoundland three times and to Spain twice, but I only want to go home to Patuxet once. I have had enough of travel."

"You are tired of travel, and I would love to go to England," said Samoset.

"Here is my friend, Thomas Dermer. He is like a brother to me," said Squanto, taking Dermer by the upper arm and pulling him forward to meet Samoset. "He is here to find a good place to start a town on the mainland. They will bring a little bit of England to you."

"Welcome, English," said Samoset, taking Dermer's right hand in his and shaking it. "Friend, Squanto; friend, Samoset. You sit my house; eat."

Dermer was a little surprised and uncomfortable with the Indian way of greeting. His impulse and training was to put his right foot forward and make a slight receding bow. He also wanted to get down to business. With Squanto as interpreter, he said, "I am supposed to meet a Captain named Edward Rowcroft here. Have you seen him or his ship?"

Samoset dropped Dermer's hand and turned away, obviously uncomfortable. He touched the bead of pollen sewn into his belt and looked beyond his house, beyond the wigwams of the village, searching for something. "Your countrymen have left only these boats," he said, nervously gesturing down the beach, still not looking at Dermer.

Pulled up on the sand were two shallops, each big enough for four men at the oars, and a gaff-rigged, five-ton pinnace, big enough for perhaps a dozen men, but hardly suitable for sailing on the high seas. Its sail was neatly furled and tied, and looked like it was in good shape.

Looking at the boats, Dermer felt helpless. "But I have orders to take Rowcroft and his ship and explore the coast of the mainland."

Samoset turned back, took Squanto and Dermer by the hands and led them up the beach to his fire and his *comaco*, as a chief's house was called. "Welcome, Captain Dermer," he said in English, then turned to Squanto to translate for him. "Come, both of you, and sit here beside me with my most trusted counselors, and we will smoke as old friends." He called out some orders to nearby warriors, who brought forth a calumet, wrapped in beaver skin and tied with ribbons of deerskin dyed red.

When the pipe was lit, Squanto whispered to Dermer, "He say, best tobacco. Big honor to you."

After the pipe had gone around the circle of counselors once, Samoset clapped his hands and called to one of his wives. "Bring boiled fish for our guest. Bring roasted duck, succotash, and corn cakes. Our guests must be hungry." He kept glancing uneasily to his left, beyond his house.

Before the women could bring the food, he called some of his warriors before the council. "It is time for the Friendship Dance. Dance for these honored guests." At once, some took up drums, others took up whistles, and began a rhythmic enactment of friends meeting after a long absence.

The food was served on small slabs of wood or in clam shells, with a root punch in gourd cups, while the dances continued.

With a slice of mallard and a corn cake in his hand, Samoset leaned toward Dermer and asked, wanting to practice his English, "You have beer?"

"Beer?" said Dermer, taken aback.

"Samoset like beer. You teach Samoset make

beer?"

"I— — I don't know how to make beer," confessed Dermer.

"Oh," sighed Samoset, settling back into his seat. "I am disappointment."

Dermer looked at Squanto, wondering if he should correct Samoset's English. Squanto explained the error in Passamaquoddy.

"Good! Good!" said Samoset, accepting the correction, while looking over his shoulder beyond his *comaco*. Then he turned back toward Dermer and burst into song:

Buck up, Billy. Put your buddy to the bar
And we drink a wee pint...

He broke off, asking in English, "What, a pint?"

"A measure," said Dermer, realizing at once that Samoset would not understand that word. "It tells how much." He held up the gourd from which he drank a dark brown root punch. "It is a cup, maybe twice the size of this cup."

"Ah," sighed Samoset, "Two, this cup." Samoset lifted his own cup and sang:

Raise the glass on high, Billy Bigh, Billy Bigh,

Tomorrow we may die.

"You teach me more of song?" he said to Dermer, smiling.

"I'm sorry," said Dermer. "I don't know that song. My friends and I don't sing it."

"Oh," sighed Samoset, again. "I am disappointment."

"And we prefer wine to beer," Dermer added, beginning to be aware that Samoset would not understand such niceties of English class structure.

Samoset glanced away, touching the protective corn pollen in his belt, neglecting to ask what wine was. To Squanto, he said in Passamaquoddy, "I don't want to spoil your welcome, but I have to tell the truth. Something on my mind has been bothering me." Then, to Dermer, he said in English, "Other white men here."

Dermer soon met a remnant of Edward Rowcroft's crew and learned from them a bizarre tale of Rowcroft's behavior. Upon arriving in Monhegan harbor, Rowcroft had discovered a French fishing barque. Declaring them to be in violation of the royal patent to "The Second Colony," the Company of Northern Virginia, he immediately seized the barque and took the crew prisoners. Besides, they were infringing upon Sir Ferdinando Gorges' fishing rights.

He sent his own ship, a part of his crew, and the French prisoners back to England, while confiscating the French barque as his own. Then, instead of waiting for Thomas Dermer to arrive, as he was instructed to do, Rowcroft set out exploring along the Maine coast. He soon found the barque drew too much water to comfortably scout the coast in shallow water.

A number of the crew began thinking they would follow Rowcroft's example and go into the pirate business for themselves. They plotted to cut Rowcroft's throat and seize the barque, but Rowcroft discovered their plot. He arrested them at the last moment before they could put their plan into action.

Instead of executing the mutineers, however, Rowcroft put seven of them ashore at Sawa-qu-a-tock, which they called Saco–

("These English have the worst time pronouncing plain words," observed Samoset to Squanto).

He left them some provisions and a few weapons. Rowcroft then sailed for Virginia. The mutineers had found their way back to Monhegan Island, where Samoset took them in, awaiting the next English ship that passed.

By Charles Brashear 193

"These are bad fellows, aren't they?" Samoset asked Tisquantum in the Passamaquoddy dialect.

"Perhaps," replied Tisquantum. "When an Englishman violates English law, he is often imprisoned in a room in a special house. The door is locked and the windows have bars across them. Sometimes, the leaders will let them out of this prison, if they agree to become sailors on explorations of distant shores. Many, but not all, sailors are criminals."

"I think these are bad fellows," repeated Samoset.

Thomas Dermer pretty much agreed with Samoset's perception, but he saw nothing to do but take these fellows into his own crew. With Rowcroft gone, Dermer would have to improvise new plans. The ship he and Squanto had come out on was commissioned to fish Monhegan waters and return to England near the end of June. Besides, it, too, was an unsuitable vessel for explorations along the coast.

The captain of the fishing vessel was anxious to get on to his business. "Wha chu wan me do wit dese goods?" Gorges had sent a hold full of trade goods with Dermer: hatchets, knives, copper buckets; coarse blankets, linsey trousers, canvas shirts, looking glasses; vermillion, ocre, charcoal, cobalt powder, colored glass beads, all of which the

Indians would accept in exchange for beaver, bear, and deer pelts; plus dried beef, bacon, and hard tack for his own use. Dermer rented a vacant house from Samoset to store the goods.

Dermer wrote a report to Sir Ferdinando Gorges, which he would send home with the ship in June. He recounted the Rowcroft incident and his own disappointment.

"If I did not have so many responsibilities here as sagamore," said Samoset to Squanto, "I would sail with these fishermen and see the world."

Squanto just laughed. "You cannot be in two places at once. As the Gypsies say, 'With one arse, you cannot sit on two horses.'"

"What is a horse?" asked Samoset with envy in his voice. "And what is a Gypsy?"

***

On the 9th of May 1619, Dermer and Squanto set out from Monhegan Island in the five-ton, open pinnace, with seven mutineers as crew, and a good supply of his trade goods. The pinnace was equipped with a descending board in the hull, which acted as a keel; so the boat could tack within about 25 degrees of a head wind. If he stayed close to the shore and caught coastal breezes, Dermer knew he could scoot along the seaboard toward Virginia, exploring the coast and looking for Rowcroft.

Standing in the prow of the pinnace with Thomas Dermer, Squanto became nervous as they approached St. George's Bay and Pemaquid. He touched his earlobe, but the good luck charm was gone. He had no talisman to protect himself from evil. "You will protect Squanto?" he asked Dermer.

"Why, of course," said Dermer, trying to calm his friend's agitation, "and you'll protect me. God will protect us both. But what are you worried about?"

"Tahanedo," confessed Squanto. "Tahanedo take Tisquantum slave once." He pantomimed dragging himself away by the neck. "Squanto not like be slave."

"Well, we'll tell him that you are a free man now, and we have English muskets to prove it."

"Tahanedo command five hundred warriors," said Squanto, doubting the efficiency of eight English muskets against so many.

But at Pemaquid, they found that very few Passamaquoddies had survived the dying time. Even those few did not know what had happened to Tahanedo. They had never heard of Skettowaroes.

Dermer coasted in and out of the inlets, southwesterly along the shore. He had a copy of Captain John Smith's map of 1614, but he and Sir

Ferdinando Gorges rather distrusted Smith's flamboyance and exaggeration. Part of Dermer's mission was to verify and add to the map, as well as chart out a desirable location for founding a colony.

They found the ruins of the Popham colony on Sagadahoc peninsula, but no one was there. The Indians had not even used the buildings for shelter. Much of the barricade had begun to rot. Other timbers were so contorted and dried that they had warped themselves out of the construction. The wood was so parched and bleached that it gave no heat when used in a camp-fire.

A few days further down the coast, they came to Sawa-qu-a-tock, where the mutineers had stayed for a while. What few natives they found still had open sores from the dying sickness. They ran from the Englishmen and hid as soon as they could, fearing some worse fate than they already suffered. The sailors were happy not to be exposed to whatever pox the natives had. Dermer agreed and departed quickly.

Squanto sat in the prow of the pinnace, withdrawn and pensive.

"What's the matter, my friend?" asked Dermer. "It's not like you to gaze at your own mocassins, instead of whatever adventure is ahead."

"Many, many, many Indian dead," said Squanto. "Many, many, many."

Dermer did not comment, but he would write to Sir Ferdinando Gorges that the natives had been so weakened by the epidemic as to be unable to put up an effective defense of their land.

29. Too many Ghosts

> A mallard hung by his feet from the roof of the wigwam. The worms had long since eaten all of the insides, and there was nothing left but dusty feathers, held together by a few shreds of dried skin. In a fishing basket was a desiccated perch, hardly recognizable as a once-living thing.
> – Alvin G. Weeks,
> *Massasoit of the Wampanoags.*, 1919.

Squanto fidgeted with eagerness, now at the prow, now at the gunwale ready to hop out and wade the rest of the way. They were entering the little harbor called New Plymouth on John Smith's map, which Squanto recognized as Patuxet. But something was seriously wrong. No one was there to greet them. There was no sound. Dermer hauled in the sail and ordered the men to row up the little waterway beside the village site.

Having no protective charm, Squanto stepped out of the boat hesitantly and looked around. Several of the wigwams had been burned, a sign that their owners were dead. Other houses were still intact, but no one was in them, no one in the whole village. Baskets, clothing, weapons, good-luck charms had been dropped hap-hazardly, as if the owners had lost all care. But there was no sign of any living being, not even a barking dog.

Squanto crept up to the wigwam of his parents, muttering "Aha, your relative," at the door in Wampanoag, to let anyone inside know that a visitor was at the door. No mat hung across the opening, nor did a stick lean across the threshold. The owners left no such signs that a visitor was not welcome.

Cautiously, he stepped inside. A mallard hung by his feet from the roof of the wigwam. The worms had long since eaten all of the insides. Nothing was left but dusty feathers, held together by a few shreds of dried skin. In a fishing basket was a desiccated perch, hardly recognizable as a once-living thing.

The platform bed had not been used in a long time. Rats and mice had carried away the pelts, bit by bit, and scattered the straw underlayment. Under the bed, he saw a strange good-luck charm, but he did not reach for it. One did not knowingly tamper with another man's medicine, for fear it was contaminated with witchcraft.

A sinew-backed bow hung on the wall by the

door. He did not recognize the markings on it. Perhaps they were the marks or brands of one of his sisters' husbands; perhaps his parents had given their wigwam to a son-in-law before they passed on. That would mean that his brothers were dead before his father, for property passed from father to son among the Wampanoag.

He picked up a clay water jar; it was empty, but he could see the rings of sediment left by the evaporating water. There was not a sound in the house, not even the creaking of the roof as it moved in the wind. He could see sky through holes in the thatch.

He left everything as it was and went back outside. Dermer and the sailors had retracted the board, pulled the pinnace out of the water, posted a sentinel, and were preparing to make camp.

"They all gone," said Squanto. "All people gone."

"They probably withdrew into the woods, when they saw us. We'll encounter some of them, if we walk a little way into the forests."

"Wigwams not use since long time."

"Don't worry, my friend. We'll find some of your people straightaway."

"My father's mark no longer in his wigwam."

"Do you think he is dead?"

Squanto bit his lip and looked away, nodding. "But not die in wigwam. Give wigwam to someone else and die outside. If die in wigwam, it be burned." He looked backward over his shoulder. He felt he was being followed by ghosts, and he had no charm to protect himself.

After the sailors made camp, Dermer hung his bag of glass beads over his shoulder, and he and Squanto walked a little way inland on paths almost overgrown with vegetation. They frightened a few wild turkeys, and squirrels scolded them from the back sides of trees, but they saw no signs of human life.

In a small clearing, they found two mats on the ground imperfectly covered with earth. Dermer scratched away some of the dirt and lifted the edge of a mat. Under it was a rabbitskin bundle, wrapped and sewn with a pack needle and bark thread. Beside the bundle was a small bow, about thirty inches long, and three small arrows. He began opening the bundle; the rabbitskin crumbled under his fingers. The bundle contained a finely ground red powder, but he could feel and see bones.

"No!" cried Squanto in alarm, when he saw what Dermer was doing. "No open. This is child's grave. Raven clan. See mark on bow. Son of head man. We not disturb dead in their resting. Evil come back with dead one."

"What is this red powder?" asked Dermer.

"Wrap dead one in red powder. Keep wolves from eat the body. One who die needs good body in heaven."

Dermer closed the grave and smoothed the dirt over it.

In another clearing, they found a fallow cornfield and another deserted wigwam. It was longer than usual, made of strong young saplings and covered on both the inside and outside with well-made mats of a coarse grass. Inside, were wooden bowls, trays, dishes, earthen pots, handbaskets made of crab shells tied together, and an English pail that had no handle, though it had ears for lifting.

Along the back wall, larger baskets contained a small amount of parched corn. Hanging from the arches overhead were deer's feet and horns, eagle claws and wings, fans made of raven tail feathers and wrapped intricately with colored sinew. On all sides, small trees and vines had begun to reclaim the clearing.

"Powah's house, holy man's house," said Squanto, indicating the marks on the baskets and dance items. A fine patina of dust covered everything.

"It looks like they just stepped out for a

minute," said Dermer.

"We go, too," said Squanto. "Too many ghosts here. Evil. I not know how handle power."

A path choked with weeds led from the clearing to a larger path. Squanto recognized it: "Trail to Nemasket. Big town, about four hour walk." He pointed inland, along the trail.

"Well, if we don't find anything around here, we'll walk to Nemasket tomorrow," said Dermer.

On the way back to the coast, they came upon a slightly larger clearing, where volunteer beans and corn grew in the empty fields. Three wigwams stood in the clearing, all deserted like the others. Near the back edge of the cornfield, they found several adult graves and the scattered bones of one man.

"E-e-e-e-e-e," keened Tisquantum in grief, as he dropped to the ground beside the man's skull. "Aa-a-a-a-a-e-e-e-e-e."

Dermer dropped to his knees beside his friend and put his arm across his shoulder. He stared at the pieces. It was not hard to figure out what had happened. The man had buried each one of his extended family, but no one was left to bury him; so wolves had scattered his bones.

***

At Nemasket the next afternoon, Squanto and Dermer met some friendly Indians. They did not recognize Tisquantum, but they had heard about him. They gave Tisquantum the bad news: Every single person of every single clan of Patuxet had died in the sickness time. Other towns and villages had been hit hard by the Indian Fever, but Patuxet had been totally destroyed. Tisquantum was the only one left to mourn the dead and burn the effects of the departed.

He withdrew in silence and squatted by the stream. It was hard to grasp. All of the people? All those he had yearned to greet again after so many years? All of them? He could hardly believe it. Surely, there were a few survivors. Surely, there were more than the uneasy ghosts he felt following him to the edge of each clearing.

Dermer found him staring at a small stick on the ground and rocking back and forth on his haunches, moaning and protesting, as if carrying on some terrible argument in his mind.

"I'm sorry," said Dermer. "God's will is sometimes hard to bear. But we just have to accept it and go on. I just don't know what to do. Tell me what I can do to help you."

Squanto looked up and focused on him. There was the trouble. The English. The white man had brought the disease to Patuxet. He felt a macabre urge to kill a white man. If he had a knife in his hand, he could slit the man's throat and leave his bones for the wolves. He sprang up and shoved the man away, so that he toppled to the ground. Squanto straightened up, poised to leap on the man and finish him off, but stopped himself. Dermer was his friend, his friend.

"I sorry," Squanto said. "I— — Leave me alone." He did not understand why he was so angry at his friend.

Dermer got up, brushing the dirt from his legs. He was not angry. How could he be angry at a friend who was in such agony? He tried to change the subject: "The people here say there is another, bigger town a day's walk on down this trail, a town called Pokánoket. They've sent runners to tell them at that place that we are here."

Squanto waited a long moment, staring at Dermer, trying to understand what he had just said. "Pokánoket big town, long day walk," said Squanto, at last, throwing his arms wide to indicate a huge town to the southwest. "Pokánoket clan is ruling clan of Wampanoag nation. Wampanoag kings come from Pokánoket clan. Pokánoket clan hate English. Hate English— Hate English— "

He could not find the words to express his anger. He wanted to hurt Dermer, to scare him, to make him creep away in fear. "Pokánoket clan have more warriors than all the Massachusetts and Nausets together. More than all warriors between here and Monhegan. Pokánoket clan kill English. Pokánoket make war, kill all white men. No peace. No peace till everybody dead."

Dermer was silent, for he realized that anything he said would be met with renewed fury. There was nothing to do but leave his friend alone until the passion for vengeance had burned itself out. "How helpless we humans are before God's omnipotence!" he thought. "How helpless and alone, when our need is greatest."

30. "No Bones for the Wolves"

> At Patuxet, he started a fire with a drill and put flames to his parents' wigwam at once. He went about the village area, picking up loose mats, bits of clothing, lances, bows and arrows, everything that he could find in Patuxet or the nearby fields. All these he piled on the fire.

Two days later, "two Kings of Pokánoket," as Dermer called them in his report to Gorges, arrived in Nemasket. One of them was Quadequina, sachem of the town of Pokánoket, the Wampanoag capital on Narragansett Bay, and younger brother of The Massasoit, great sachem-in-chief of the Wampanoag Confederation.

The Wampanoag leaders wanted to know what the intentions of the English were.

"We come in peace," Dermer assured them, with Squanto as translator. "We only wish to trade with the Wampanoag people. We have buckets and hatchets, knives with iron blades, blankets, shirts, trousers— all things the Wampanoag want to live in comfort and ease. The Wampanoag have beaver and otter skins, deer skins and bear skins, corn and beans— all things which the English want to make their lives easier. If the English and Wampanoag exchange these things, both will be richer."

Quadequina liked Dermer's speech. It was his intent, also, to be at peace with the English. If the English would promise not to kidnap the Wampanoag people and carry them away, the Wampanoag would meet the English ships at the coast and trade.

Quadequina gave Dermer a flint knife with a tight raw-hide handle. To Tisquantum he gave a necklace of power-shells from Narragansett Bay, saying, "This will protect you from most evils."

As he put the necklace over Tisquantum's head, Tisquantum could feel the magic of the shells tingling across his skin. What a wonderful development, thought Tisquantum. The Manitou was smiling again on him and his projects.

Then Quadequina called on the people of Nemasket for a banquet to purify all hearts and dedicate them to peace and friendship.

The people of Nemasket cooked perch on willow grills over open fires and boiled corn, beans, and squash together. They had corn cakes sweetened with maple sugar and a bitter, brown beverage made of marsh roots, which went with the food nicely.

Quadequina himself danced in honor of Dermer and their agreement to be friends. Squanto could feel the power of the necklace burning into his chest, and he was warmed by the rituals that he recognized. Realizing that Dermer would not understand his obligation to reciprocate, he pulled his friend to his feet and insisted he go through the motions of a dance.

Quadequina brought with him fifty warriors and a Frenchman who had survived a shipwreck, only to be held captive by the Indians and transported from place to place to be exhibited as a curiosity to the people. The man had learned some Wampanoag, and Dermer knew some French and Latin from his school days; so both his urge to free a fellow European and his calculation that the man might be a good servant in his own crew prompted him to ransom the Frenchman.

Dermer gave Quadequina a good belt knife, a hatchet, a bracelet of white beads, and a cut-glass pendant on an ear-ring. And Quadequina delivered the Frenchman into Dermer's hands.

When the two groups finally parted, each had great confidence in the other's good will.

***

Back at Patuxet, Squanto would not

acknowledge the abandoned wigwams. He went directly to the pinnace and insisted they leave at once. "Bad place," he said. "This, bad place. Dead people walk around. Too many ghosts.

"And men must leave things they pick up: baskets, bows, good luck charms, everything. Belong to ghosts."

Dermer was surprised, for he had not noticed his friend was afraid of the dead. However, the important thing was that Squanto wanted to leave Patuxet, wanted to leave as badly as he had wanted to arrive. For whatever reason, Squanto was anxious to continue his travels with Thomas Dermer.

Dermer touched at Cape Cod and, with Squanto's help, ransomed another French shipwreck victim from Aspinet, the sachem of Nauset. This one had been in captivity for three years, transported from village to village for public punishment in town dance squares. Numerous scars, some of them not wholly healed, testified to his tortures. He had to be restrained from taking vengeance as soon as he could get his hands on a sword.

"Be sensible," said the first Frenchman. "You'll get us all killed. Be happy that a civilized man has rescued you. Be content simply to leave the savages to their savagery."

By Charles Brashear 211

At Capawack, the big island south of Cape Cod, Dermer collected dirt samples from holes he found partially dug out, thinking this was the island where gold was reported.

"This island, Capawack," said Squanto. "Where Epanow live. We find Epanow and say hello?"

"If we find him pretty quickly," said Dermer. "I've got to get back to Monhegan before that ship leaves for England."

He also collected samples of plants and rocks to send to Sir Ferdinando Gorges. Then he hastened back to Monhegan Island, arriving on 23 June 1619. He found the fishing ship loaded with quality fish and ready to sail for England.

Dermer wrote a report for Gorges, including a journal of his explorations from the Penobscot River to Cape Cod, and sent his samples of dirt, rocks, and the plants he thought might prove valuable.

The tortured Frenchman and some of Dermer's crew chose to ship for England, but the other Frenchman stayed with Dermer, who had so few men he could hardly leave an adequate guard with the pinnace when he went ashore for wood, water, or food.

Captain Rowcroft had not returned; so Dermer still did not have the means to explore the way he and Gorges had agreed upon. *The Sampson,* a ship from Cape Ward, Virginia, was then in Monhegan harbor; they had been catching fish off the mainland and were ready to return to Jamestown. Dermer sent his surplus supplies to Virginia with them; then he and Squanto set out in the pinnace again, determined to sail to Virginia and find Rowcroft.

At Sawa-qu-a-tock, Squanto wanted to be put ashore. "You mean you want to leave me?" asked Dermer, unable to understand.

"Yes," said Squanto. "Something I must do."

"You've been acting awfully strange, my friend," said Dermer. "Ever since we left Nemasket, you've been acting crazy, like the moon had gotten to you. What's the matter? Tell me what's wrong, and I'll try to help you."

"No. No help. Tisquantum must do alone."

"You're not making sense, Squanto. We've been through a lot together, haven't we? You and me; you protect me and I protect you, right?"

Tisquantum touched the necklace Quadequina had given him and silently recited a little charm. "You give me bag of beads? I trade for food."

"Yes, of course. You've certainly earned our many thanks. But why won't you stay with us?"

By Charles Brashear 213

He would sail with Dermer again, but now, he didn't want to wait for his capricious little boat. Dermer and his pinnace could be carried backward by tides, or cracked on the rocks in a storm. Tisquantum couldn't wait for such delays.

By keeping at it, day and night, he traveled to Patuxet in three days.

At Patuxet, he started a fire with a drill and put flames to his parents' wigwam at once. He went about the village, picking up loose mats, bits of clothing, lances, bows and arrows, everything that he could find in Patuxet or the nearby fields. All these he piled on the fire.

He pulled burning brands from the fire and put them to the vacant wigwams. He threw in the baskets, broke the clay vessels, destroyed and burned everything. And when the ashes were cool, he scattered them, so that soon no one would know there had ever been a village there.

He went inland, along the same choked path he and Dermer had explored. At the Powah's clearing, he set fire to the wigwam, piled on all the bits of clothing, mats, weapons, ceremonial items, everything he thought might have belonged to the shaman. With brands, he fired the other wigwams and storage huts.

Then he returned to the corn field where he and Dermer had found the scattered bones of a man. Again, he set fire to the wigwam and piled on all the artifacts in the clearing. When the fire was high, he gathered what bones of the man he could find and threw them on the fire. At least, the man's spirit would have the bones the wolves hadn't eaten.

Then Tisquantum followed other trails to other clearings. He burned every wigwam he could find. And in each clearing, when the ashes were cool, he scattered them, so that soon, after a few storms, after a few seasons, no one would know that houses had once stood here and happy people had walked among friends and relatives.

At last, the ghosts of his family would not be homeless in heaven.

And there were no bones for the wolves.

31. Another Kind of Rope

His wrists had been tied many times with small ropes, his shoulders with large ones. He had controlled John Slaney's ponies with a rope, just as Slaney had controlled him with an imaginary rope. He had hauled sail with a rope, and the same ropes had pulled him across the ocean four times. And now, The Massasoit was putting yet another kind of rope on his life. His necklace felt like a rope.

Tisquantum had slumped to his knees amid the ashes of Patuxet and was keening for the dead. Others came into the clearing, but he made no move to defend himself.

"We saw the smoke from far off."

Though he looked up, Tisquantum said nothing. He saw a man in front of him. The man wore a yellow feather, and there was a mulberry thumb-print on the little stick he carried, but those things did not mean anything to Tisquantum. In the end, all, everything, everyone came to ashes. No more than that. Nothing had importance. Nothing had meaning.

The yellow feather turned, nodding in approval. "It was a great task, doing service for so many dead relatives. You must be exhausted from the sorrow."

The man shifted on his haunches, facing Tisquantum. "I have made inquiries. No person of your clan exists. No person of this town survives. You are the last citizen of Patuxet."

Still, Tisquantum did not respond. The English purse of beads swung on its strap over his neck and shoulder, but what of that? It, too, was meaningless. He looked at the ground between his knees, where a small stick lay beside a few pebbles. The stick would rot and become earth, or burn and become nothing more than air and ash, but the pebble would survive all. He must study pebbles. From pebbles, he could learn survival.

Without looking, yellow feather signaled to his retainers, and a woman came forward with a deerskin bag which contained Johnny-cakes and slices of venison. He took a corn cake from the bag and offered it to Tisquantum, saying, "We know you have not eaten since you started the burnings. Here is food."

Tisquantum made no move to take the Johnny-cake. He was studying the pebble.

The man reached out and turned Tisquantum's wrist, so that his palm was extended. He put the corn cake in the hand, closed it, and guided it to Tisquantum's mouth. "Eat," he commanded gently. "Eat, for you must live."

Tisquantum watched in amazement as his mouth bit into the corn bread and began chewing. And there was someone's hand, holding a bit of sliced venison in front of the mouth. The mouth opened and took the meat.

The teeth chewed. The throat swallowed. The stomach awakened and told Tisquantum that he was hungry. The hunger made his eyes focus. There was Ousa Mequin, The Massasoit, sachem-in-chief of the Wampanoag Confed-eration, on his knees in front of him.

Tisquantum bowed at once. "Forgive me, Great Sachem. My eyes hardly know what they see."

"I understand," said The Massasoit. "Sorrow for even one relative can blind a man or woman, and you have lost many."

Tisquantum looked at the pebble again. "All? Did none survive?"

"None. If you had not been kidnaped by the yang-kaysh, you would not be here."

Tisquantum looked at the ashes of many wigwams. Soon, in a season, there would be hardly any sign that a village once stood here. Soon, there would be no sign that many people had walked these paths, going about the business of daily life. "The ghosts of Patuxet will be lonesome," he said to The Massasoit. "Who will keep company with the ghosts of Patuxet?"

"You will, my son," said The Massasoit, putting his hand on Tisquantum's shoulder and making a point of touching the power necklace. "It is your duty."

"Come," said The Massasoit, standing up and pulling at Tisquantum's arm to get him to stand up also. "I will take you into my clan. My relatives will be your relatives. I will adopt you. As my son, you will have relatives in every village and town of the Wampanoag Confederacy."

He looked around at his traveling companions, his counselors. They nodded their agreement.

Tisquantum looked at The Massasoit. The Great Sachem was no more than nine or ten years older than Tisquantum. It would be hard to think of him as a father. Yet, the invitation could not be denied. "May it be so," said Tisquantum. He could feel the necklace glowing again.

"Follow me," said The Massasoit, leading Tisquantum. "I have a wigwam less than half a day's walk to the southwest from here. It is located near a nice little pond where perch and bream are many. Deer come to the water's edge to drink.

Ducks and geese swim among the reeds. The earth will provide for you there, if you will do your part."

***

The wigwam was set among trees on high ground, away from the fog and mist that formed on the water's surface when the temperature dropped. It was a small wigwam, in good condition with a woven mat for a door, but quite empty. Tisquantum looked at the door post. There was the mark of a man he did not recognize and, below it, the mulberry thumb-print of The Massasoit.

The Massasoit saw Tisquantum looking at the signs. "The man who owned this wigwam was considerate enough to die outside, so the wigwam did not have to be destroyed," he explained. "Also, he gave me the wigwam, so that it was my personal property when he died. I now give it to you. We will put your mark on the door."

Tisquantum did not move.

"What is your mark?" asked The Massasoit. "I will put it there myself."

"I do not have a mark," said Tisquantum. "I was only fourteen when the Passamaquoddies first kidnaped me. I had not earned a mark."

"Well, let us choose one for you. What would most identify you?"

Tisquantum thought for a while, touching his necklace for inspiration. He was aware of the great honor in being permitted to choose his own emblem. But the usual totems of Wampanoag life seemed distant; he had hardly lived among them. He had spent half his life, the half he remembered best, among the English, on the waves, pulling ropes to hoist sails, or being pulled by ropes wrapped around his arms and shoulders.

The Massasoit was waiting, looking at him. "What will it be? What thread of meaning will tie you to your past?"

What had tied him to his past? His wrists had been tied many times with small ropes, his shoulders with large ones. He had controlled John Slaney's ponies with a rope, just as Slaney had controlled him with an imaginary rope. He had hauled sail with a rope, and the same ropes had pulled him across the ocean four times. And now, The Massasoit was putting yet another kind of rope on his life. His necklace felt like a rope.

"Let my mark be a rope," said Tisquantum. "All my life I have been controlled with a rope."

"So let it be," said The Massasoit, and, taking paint and a chewed twig from one of his followers, he drew on the door post a row of double ogive curves, linked to represent the twisted strands of a rope. "This house is now your house."

A man scooped the sand and ashes from the fire-pit and began to kindle a fire. A woman came forward with a bearskin blanket and spread it across the raised bed frame. Another placed a shallow basket of parched corn in the food-storage corner. "Now you have a place to hang your possessions," said The Massasoit, indicating the English bag swinging beneath Tisquantum's arm. "And your new aunt, Miana-mohahas," he added, indicating the woman with the bearskin blanket, "will clean your house and fix your food until you have a woman of your own."

Tisquantum took the bag off his shoulder and hung it on a short branch that had been left on the framework of the house as a peg. He opened the bag. He still had a few beads that Thomas Dermer had given him. He gave a red bead to the woman who was spreading his bed, and a blue one to the man who had kindled the fire. To The Massasoit, he gave a cut-glass pendant that caused the light to sparkle like sunlight caught in a dew drop.

He looked around at his new home. It would do. It was pretty isolated, so he would be alone with his thoughts, which he preferred. Yet he was not far from the path that led from Manomet to Nemasket; so he would often meet travelers. And the fallow field nearby was ready to be planted again.

"I will need a bow and arrows," he said. "I

will have to hunt. Learn how to hunt. Can I buy a bow and arrows from someone?"

A man stepped forward, offering his bow. It was marked with a symbol to represent a wildcat. Tisquantum gave the man three beads, which pleased him as a rich exchange. "I will mark this bow and quiver with a rope," the man said loudly, to all around, "so that whosoever sees them will know that they belong to Tisquantum."

"We shall leave you now," said The Massasoit, grasping Tisquantum by the upper arm. "Come to Sowams at Thanksgiving. We will perform the ceremony of adoption."

32. The Murderers

"That is why we need to know everything we can about the white man. Only by good knowledge can we form a workable defense." —

Ousa Mequin (Yellow Feather), The Massasoit

Tisquantum spent the next months at Sowams, where The Massasoit adopted him into the Pokánoket clan. The Great Sachem wanted to learn everything he could about the English. "Tell me about their houses and clothing and foods, - their treatment of enemies, their methods in war."

Their ships were terrifying miracles, as were their long knives, and, above all, their matchlock muskets. A dozen little wars showed that a small number of Englishmen with armor and muskets, perhaps as few as fifteen, could withstand and, indeed, conquer a thousand warriors with bows and arrows or lances. "How can even a brave and worthy Wampanoag deal with such power?"

Talking about the English made Squanto homesick. He missed blood puddings and beef pot-pies. He missed shirts, and trousers, and boots that came up to his knees. He missed speaking their language, and laughing with comrades, and singing songs while drinking their beer.

"Your mind is constipated with these longings, my son," The Massasoit pointed out. "They need no rope to enslave you. You have given them your heart."

"No, no," protested Tisquantum. "I care nothing for most of them. They could vanish for all I care."

That was true for Sir Ferdinando Gorges, and Captain John Smith, and John Slaney; he saw that such men were interested only in their own profit. But he admitted that he loved Thomas Dermer as a brother, and he would do all he could to help his brother with his designs.

"Come," commanded The Massasoit, "we will wash this trash from your body and mind." The Great Sachem led Tisquantum and others to the bath house on the banks of the Kickemuit River. Its stone floor was heated the same way a pit for baking clams was heated.

When the coals and ashes were raked out, the hot stones were covered with seaweed, and people sat in the house until they had sweated a great deal. After they jumped into the river to wash off, they came out re-newed, young again, with minds fresh and eager to celebrate the sunlight sparkling in a dew-drop on a leaf.

By Charles Brashear 225

The good feeling made Tisquantum think of Thomas Dermer. He and Dermer had arranged to meet in the spring at Sakonnet, and Squanto would sail away with Dermer again. The thought of it lifted his spirits.

***

In the time of budding leaves, news came of a massacre at Pocasset, a village on Buzzard's Bay. A ship's captain had invited a great many Wampanoags aboard his ship for a demonstration of his fire-power. The white man loaded his small cannons, called "murderers," with grape shot and shrapnel and fired them into the line of Indians standing along the rail.

At least forty were killed, many others wounded, and the survivors had a hard time coming away in their canoes, for the musket balls kept making little water-spouts in Buzzard's Bay.

With a hatred to feed his foolhardiness, Corbitant, the sachem of Pocasset, led a party of warriors against the ship, vowing that he would slay every white man he could catch. He killed only a few before the ship's fire-power forced him to withdraw. A great many of his warriors were killed or wounded.

"How is one to deal with such treachery?" The Massasoit wondered, fingering the yellow feather that was his name-sake. "Are all the

English like that?"

"No, No. Those weren't English!" exclaimed Tisquantum. "They must have been French or Spanish. My English do not kill like that."

"Aren't they all alike?" asked The Massasoit. "All I've seen look alike. All I've heard about do the same things. English, Dutch, French, Spanish—all white men are alike."

"When you get to know a few of them," said Tisquantum, "you can tell them apart."

"Well, I'm not sure I want to know any of them. They are dangerous."

Several of his followers grunted their agreement.

"But how are we to deal with them?" The Massasoit went on. "Corbitant was clearly courageous to attack them, no doubt about that, but the results were disastrous. If the whites attacked Pokánoket, a resistance like Corbitant's would only bring another massacre. The white men can repeat the murders any time their whim moves them.

"That is why we need to know everything we can about the white man. Only by good knowledge can we form a workable defense. Tell me more about the English."

"I hardly know what else to say," responded

Tisquantum, lifting the front of his necklace to loosen it. And he felt jealous. He wanted to keep his memories to himself, not share them with The Massasoit. It was almost as if The Massasoit were commanding him to betray his friends. He felt the strong urge to say, "I prefer not to."

33. "My Savage Entreated Hard for Me"

> "We had not now that faire quarter amongst the savages as before, which I take it was by reason of our Savage's absence, who desired (in regard of our long journey) to stay with some of our savage friends at Sawa-qu-a-tock..."
> — Thomas Dermer, letter to
> Sir Ferdinando Gorges, 27 Dec 1619

Tisquantum sat on the ground in front of his wigwam, bending and tying willow branches to make a chair. Perhaps it was foolish of him, but he had come to prefer sitting in a chair to sitting on the ground, just as he preferred cloth garments to skins.

Without stopping his work, he and his aunt watched a man coming up the sunlit path to his house. It was a messenger. Miana-mohahas would give him a handful of parched corn and a drink of water, and the man would tell them the news.

The messenger did not know the name of the

Englishman he described, but Tisquantum recognized Thomas Dermer from the details. Dermer's little pinnace had been caught in a storm off Cape Ann and was driven toward the crags. By a great effort, Dermer managed to miss the boulders, only to be lodged in the rocks. The keel, or plank, was damaged on a submerged bar.

The men got off safely and waded ashore, but they lost many of their provisions, especially their dried beef and cider. Yet, when the sky was clear again, they pulled their boat free of its trap, salvaged some of their trade goods, repaired the plank, plugged the few leaks, and set out again.

"One has to admire these fellows," remarked the messenger. "Many would give up in the face of so many troubles, but these yang-kaysh... I wonder if there is anything that will stop them? You have been among them, my friend. Have you seen anything that will stop them?"

"Only their gold," said Tisquantum. "Or rather lack of it. The only thing I have seen stop them is lack of their money."

Dermer and his little party had made their way slowly down the coast and were now on the lower part of Cape Cod peninsula. They had almost nothing to trade— they had saved only their muskets, lead, and powder, from their shipwreck, plus a parcel of hatchets and butcher knives— yet they seemed to expect Indians to supply them with corn and venison, as well as clothing. They were having a hard time.

The English in their pitiful little boat had no fuses to light their matchlocks, so it would have been easy to simply kill them. But Iyanough, the sachem of Cummaquid, had dissuaded the belligerents, saying that if they killed these Englishmen, the ship they came from would surely send more, and the invaders would surely have fire to tinder their powder. It was not wise to provoke the English to revenge.

In the end, reluctantly, the people of Cummaquid gave the English a supply of corn and beans in exchange for a few hatchets, and the English moved further out on the Atlantic coast of Cape Cod, where they camped for several days on a beach. They killed some game, cured the meat, rested, and repaired their equipment. Then they went on.

"But they will meet only trouble," said the messenger. "Mano-Kiehtan of Manomoyack has prepared a trap for them. He will capture them, and he will not be so mild as Iyanough of Cummaquid. Mano-Kiehtan will torture the English several days, before killing them."

After the messenger had gone, Squanto sat aside his unfinished willow chair and gazed long hours into the twilight, thinking about the situation of the English. They were such helpless children. They could do almost nothing for themselves, but required constant care and attention.

Yet, they were powerful. Their guns were dangerous and their persistence was terrifying. It would be good to be rid of them for once and all. Still, Thomas Dermer was Squanto's friend. They had traveled together, eaten together, slept in the same cramped space, provided for the safety of each other, as if they were brothers.

"I must have supplies for traveling at dawn tomorrow," he told his aunt, Miana-mohahas. "As much as I hate to leave home once more, I must go and get my Dermer out of trouble again."

***

When Squanto reached Manomoyack Harbor, a farce had been in building for several days. Squanto knew that even Thomas Dermer would have thought it comic, had he not been in the middle of the action— and all of it threatening to become tragic at any moment.

ThroughMano-Kiehtan's ruse, in which Dermer thought the Nauset warriors were trying to murder the guard at the pinnace, Mano-Kiehtan succeeded in capturing Thomas Dermer and demanded ransom for him.

Dermer bought his freedom with a bundle of five hatchets, but, when the hatchets were delivered to Mano-Kiehtan, Dermer found himself no more free than he had been before. The messenger was taken prisoner.

In fury, Dermer grabbed Mano-Kiehtan himself in a hammer-lock and half-nelson, then knocked him out. He managed to get his hands on his own sword and musket, as well as a twig from the fire to light his matchlock. The Indians were terrified of English muskets; so the main body of the warriors ran to take cover in the trees. Dermer and the messenger then took Mano-Kiehtan and two of his advisors back to the pinnace and held them hostage.

For safety, the English rowed a furlong off the beech. Mano-Kiehtan tried to jump overboard, but an alert sailor grabbed him and tied his wrists behind the mast. At gunpoint, they tied the others to the gunwale. Dermer demanded a canoe full of corn as ransom for the three Nauset leaders.

When Squanto arrived, the corn was being delivered, but a plot for another ambush was under way.

"Stop! Stop!" he yelled in both languages. "This quarrel has no good end for either of you."

"Squanto?!" cried Dermer. "How did you get here?"

"Stay out of this, Tisquantum," said Mano-Kiehtan, still tied to the mast, "or I will have to kill you at the same time I kill all the other yang-kaysh."

"This Judas planned to exhibit me like a savage in all his dirty villages, then take off my head," said Dermer. "Damn me, but I will have his life! I will have his life, or he mine."

"What the benefit to you, my friend, if Mano-Kiehtan die? You slay him, you forced ever after steer wide of this place. Always be careful that none from here come near you." Squanto paused to let them understand that.

"Others enjoy Monomayack's grain, deer and turkey, water, wood, but not you. Why a man of thought give himself such a handicap? That side of your spirit that love evil rejoice. But side of your spirit that love good fellowship and honesty surely grieve."

And to Mano-Kiehtan, he said, "What gain to you, Grandfather, if you win this squabble and kill these Englishmen? Your deeds in battle and your fame among your people do not need the conquest of five puny men in a leaky boat." Again, Squanto paused.

"Would a great leader be not greater, who has a spirit to forgive enemies, rather than seek their destruction by whatever means?

"And afterwards, as your friends, these former foes can bring you knives, blankets, hatchets— Oh, I tell you, Grandfather, they have so many wondrous machines, as well as cloth for blankets and clothes and metal knives and cooking pots. These can all be yours in trade.

"Would not a man of vision give himself that glory, that leads his people into a better life?"

Both Mano-Kiehtan and Dermer were silent, thinking over what Squanto said. But neither was ready to relent.

"Look," Tisquantum said to both of them, speaking first in one language, then in the other, "Captain Dermer has hatchets which Mano-Kiehtan needs. Mano-Kiehtan has corn which Captain Dermer needs. Better that you both win, by accepting in peace what the other has. Is it not better to make profit of this conflict, rather than loss?"

Both leaders were still silent, but Squanto saw that they had yielded.

"Take the corn from the canoe into the pinnace," said Squanto, like a captain, feeling the warm strength in his necklace. "Put the hatchets into the canoe. Then Mano-Kiehtan and his Panisees can return to Manomoyack, and Captain Dermer can continue toward Virginia."

"So let it be," said Mano-Kiehtan.

By Charles Brashear 235

"All right," said Dermer. "But leave them tied until we have moved the corn."

"There is no peace while one man is in a rope," said Squanto, surprised that he sounded again like his old friend, Draghan. Slowly, deliberately, he untied Mano-Kiehtan's hands and loosed the others from their bonds.

Mano-Kiehtan stood near the mast, rubbing his wrists where the rope had chafed. Dermer stood at the stern of the pinnace, his musket at the ready. It was an awkward truce, until the exchange had been made and the Indians were on their way back to shore in the canoe.

Squanto stayed with Dermer. "I'll swear, Squanto, King James needs a man of your skills in his foreign service. But," he added after a moment of thought, "he would be too childish to recognize it."

To his employer, Sir Ferdinando Gorges, Thomas Dermer wrote on 27 Dec 1619 that he came away with his life, only because "my savage entreated hard for me."

34. "If he comes again, I Shall Have to Kill Him"

> "I do not know how long I could be civil to an Englishman, even one who is your brother. Tell your Captain Dermer that he should not come back here. If he comes again to Capawack, I shall have to kill him."
>
> —Epanow, Sachem of Capawack

"Greetings, Grandfather," said Tisquantum in Wampanoag, as he kneeled before the near-giant Epanow, sachem of Capawack Island, where Dermer had stopped for water and wood. "As I once said—when I am on Capawack, I will bend my knee to you."

"Stand up, Tisquantum. You have no need to cower beneath any sachem. Least of all, me. You gave me good advice, though I did not know it at the time. I am heartily glad to see you again. But who is this fellow with you?"

"This is Captain Thomas Dermer," said Squanto in English. "He is my friend. Like a brother to me."

"Welcome to Capawack," said Epanow, who, as Dermer reported to Gorges, spoke 'indifferent good English.' "Friend of Tisquantum, friend of Epanow." He made the hand-language sign for friend and pointed to Tisquantum; made it again and pointed to his own chest. He extended his huge hand and shook hands with Dermer, who was getting used to this Native American way of greeting.

Epanow led them to his *comaco,* invited them to sit beside his fire, and called for his pipe and tobacco. After they had smoked, Epanow called his women to serve them Johnny-cakes, succotash, and roasted mallard.

When they had eaten to the first pause, Epanow asked Dermer: "So. Why ... you here? What ... business?"

"I must get to Virginia soon," said Dermer. "There is a ship's captain, Edward Rowcroft, whom I must meet. We are to explore and trade together."

Epanow pointed to Dermer's chest: "Work for Rowcroft?"

"No, we are supposed to work together."

"Good man?" asked Epanow.

"I don't know," admitted Dermer. "He violated his orders and went on to Virginia without authority. Still, Sir Ferdinando Gorges trusts—"

"Gorges?" asked Epanow in surprise. "You

know Gorges?"

"Why, yes. I work for Sir Ferdinando."

Tisquantum could feel the tension mount suddenly in the big sachem of Capawack Island. Epanow could hardly disguise his disturbance. "How do you do, Sir Ferdinando?"

Dermer understood that Epanow was inquiring after Gorges. "He is in good health, though he eats too much rich food. And he is excited about colonization and fishing and trade, as much as ever."

"Find plenty gold?" asked Epanow. "Satisfied with gold?"

"Hardly," said Dermer, laughing. "No man ever has enough gold. And Sir Ferdinando spends his on new voyages as quickly as he acquires any. Not that he is a wastrel, but he keeps his resources invested. As one of his friends, Sir Francis Bacon, says, 'Money is like muck—no good unless it be spread.'"

Tisquantum had to explain to Epanow how the English spread their barn wastes on their gardens to make them grow, because they had no new land to move to, and they had to fertilize what little they had, to get any produce at all. In a similar way, they planted their money in schemes to make more money. And they always hoped their harvests would make them rich.

By Charles Brashear

Epanow was amazed and amused. These English! He had seen many wondrous things in England, but not a man feeding the ground to make the corn grow.

Epanow asked about Tisquantum's plans: "Do you go to Virginia with this Dermer?"

"No," said Tisquantum, shifting over to Wampanoag. "I must attend The Massasoit at Sowams for Thanksgiving. Perhaps you have heard, he has adopted me…"

Epanow nodded. He had heard as much. A messenger from Pocasset had come before Tisquantum to Capawack.

"Master Dermer has agreed to put me ashore at Sakonnet. He does not know where Sakonnet is, but he will leave me there, and I will walk to Sowams."

"With a stick in the sand, I will draw him a picture of the coast line," said Epanow.

"He will thank you. I will thank you."

"You must give my greetings to Awashonkas, the squaw sachem of Sakonnet. She leads with a wise head and a strong hand. Her dead husband did no better. Tell her that Epanow of Capawack is ever her friend."

"You," Epanow pointed his chin to Dermer's chest, "you look … gold?"

"No," admitted Dermer, "not this time. I have no time to stop and prospect now. I have to get on to Virginia and find Mr. Rowcroft."

"I give corn ... dried venison ... to speed journey."

"Sir Ferdinando Gorges will thank you. I will thank you."

"Keep the thanks of Gorges," said Epanow in Wampanoag, his face flashing anger. "If I ever see him again, I will do my best to kill him."

By the time they had finished the meal, Dermer's sailors had gathered as much wood as they could carry and filled their few containers with fresh water. Epanow ordered his women to bring the men food, as he had promised. It was time to depart.

As they were walking to the pinnace to leave, Epanow talked with Tisquantum in their own language. "I thought I would never see you again, my friend; so you may imagine my surprise when you walked up my beach. So few of those captured ever get back to their homes. You must come again to Capawack. I want you to sit with me and tell me your adventures. And I will tell you mine."

"I would be honored, but now we have no time to tarry."

"That is as well," admitted Epanow. "I do not know how long I could be civil to an Englishman, even one who is your brother. Tell your Captain Dermer that he should not come back here. If he comes again to Capawack, I shall have to kill him."

35. This Time, That Place; What Does it Matter?

> His friend and brother was dead, destroyed early by the indifferent world that breaks both hero and coward in time; but taken out of time, out of season; taken in his prime, leaving Tisquantum only a vacancy.

On a warm summer day, a large Narragansett canoe came slowly into the inlet and glided toward the beach below Sakonnet. There were eight men aboard, six of them paddling. The leader, a tall, sturdy man, stood near the front, holding a lance, but its point was held downward. They were coming to talk.

In spite of the family ties between the Sakonnet people and the Narragansetts, the warriors of Sakonnet picked up their bows and quivers, because many of Sakonnet also had ties with the Wampanoag. Was not their queen a relative of The Massasoit and also widow of a Narragansett chief? Because of their divided allegiance, the Sakonnet people were often used as go-betweens in contact of one tribe with the other.

Still, a wise Sakonnet man had to be on guard; he never knew when peace talks with Narragansetts would break into flying arrows. The warriors stood in a loose row near the upper edge of the sand, waiting.

The Narragansett canoe came still slower, almost floating at a standstill. They were making sure that the Sakonnet people got a good look at them. Their gesture was saying, 'we carry no surprises.'

When at last the canoe came to land, a single man, not the leader, stepped out and walked slowly up the strand. The leader stood in the canoe, his lance still conveying the same, peaceful message. One other man got out of the canoe to hold its side rope and keep it from drifting. The messenger stopped half way up the beach.

The queen herself, with two of her bodyguards, walked down the beach to meet the man. "Greetings, stranger. Awashonkas, the squaw sachem of Sakonnet and widow of your brother, welcomes you to Sakonnet. Let our people be at peace."

"May it be so," said the messenger, opening his hands in front of him and leaning slightly forward. "I am Beaver-skat, of the lower Connecticut people near Hell Gate. I come with a message from a dying man. Is there here a man of The Massasoit's nation, called Tisquantum?"

"I know him," said Awashonkas. "He has been here— and will come again. He waits for an Englishman he calls brother."

"I bring news of that Englishman."

"Come up to our fire. We will smoke to the spirit of First-Mother's breath and eat of her flesh. You are welcome to Sakonnet." She made a gesture, and one of the bodyguards went down to the canoe to extend the same invitation to the others.

After the calumet had gone around the council and food had been served to all the guests, the messenger told his story.

Thomas Dermer had put a deck on his pinnace during the winter in Virginia, then set out northward with the first good weather. A sudden spring storm had blown his little boat past Sakonnet and all the way to the shallow banks off Nantucket Island before the gale had turned him loose. There he waited for fair winds to return to Sakonnet and pick up Squanto. He stopped at Capawack to visit again with Epanow.

"Captain Dermer told me to say this," said the messenger. "That Epanow treated him with arrogance. Epanow laughed in his face and gloated how he misled Sir Ferdinando Gorges and Captain Edward Harlow. He fooled them, tricked them, and managed his own escape from enslavement.

"When Captain Dermer turned to leave, Epanow laid hold of him, saying he would hold Dermer hostage until Sir Ferdinando Gorges rewarded Epanow, or he would keep Dermer as his personal slave. Captain Dermer managed to wriggle from Epanow's grip, drew his sword, and resisted.

"Captain Dermer was wounded fourteen times in the fight. Three of the English sailors were killed, two more were wounded, but Captain Dermer and the three remaining managed to escape and get their pinnace sailing. They returned to Virginia, where the two wounded sailors died, but Captain Dermer recovered from his wounds and sent talking papers to Gorges in England.

"Then, weakened by his time of inactivity, he fell ill of the malady of that swampy place; his chest gurgled and his forehead burned. And he died. This was his message to Tisquantum: That because of his death, he would be unable to return and meet his brother at Sakonnet."

Would Queen Awashonkas become custodian of the message? The Narragansetts were uncomfortable with traveling further into the Wampanoag Confederacy.

***

Tisquantum slumped to the sand and looked away. His first impulse was to ask "What?" "How?" But even that was useless. He did not doubt the messenger's word. His brother was dead, destroyed early by the indifferent world that breaks both hero and coward in time; but taken out of time, out of season; taken in his prime, leaving Tisquantum only a vacancy. He threw away his worthless necklace.

He could not get the scene out of his mind. He could see Epanow taking Dermer's arm, Dermer jerking the arm upward and forward, wrenching it out of Epanow's grip. He could see Epanow coming again, determined to make the white man a slave.

Dermer would draw his sword to defend himself. He probably killed one or two of the Capawack men before they backed off. But his sailors were full of arrows by that time, and Dermer, too, had some arrows in his arms, above his breast-plate, and perhaps in his chest. He would be weakened.

Epanow could dash in behind the swing of Dermer's sword and ram a knife into the soft part of his side. Perhaps Dermer had fallen to the ground, but bounced up quickly, swishing his sword to keep the Indians back.

By that time, the other sailors were running

up from the pinnace, their matchlocks already smoking. Then the Indians would run from the muskets, and the sailors could drag Dermer and the dead and wounded men to the pinnace and get under way.

Fourteen wounds. Squanto felt them on his own body, sprinkled across his chest and upper arms, and that deep slash in the soft side. Each wound ached with a fire that would not be quenched. But the pain refused to clarify how his friend had recovered from the wounds, only to fall before the consuming fire of the Virginia lung sickness.

Squanto was left alone in the world again; that was the greatest hurt.

That fact kept getting larger and larger in his mind. He was alone. It did no good to invest another human with your love; he would die and leave you alone. Nothing had meaning. All fell before the sure-destroying-power of Death. All perished and left you alone. We are all alone.

Queen Awashonkas tried to comfort him, but he had trouble understanding what she was trying to say. "You have suffered a great loss, that is true. But you also have still immense wealth. You are The Massasoit's adopted son; you are famous and loved and respected in hundreds of villages, from the Penobscot to Narragansett Bay; you have the bounty of the world to enjoy— all beasts of the forest, fishes of the waters, fowl of the skies, corn of the fields, the glitter of morning dew on leaves..."

The sunlight still struck the dew drops, but what of that? It was a nothing. An accident. Something that happened in this time, at that place; what did it matter? Nothing lingered, and one was alone again. Abandoned.

His mind hurt with its memories. Thoughts that once caused his heart to surge with joy now caused it to ache. The possibility of happiness was revoked, annulled, destroyed. He had once felt pain, but lost even that. Pain had negated pain, rescinded sorrow. One's existence was abolished, detached; hope was canceled; the mind disengaged itself from its memories.

Tisquantum wished to be alone with his misery. Awashonkas understood and sent two men of Sakonnet to take him back to his wigwam on the little pond near Patuxet.

Detached from his self, he failed to recognize what the glitter was. He watched as someone walked along a path, simply because it was there, but hardly knowing that it was a path. One came to a wigwam by a pond and lay down, because there was nothing to do. There was nothing to expect. Anguish erased the future.

He looked at his hands and wondered who

they belonged to. That, too, was unimportant, because he had forgotten who he was.

The two men of Sakonnet put food in the mouth, saying, "Eat, Tisquantum, or you will starve."

But he could not determine who they were talking to. All he wanted was to sleep. It did not matter that he urinated on himself and fouled his bed with feces.

At last, one forgot why he hurt. Vacant, his mind and heart slept. Paralyzed, he was isolated, but what of that? It was a nothing. An accident. Something that happened. In this time, at that place; what did it matter?

36. "There are Some English at Patuxet," 1621

> They wear black, red, and purple coats, and wide-brimmed hats, and shoes with buckles as big as bull-frogs. They are unlike any English I have seen. They have their women and children with them. The women do not have legs, but only a big column of cloth that rests on the ground. They slide around on the big column of cloth.

Samoset walked up the path to Tisquantum's wigwam with his Passamaquoddy traveling companions. He found Tisquantum in a trance, nearly emaciated, his skin turned a dull purple. The aunt who lived with him was feeding him, as if he were a baby; for he would neither eat nor drink on his own, and his eyes, though they seemed to be looking at things, were unseeing. Samoset passed his hand with open fingers across in front of Tisquantum's face, but his eyes did not follow the hand, nor even register that it was there.

"Wake up, my friend," said Samoset, taking one of Tisquantum's shoulders in his hand and budging it, thinking that the physical movement would stir him to consciousness. Tisquantum was like so much clay: his shoulder retained the position it was last molded into.

"He has been like that for weeks," said the aunt, Miana-mohahas. "It is a wonder that his mouth works when we put food into it. Even so, we have to mash the succotash to a mush, and he sometimes forgets to swallow, so the food falls out on his shirt."

"Come up, Tisquantum," said Samoset, pulling him to his feet, "this is no way to survive." Tisquantum allowed himself to stand erect, to shuffle forward when he was led, but when Samoset turned his arm loose, Tisquantum crumpled into a heap on the earth.

"I have become a squaw," said the Sakonnet man who had stayed to hunt for Miana-mohahas and Tisquantum, "feeding a baby soft food, wiping his butt, tucking him into the pelts at night. And we lie beside him to keep him warm and quell his bad dreams."

"He causes us to neglect our own families," said the other Sakonnet man, with a touch of bitterness. "We do it willingly, because it is our duty. But I wonder who is comforting my wife at night."

Samoset sent a runner with the news to The Massasoit. The Sakonnet men were relieved to go home.

But still Tisquantum was comatose. He had apparently lost all sense of self and surroundings. His eyes were out of focus. His movements were not even automatic, for he had to be pushed and molded into a semblance of a living man.

"Come, come, old chap," said Samoset in English. He began singing:

> *Buck up, Billy, put your belly to the bar,*
> *And we'll drink a wee pint for auld lang syne.*
> *The birds, they're asinging, the sun he's ashining,*
> *We're all of us fed, they've stopped the ole war;*
> *So raise the full glass on high, Billy Bigh, Billy Bigh,*
> *We'll all of us live to a hundred and nine.*
> > *Yea, raise the glass on high, on high, on high;*
> > > *tomorrow we may die.*

As Samoset sang, Squanto's eyes began to focus. His ears detected a familiar language and a familiar voice. But he could not recognize them. He was aware, without any urgency, that he should know them, but it was too much work to untangle the noises. He let them slip back into the void, something, in this time, at that place, nothing mattered.

But Samoset was still singing the song. The sound pressed in at his ears.

Yea, raise the glass on high, on high, on high;
tomorrow we may die.

Tisquantum saw black, diagonal bars on a face. Where had he seen that before? What did it mean? And the song, the voice... why were they there?

"This singing makes me thirsty," said Samoset. "I wish we really had a pint. That'd lift your chin, wouldn't it, old chap?"

Tisquantum saw the mouth moving beneath the black, diagonal bars. It was the most interesting thing in the universe. Why was it interesting?

Samoset saw in Tisquantum's eyes that sentience was returning.

"Thatta boy, 'Squanto," said Samoset, nudging his shoulder. "You're among friends." And he sang again:

Buck up, 'Squanto, and swallow your beer;
The landlord's left and we're in charge.

The maids are free, the glass is large,
And we've no more work the rest of this year;
> *So raise the glass on high, Billy Bigh, Billy Bigh,*
> *We'll all of us live to a hundred and nine.*

Yea, raise the glass on high, on high, on high;
> *tomorrow we may die.*

The song was the funniest thing in the world to Tisquantum. He felt a grin tugging at his cheek. The black, diagonal bars and the mouth were in a face. He knew that face. He knew about that face. He struggled to decipher what he knew about that face.

Samoset grasped each of Tisquantum's shoulders in his hands. "Come on, now, 'Squanto. You've got to sing with me. Let's do the first verse again."

Buck up, Billy, put your belly to the bar,
And we'll drink a wee pint for auld lang syne.

Tisquantum smiled with the song, as if the smiling were a sing-along. The black, diagonal bars on the face had two feathers behind them. Somewhere in the past, Samoset was leaning

---
By Charles Brashear 255

across a fire toward Tisquantum and saying, "Now, teach me the second verse."

The non-world retreated, and he could see a head in a tunnel, a head he recognized. "Samoset?" he asked, tentatively, hoarsely. He wanted to say more, but could not command his own mouth.

"Yes, it is Samoset. Come on, old friend. We'll pretend this water is beer and we've no more work the rest of this year." He put a gourd-mug in Tisquantum's hand.

The tunnel moved and focused on his hand. He knew it was his hand. How did he know it was his hand? The mug made no sense. Samoset's hand— how did Samoset's hand get there?— Samoset's hand was lifting it to someone's mouth. The mouth drank.

The cool water invented the gullet as it washed down and defined his belly. He could feel the water as it created the sides of his stomach. Tisquantum became aware that he was hungry.

He looked around. A woman— he recognized her; why did he recognize her?—was dipping succotash into a clam-shell bowl. She handed the bowl to Tisquantum, along with a wooden spoon. He took the succotash and began eating.

He tasted the succotash as he ate it. Corn, beans, squash—the first food of creation. It warmed his soul.

***

It was a winter day. Tisquantum was aware that it was a winter day, but he could not make sense of the willow construction. He had learned to recognize the woman and call her by her name, Miana-mohahas. She kept his fire, prepared his food, and covered him at night with a bearskin. But he could not understand the willow.

He held the thing in his hand and ran his fingers along its legs. He traced each of the windings that held the seat to the legs, but he could not decode the mystery. He felt that it was urgent to understand the willow. He ran his fingers along its legs again and again, traced its bindings again and again, as if his fingers would miraculously define the willow and tell him what it was.

Even as he talked with Miana-mohahas, he tried to fathom the willow. Sometimes, he forgot to respond to her, because his finger was tracing the winding on a leg and the seat. He had to comprehend the willow.

When Samoset crouched beside his fire, Tisquantum asked him what the willow was.

"I think it is a chair you started," said Samoset. "But you never finished it. See? The willow of the back is too dry to bend into position now. It will never be a usable chair."

Tisquantum looked at it. It was too much to understand. And yet, he had to grasp its significance. He had to.

Samoset had other news. "There are some English at Patuxet. They wear black, red, and purple coats, and wide-brimmed hats, and shoes with buckles as big as bull-frogs. They are unlike any English I have seen. They have their women and children with them. The women do not have legs, but only a big column of cloth that rests on the ground. They slide around on the big column of cloth."

Tisquantum was not very interested. How would the English at Patuxet help him to understand the willow? He ran his finger along its bindings while Samoset talked.

"They stayed on their ship for thirteen days," went on Samoset. "They came ashore to put together their shallop, and to get wood and water. But they were living on the ship. We hardly know what to make of it.

"Their men slept on the beach near Nauset one night near the beginning. Aspinet and twenty of his best warriors thought they would surprise the English and kill them all. But the yang-kaysh had put up a small breast-work of logs and kept one on-guard, so they responded to the attack. Aspinet and his men let fly a great many arrows from behind the trees, but the English were ready to shoot their muskets in a matter of moments; so Aspinet and his warriors withdrew from that First Encounter."

"English?" asked Tisquantum, baffled. How was this going to help him understand the willow. And what was a chair?

"Aspinet thought he had driven them away. They went back to their ship and moved it to another place. We thought they were leaving. But their women came ashore and washed their clothes. Then we saw that some of the women have legs under the column of cloth. Their men found some of Aspinet's corn and took it.

But always, they went back to their ship and acted as if they would leave. This is going to be a hard winter. It's a stupid time to be trying to come ashore. We thought the English might understand that. For several days, we thought that maybe they would discover their own stupidity and would go on to Virginia to be with the others.

"But when they came to Patuxet, they carried ashore their chests and tools. There are about a hundred of them. They have cut trees into slabs and have constructed square wigwams of the pieces. Some of them have died, and they buried their dead there at Patuxet. Some say that is a bad sign. They will not want to leave the graves of their dead.

"They look like they are cold and hungry. But I think they brought neither fish-hooks nor nets, so they seem unable to take fish. They have shot a few geese and mallards, but, of course, the other animals like the deer know better than to be out at this time of year. The English act like they want to stay at Patuxet, but they are such helpless babies."

Tisquantum did not respond.

"I think it would be fun to go and talk to the English. Let's go and visit the English," urged Samoset.

Tisquantum was still trying to understand the willow. He said only, "I prefer not to."

37. Pow-Wow at Pokánoket

> If their muskets are to fire, let them fire at our enemies. We need an alliance of mutual protection and peace with the English at Patuxet. We are forced to become friends with the English.

At the first sign of spring, 1621, The Massasoit called a pow-wow at Pokánoket to discuss "What are we going to do about the English at Patuxet?" They had been there three moons now and were building houses; they did not act like they would return to their ship and go away, as all the other English had.

Samoset, the Passamaquoddy sagamore of Monhegan Island, was visiting, pulling Tisquantum along, trying to cheer him up by conversation with everyone. Tisquantum was still so sick at heart that he was widely regarded as useless. For long hours, he sat cross-legged on the ground and stared at the earth, neither hearing, nor giving sign that he listened.

Samoset had been talking with him in the English language, and his mood had improved some. The Massasoit invited them to come to the pow-wow. "You'll see some old friends," said The Massasoit, "and perhaps the pow-wow will bring Tisquantum out of his trance."

The Massasoit, Samoset, and Tisquantum left Sowams on the northeastern shore of Narragansett Bay and walked to the council house at Pokánoket, the adjoining town and capital of the Wampanoag Confederation. The Massasoit's best warriors accompanied him, for he felt the need to travel with some strength; both the Narragansetts to the southwest and the Abenaki-Tarentine Federation to the north of the Massachusetts tribe often sent war parties into Wampanoag territory.

He was received at Pokánoket with honor and ceremony, for the town was the home of his clan, the ruling clan of the Confederation. His younger brother, Quadequina, was sachem at that place.

In addition to Hobamock and the elders' council of Pokánoket, sachems from several towns were present: Ohquamehud of Lower Nauset, on the outer hook of Cape Cod; Epanow of Capawack, the island off Buzzard's Bay; Cawnacamón of Manomet, the village south of Patuxet and inland from Cape Cod Bay; Corbitant of Pocasset, the town at the head of Buzzard's Bay; Obbitinuat and Chicka-taubut, from villages belonging to the

Massachusetts tribe; Nattawahut of the Connecticut tribe, and others. There had not been such a gathering of leaders since the big Narragansett-Abenaki civil war five years ago had made it necessary for them to form the Wampanoag Confederation for their mutual defense.

After the calumet, filled with their best mixture of tobacco and cedar, had gone around the council and all present had touched the Spirits through First Mother's breath, Ousa Mequin, The Massasoit, opened the proceedings with a prayer to the Great Spirit.

He was a tall man, forty-one years old, and a veteran of much warfare, through which he had acquired his great status so early in life. His face was painted a dull mulberry red and oiled. He carried a small stick covered with rune-like symbols, which told the story of his ancestors from whom he had inherited power. It was his scepter of office.

Closing his wildcat-skin cloak and sitting down, he announced, "We will hear first from those who have had experiences with the English."

Many eyes turned toward Corbitant of Pocasset, for he was known to be the most hostile to the English. He had lost members of his family in the recent massacre at Pocasset and had himself fought back. He opened his wildcat-skin cape to show he had nothing to hide and let it fall behind him.

He was a tall man, in his mid-thirties, young to be a sachem, but he had earned the rank, both in war against the Narragansetts and the English. He had painted yellow, zig-zag lightning bolts on each cheek and oiled his face and head. "I say, kill the brutes," he shouted. "True, they have a few muskets. But once those are discharged, forty or fifty warriors can race in and overpower them easily. Epanow has shown that it can be done."

"They have their women and children with them," said Hobamock of the Pokánoket elders' council. "Would Corbitant become a woman-killer?"

"Aagh!" he scoffed. "Take them prisoner. Let each warrior take as many as he likes and sell them in whatever village he likes. They would make good servants, for they are hardy people. Their surviving this winter has shown that they are strong. Kill all the men and the boys that are near the warrior age, and sell the women and girls as Wampanoag wives and servants."

"We already have too many women," said The Massasoit. "Corbitant knows that. Many men have left widows and orphans to become other men's duty. I myself have five wives, as you know.

Sometimes, I have trouble keeping meat before them."

"Let the English women become part of our nation and breed hunters and warriors."

"It takes fifteen years for a child to reach warrior age," was muttered around the council.

"They can take care of themselves with their work," Corbitant went on, "and produce sons to become warriors. You all know we will need much strength for the coming war."

The council was silent a moment, in deference to Corbitant's point of view, but not all shared it.

Quadequina got up to speak. In his mid-thirties, he was shorter than his brother and tending toward a loose fattiness in his body. He wore four feathers in his hair, but his face was not painted. "Reports are that they have many reserves. If you kill some of them, they will send more from England. There seems no end to the number of warriors they have.

"Epanow, who was their prisoner, can tell you that they have many warriors.

"Samoset, our distinguished visitor from Monhegan, can tell you they have many ships, for he is acquainted with most of their sea captains.

"Tisquantum, before his mind went blank,

told us of their huge towns, where thousands upon thousands of men walk with little to do. They can easily give each of them a musket and send them all to war with Corbitant."

"Let the come," muttered Corbitant.

Cawnacamón of Manomet got up to speak. He was an older man, tending now toward paunchiness, having been in his mid-fifties when Captain Edward Harlow had kidnaped him, Epanow, and three others in 1611. "I, too, have seen their strength, for I was their prisoner at the same time as Epanow, as you all know. I acknowledge that Epanow effected my release and his own escape." He paused and looked toward Epanow, bowing slightly. He allowed a moment of silence for all present to honor Epanow.

Cawnacamón went on: "I grant you, I am rather too old to be of much use in battle, but I believe that death in battle against the English would be not so much a good cause as a futile effect. They would slaughter us, like fish in a basket. I do not see much honor in that kind of death."

He paused, waving his hand in a gesture of dismissal, then went on. "Compared with English numbers, we are strong. But compared with English muskets, our weapons are weak. If we were allies, not enemies, with the Narragansetts and Abenakis, we might have strength enough to delay the English a generation. A confederation of all the Algonquin tribes might have some chance." He paused to let the council absorb his point.

"But we are at war with the Narragansetts," he said. "And our friends, the Massachusetts, are always at war with the Abenaki-Tarentine Federation. The Narragansetts are a war-axe coming up from the south; the Abenaki-Tarentines are a lance coming down from the north. What are we to do to avoid being smashed in the middle?

"Plus the English are an explosion of muskets coming at our side from the sea. I can see the poor Wampanoag being squirted westward toward the Mohawks, where we will meet another set of lances and arrows. I do not know what to do, but I do not think it wise to die in battle."

"What does Epanow say?" asked The Massasoit. "He and his warriors have wounded and killed more of the English than any of us. What does Epanow counsel?"

All attention turned to Epanow, who got up slowly and opened his cape. He was a huge man, well over six feet tall and still as well-muscled as in his youth. He wore a loose, English sailors shirt and a breech clout.

"I am reluctant to recommend anything, for I am of two minds. I think there can be no peace with the English, for their greed exceeds everything any Algonquin can imagine. The only thing stronger than their greed is their determina-tion to satisfy it.

"It is true that I and my warriors have killed a few of them, but we cannot hope to win a war against them, not even if we had an Algonquin Confederacy. It would be like standing in a river to stop the flood. We would all be swept away."

He paused to let his point have its effect. Everyone knew that Epanow had well-proven his courage and cleverness.

"They are many," Epanow went on. "I have walked in the streets of their towns, and I can tell you, they are thick with people. Cawnacamón can tell you their streets are thick with people. Tisquantum has told us that they have towns a man cannot walk across in a day, and those streets are thick with people."

Cawnacamón nodded his agreement. Samoset tugged at Tisquantum's arm and whispered in his ear. Tisquantum roused from his trance and nodded his assent.

"They have poisoned their air and water," Epanow went on. "They are looking desperately for some new place to go. They want room to live. And they will have it. Room to live. By their greed and their muskets, they will have room to live. I see no difference if we die by war with them, or die by peace with them. I have no recommendation."

In the pause that followed Epanow's pessimism, The Massasoit looked around the council. He could see that Epanow's despair had affected most of the leaders; even Corbitant seemed sobered by it. He could see that almost all agreed about the tremendous power of the English and that a war with them would be disastrous. The only hope lay in maintaining the peace for a while, appeasing the English until some new, yet-unforeseen solution could be worked out.

Hobamock spoke for the Pokánoket council of elders. "Many of us think it is better to lie quietly on our beds at night, than to be ever-fearful of an English attack.

"We created this grand alliance, the Wampanoag Confederation, as a way of maintaining peace. And it has been our protection against Narragansett and Abenaki alike.

"We elders of Pokánoket recommend that we take the English into the Wampanoag Confederation. That way, we can be assured that they will not join the Narragansetts or the Abenakis against us. If their muskets are to fire, let them fire at our enemies. We need an alliance of mutual protection and peace with the English at Patuxet. We are forced to become friends with the

By Charles Brashear 269

English."

The Massasoit waited a long moment, but none else rose to speak. He could see Corbitant shift uncomfortably in his place, but he, too, recognized that a consensus had arrived and that his voice against a treaty with the English would be no more than a wind in autumn.

"Very well," said The Massasoit at last. "We will seek an agreement with them. I, myself, Ousa Mequin, see no other hope; so I cast my voice with the elders' council."

A murmur of assent went around the assembly.

"I suggest that Quadequina and I go to meet them first. When we have worked out a good agreement, the other sachems can go later and pledge their support of the agreement."

Again, a murmur of assent went around the meeting.

"We will need warriors and counselors to perform certain tasks. Hobamock, Quadequina, and I will act as a council of ambassadors to work out the agreement. We will need a tongue to speak for us. Will Tisquantum be our tongue?"

Tisquantum was staring at the ground. Samoset tugged again at his arm and whispered in his ear. Tisquantum lifted his head, but his eyes still looked vacant. "I prefer not to," he said, sounding weary. He turned his eyes back down, to study the nothing he was gazing at.

A wave of shock went around the council. It was unheard-of that a man of the tribe and especially an adopted clan-son of The Massasoit should refuse to do what The Massasoit asked of him, even if he were sick.

Quickly, Samoset rose and opened his arms. He wore two feathers in his graying hair and black, diagonal bars on his face. "Let me be your tongue for the first contact," he said. "I have met many of the English. I will go ahead and soften their hearts to your wishes."

A wave of protest passed around the council. "But you are our visitor and our guest," said The Massasoit. "It is not your duty to do our work."

"That is no matter," said Samoset. "I rather like to talk to them. I'd probably stop by there and chat with them on my way home. Let me be your tongue for your first contact with the English."

38. Ambassador

> "All the afternoon, we spent in communication with him. We would gladly have been rid of him at night, but he was not willing to go this night. Then we thought to carry him on shipboard, wherewith he was well content, and went into the shallop. But the wind was so high and the water so scant that it [the shallop] could not return [to the ship]. We lodged him that night at Stephen Hopkins' house, and watched him."
>
> William Bradford, *Of Plimouth Plantation*, 1647.

On the 16th of March, 1621, the Pilgrim men were astonished to see an Indian walk into Leyden Street, the only street of Plimouth Plantation. He was a tall and handsome man, naked except for a very small breech clout, two feathers in his hair to indicate rank, and black, diagonal bars painted on his face. He carried a bow and two arrows, one of them with a stone head, the other without.

He walked rapidly, looking in the doors of all the buildings, and came to the community house. William Bradford thought he would have entered, had not a man stood in the way. The native took Bradford by the hand and said, "Welcome, English!

You got beer?"

"B—Beer?" said Bradford, non-plussed. In three and a half months, they had not so much as seen a native up close, and now one walked in and asked for a beer.

"Yes, many times ... drink beer with English friends."

"Friends?"

"Yes. Samoset friend with English," he said, patting his own chest. "Monhegan Island ... Five days much walk by land—" he held up five fingers and pointed northward up the coast—"and one day sail—" he pointed eastward— "with great wind. English Captains stop. Visit Samoset. Get wood and water for ships. Give Samoset beer. Samoset like beer."

"Well, how do you do, Mr. Samoset," said John Carver, making a sweeping bow. He had taken off his ruff and his collar was open, for the men had all been working on their houses. His dark, knee-length breeches were soiled, but his lace cuffs were still clean. "I am John Carver, governor of this group."

"Gov--?" Samoset was baffled.

"Leader," explained Carver. "Head man."

"Oh, head man," said Samoset. "Sagamore—" he patted his chest again. "Samoset sagamore, Monhegan Island."

Many of the other men, Elder Brewster, Edward Winslow, Myles Standish, Isaac Allerton, as well as the women and children, had collected about the group by this time.

"Elizabeth," said Carver, "bring our friend a mug of strong water. And a biscuit."

Elizabeth Carver did as her husband commanded.

The Pilgrims all assumed that Samoset had an aversion to water, as they had, because it was polluted. Among the Pilgrims, alcoholic content was regarded as water purification, and a brewer was as necessary a member of a community as a carpenter. The Pilgrims did not have beer, since they did not have the ingredients, but they made a "strong water" of dried fruits fermented in boiled water.

"Patuxet," said Samoset, pointing to the ground. "This place, Patuxet."

"Patuxet," repeated William Bradford.

"Yes. Wampanoag village, long time. Many grandfathers. No more. Four winters"— he held up four fingers and pointed backward over his shoulder— "great sickness. All people die. Wampanoag no want live here."

"Do they mind if we live here?" asked Carver.

Samoset only partially understood Carver, but he went on. "Wampanoag say Patuxet, bad place. Bad spirit place. No want wigwams or longhouse here ... bad spirit place."

"So that's why we haven't seen any natives," said Myles Standish. "And why none has come to attack." He was a very short man, hardly over five feet, but stocky and quite strong. He had been elected captain of the Pilgrims' militia.

Elizabeth Carver returned with the mug of "strong water" and biscuit. She was slightly apprehensive to hand them to the near-naked and dusky-skinned Samoset directly; so she gave them to her husband, averting her eyes from the primitive man. Carver handed the mug to Samoset, saying, "This is what we drink instead of beer."

Samoset took the mug, tipped it up, and drained half the pint in several big gulps. "Ahhh. Good," he said, smacking his lips. He drained the mug and handed it to Elizabeth, making a pouring motion into the mug to indicate that he wanted more. Elizabeth took the mug and looked at her husband, for the Pilgrims' supply was short. Carver nodded his assent.

"All Patuxet people die," Samoset went on. "Only one live. He carried away on ship to England before all Patuxet people die. He, more English talk, than Samoset."

"Does this Patuxet man live here?" asked Edward Winslow.

"No far," said Samoset. "Tisquantum live alone. All mothers and fathers die. All brothers die. All die. Tisquantum sad. Tisquantum sad-sad," he added for emphasis, unable to convey Tisquantum's depression.

"Do you know other natives of this place?" asked Myles Standish.

"Oh, sure," said Samoset, with one of those idioms that people pick up as they learn a language. "Many, many Wampanoag. Ousa Mequin is The Massasoit of"— he flashed all his fingers four times— "many, many villages."

"Massasoit?" asked Bradford. "What is a massasoit?"

"Great sagamore," Samoset explained. "Ousa Mequin is great sagamore over many, many villages." And he flashed all his fingers again four times. "Wampanoag word sachem, same as Passamaquoddy word sagamore. Wampanoag say massasoit ... mean great leader."

'So they've got a nation,' thought Myles Standish. He calculated quickly that if each of forty villages had twenty-five warriors, that would make an army of a thousand men. He hoped he did not have to lead his fourteen-man "army" against such a nation. Against one village at a time, they might have a chance; but they couldn't hope to defeat the whole nation at once.

It being near mid-day, the Pilgrims brought Samoset more "strong water" and biscuit and butter, with cheese and a piece of mallard, and pudding, all of which "he liked well," as William Bradford reported, in *Of Plimouth Plantation*, 1647, adding that Samoset had been acquainted with all these foods from the English sea captains.

When a slight breeze came up, the Pilgrims put a maroon horseman's coat around Samoset, to the great relief of both the Pilgrim men and women, for they were acutely embarrassed by Samoset's nakedness.

The Pilgrims asked Samoset many questions about the natives nearby. Affected a bit by the wine, he tried to make them fear The Massasoit's Confederation. "Aspinet, sachem of Upper Nausets. Lead hundred warriors. Nausets angry-angry."

Seven of the Nauset people were kidnaped in 1614 by Captain Thomas Hunt, along with twenty Patuxet men, and taken to Spain, where they were sold into slavery. Aspinet's Nausets had killed three of Sir Ferdinando Gorges's men only five months ago. It was the Nausets who had attacked the Pilgrims at First Encounter.

The Pilgrims mentioned some tools the local natives had carried away, drawing rough pictures in the sand and pantomiming their use when they did not have a sample to show. Samoset promised he would inquire about the tools.

"All the afternoon, we spent in communication with him," wrote Bradford in his history, *Of Plimouth Plantation*. "We would gladly have been rid of him at night, but he was not willing to go. Then we thought to carry him on ship-board, wherewith he was well content, and went into the shallop. But the wind was so high and the water so scant that it [the shallop] could not return [to the ship]. We lodged him that night at Stephen Hopkins' house, and watched him."

The next morning at daybreak, Samoset was up and ready to leave. Governor Carver gave him a knife, a bracelet, and a ring, pledging his and the Pilgrims' friendship.

Samoset accepted the gifts, saying, "Samoset come, two, three nights.... Bring some ... Wampanoag people."

***

The next day, Sunday, Samoset returned with five men from Nemasket, all tall, sturdy men, as Bradford reported. They were dressed ceremonially, with their hair cut short in front, long behind; some wore their hair trussed up with a feather, some spread out in back like a fan, some like a fox's tail hanging out.

"They had every man a deer's skin on him," wrote Bradford, "and the principal of them had a wild cat's skin or such like on one arm. They had, most of them, long hose up to their groins close made, and above their groins to their waist another leather. They were altogether like Irish trousers."

These men brought back the tools which the English had left lying in the woods, and a few beaver and deer skins. They offered these skins in trade.

"No," said Elder Brewster, holding up his hands in defense. "Explain to them, Mr. Samoset, that we cannot trade on this day. 'Tis the Sabbath. This is the day we talk to God, and he would be very angry with us if we conducted earthly business today."

The Indians were curious and asked for further explanation.

"On the Sabbath," explained Brewster, "we cannot do anything but God's work. Else He may come and work His wrath on us all. Come tomorrow, and we shall be happy to trade. But we cannot trade today."

The Indians looked around, to see where so powerful an enemy was hiding, but they saw nothing but signs of spring—the buds on the trees making them look like a green mist in the winter branches, the wind roughing the new grass as a man would fondle his son's hair.

"Nevertheless, you are welcome to New Plimouth," said William Bradford, opening his arms in a gesture of welcome. "We are very happy to meet our red brothers."

The Pilgrims gave them bread and goat cheese and a mug of 'strong water.' The Wampanoags looked suspiciously at the food, but Samoset assured them he had eaten the same many times with English sea captains. At last, they ate the food and found it pleasant.

They put aside their extra clothing and danced to honor the English, not knowing that the Puritans thought dancing ungodly. "Stop! Stop!" cried Brewster and Carver in unison. "Stop, before God sends a thunderbolt and annihilates us all. You make God very angry with such unGodly behavior."

Bradford, Winslow, and Standish, however, tried to smooth over the tiff. "Here are some small gifts," said Bradford, "tokens of our love and good will toward you." The English gave each man a small bracelet of green and red beads and a double pinch of rouge.

The Wampanoags were greatly pleased by the tokens. They began tying the bracelets on their wrists at once.

"Come again tomorrow," said John Carver,

turning the leaders by their shoulders and escorting them toward the edge of the town. "Come again tomorrow, and we will be better willing to trade."

In spite of the Pilgrims' protests, the Wampanoags left their beaver skins with the English, saying they would come the next day with more and better skins.

Samoset again insisted on spending the night. Then he feigned illness until Wednesday morning.

Bradford and Carver gave him a hat, a pair of stockings and shoes, a shirt, and a piece of cloth to wear around his waist. "We want you to go and find those men of Massasoit's and ask them why they have not come again as they promised they would."

39. The Massasoit and the Peace of Patuxet

"There is nothing in his [The Massasoit's] career as far as it is revealed by the white man's history, to appeal to the fiery ardor and enthusiasm of youth like the exploits of his son Pometacom or Metacomet, the King Philip of history, or Red Jacket, Joseph Brant, Pontiac, Tecumseh, or scores of others whose deeds of valor have fired the imagination and thrilled the hearts of our young men for generations; but to the man in middle life, whose blood has been cooled to some extent by the snows of many winters, to the student of human character, there is something about the calm and dignified demeanor of that great chief that brings a feeling of regret that the colonists should have looked upon the continued existence of his race as an insurmountable barrier to the fruition of their ambitious designs..."—

Alvin Weeks, *Massasoit of the Wampanoags*, p.91

On Thursday, the 22nd of March, 1621, Samoset returned, with Tisquantum and three others. Samoset wore the hat and shirt the Pilgrims had given him, but not the shoes and stockings.

Tisquantum, a healthy man of medium stature and about thirty three years of age, wore a deerskin shirt and leggings, without decoration. He had to be guided, almost like a blind man.

The others wore breech clouts and carried a few skins to trade "and some herrings newly taken and dried, but not salted." They took their flint knives from their waist-bands and cut the food into pieces, as they had seen the English do, then offered the Pilgrims bits of the food.

"Ousa Mequin, The Massasoit, near by," said Samoset. "Short walk." He indicated with his chin a direction a little to the north of west. "Quadequina, Hobamock, with. Make pow-wow."

"Pow-wow?" asked Carver and Bradford, almost at once, for they did not yet know the word.

"Talk, talk," said Samoset, turning to Tisquantum.

"A discussion," Tisquantum said, hardly lifting his eyes. "A conference."

"You know English so well?" said Carver, astonished.

"Are you the fellow who lived a while with Master John Slaney in Cheapside?" asked Bradford.

"Yes," said Tisquantum, looking up and meeting Bradford's gaze. Bradford wore a full, dark beard and hair that came down to his shoulders, though he had very little on the top of his head. He seemed a kind and honest man. "You know Master Slaney?"

"No, but I've heard of him," said Bradford. "A merchant, right? With a good amount of money?" He thought Tisquantum's complexion rather like an English gypsy's.

Tisquantum nodded, flattered and pleased to find a common ground between himself and these English. "Tisquantum take care of Master Slaney's horses. You have horses to ride? Pull your carriages?"

"No," said Bradford. "We don't even have cows. We have only a few pigs, some goats, and a few chickens. The Lord hath not pleased to send us cows or horses, yet."

Tisquantum shook his head in wonder at how ill-prepared the English came. They seemed like children in a wilderness. At the same time, they were marvelously capable: they had sawed logs into boards as thick as two fingers and built several board and batten houses with low, thatched roofs. Some even had window shutters on leather hinges. He saw Bradford watching him. He felt a warmth for this serious man with hair on his chin, but little on top of his head.

"The Massasoit come," repeated Samoset.

Bradford reported that they talked with the natives for about an hour, not able to understand what they wanted. Then suddenly, the Pilgrims saw about sixty Indians at the ridge of Watson's Hill, across Town Creek. A few of them stood out as leaders by the wildcat skins and feathers they wore.

The Pilgrims' first impulse was to check that their muskets were loaded, their fuses lit, and the militia ready.

"No war," said Tisquantum, alarmed because he understood the intent in the English preparations. "The Massasoit want peace."

For some time, the two sides stood, gazing at each other, each unwilling to approach the other. "Well," said John Carver, at last, touching his gray, Van Dyke beard, as if it were a good-luck talisman. "I suppose I will go out and see what they want."

"No," said several of the Puritan men at once: Myles Standish, Edward Winslow, Elder Brewster. "You are the Governor," said Myles Standish. "We can't afford to lose you."

"There would be another governor," said Carver, "should God choose to call me home."

"Let's send Squanto to ask what to do next," suggested Bradford, using the mispronunciation of Tisquantum's name that would follow him the rest of his days.

Tisquantum looked at Bradford, as if for the first time. He seemed a healthy man, in his early thirties, the age of a next-younger brother, and he seemed a man of courage, ability, and industry— one could depend upon him to get a job done.

Squanto rather liked him. He even liked the idea of being called 'Squanto,' the way John Smith and Thomas Dermer had called him. It was the right name for a new man.

The other Pilgrim men were looking at Squanto, waiting, as if a real question had been asked. "Yes," said Squanto. "I will go."

Indicating the Indians on the hill opposite, John Alden asked, "Is this ... this Massasoit? The King of the Wampanoags?"

"Yes," said Squanto. The English, slightly misunder-standing, would ever after use his title, The Massasoit, as his name.

All waited with some apprehension while Squanto went to The Massasoit and came back. "The Massasoit say, 'send one of your men to speak, not Tisquantum.' He would know your mind and will."

The Pilgrims seemed caught by surprise and delayed some time, before choosing Edward Winslow as their spokesman. Almost as an afterthought, they sent gifts to the leaders: "to the King, a pair of knives and a copper chain with a jewel to it," as William Bradford later wrote in his history, *Of Plimouth Plantation.*

"To Quadequina, we sent likewise a knife, and a jewel to hang in his ear." They sent also "a pot of strong water, a good quantity of biscuit, and some butter," which they had brought with them from England, conserved in tubs.

After presenting the gifts and the food, Ed Winslow spoke through Squanto, the interpreter: "King James, our King in England, salutes you with words of love and peace. Our governor and all of his men would gladly be friends and allies with Massasoit and all his people."

He paused while Squanto translated. The Massasoit seemed pleased with this message.

"We English would gladly live at peace with our red brothers on this land and trade with them, such things as each side needs and likes. Our governor desires to see King Massasoit in person, so that he can confirm a peace with him as his next neighbor."

"You stay here," The Massasoit said to Winslow, "with my brother, Quadequina, and his warriors; if harm comes to me, you will pay with your life. I will go and talk with your Head Man."

Squanto was pleased to be interpreting between the languages again. It made him feel valuable. Perhaps life was worth living, after all. He felt a sense of power, for he was the voice of The Massasoit when he instructed the English: "The Massasoit lays his weapons on the ground. English do same."

Then The Massasoit and about twenty of his men, all unarmed, crossed the brook.

Bradford wrote: "Captain Standish and Master Allerton ... met the King at the brook, with half a dozen musketeers. They saluted him and he, them. So ... one on the one side and the other on the other, they conducted him to a house then in building [still under construction] where we placed a green rug and three or four cushions.

Then instantly came our Governor with drum and trumpet after him and some few musketeers. After salutation, our Governor kissing his hand, the King kissed him, and so they sat down. The Governor called for some strong water and drank to him, and The Massasoit drank a great draft that made him sweat all the while after."

Carver called for fresh meat, a bit of carved goose, and The Massasoit and his followers ate willingly.

William Bradford

The English were fascinated by the appearance of The Massasoit and his body guard. The Massasoit was strong and alert, a dignified man who carried himself with authority.

His escorts were all young, sturdy men. Some wore wildcat-skin capes with thick, soft fur still on the delicate leather, some were dressed in deerskins; all were painted: some black, some red, some yellow, some white, some with crosses on their faces, or other "antic works" of decoration.

The Massasoit was "of an able body," as Bradford described him, face painted a dull mulberry red and greased, "grave of countenance and spare of speech. In his attire, he was little or nothing different from the rest; only in a great chain of white bone beads about his neck." The Massasoit had a bag of tobacco with him, from which he and Governor Carver smoked together.

Then, through Squanto as interpreter, The Massasoit and Governor Carver worked out what the English thought of as a treaty.

"Ousa Mequin, The Massasoit of the Wampanoag Confederation, pledges to the English that neither he nor any of his people will injure or do hurt to the English." He waited for Tisquantum to translate, and Governor Carver to return the pledge.

"Ousa Mequin, The Massasoit of the Wampanoag Confederation, pledges to the Governor that if any Wampanoag does hurt to an Englishman, I will send the offender to you to be punished. Will Governor Carver do the same?"

John Carver quickly agreed. "Yes, none of ours will do any harm to any of yours."

William Bradford sat beside the Governor, writing down all the terms of the agreements, as Squanto translated. Squanto watched, admiring this young man and his Englishman's ability to make paper talk with the words which he, Squanto, told him.

The Massasoit's next point was: "I have caused the tools that were taken from you to be returned to you. We expect that, if any of your people should take things belonging to a Wampanoag, the Governor would cause them to be returned."

Governor Carver agreed, and Bradford wrote the article into the agreement.

"Ousa Mequin, The Massasoit of the Wampanoag Confederation, pledges that if any tribe unjustly wars against the English, the Wampanoag will come to your aid. And we ask that if any tribe wars unjustly against the Wampanoag, the English will come to our aid."

"We are a peace-loving people," said Governor Carver. "We take up arms only in cases of injustice. We like well this pledge."

"Good," said The Massasoit. "I will send word

The Peace of Patuxet

to all the towns that follow my commands and tell them of this. Knowing this pledge, they will not wrong you, but will understand that the condition of peace, friendship, and mutual defense exists between our two peoples, and they will live by it."

Carver assented, and Bradford made a record.

"Finally," said The Massasoit, "because we are friends, our men will leave their bows and arrows and other weapons behind them, when they come to visit you; and we expect that the English will leave behind their muskets and swords when they come to visit the Wampanoag."

"Yes," agreed Carver. "And since Massasoit and the Wampanoag people do all this so willingly, King James in England will consider you his friend and ally, forever."

That was what The Massasoit had come to hear. He wiped his thumb in the greasy paint on his forehead and touched the paper on which Bradford was writing, leaving a mulberry thumb print. "Ousa Mequin, The Massasoit of the Wampanoag Confederation, has given his word and made his mark."

John Carver signed his name, saying, "All the English at this place have given their word."

As The Massasoit and his warriors prepared to withdraw, he commented through Squanto as interpreter, "In one week, some Wampanoag will return to plant and till the cornfields nearby. Do not be alarmed. They do ordinary work. We will come again," he added, "to visit our friends, when the planting time has passed. Now, there is work to do."

Within a short time, The Massasoit had departed, and Quadequina came for a short visit. Shorter and pudgier than his brother, he wore four feathers in his hair. He, too, wanted to see the English up close, learn to recognize the leaders, and receive food and gifts.

Then, as quickly as they had come, the Indians returned to the ridge of Watson's Hill, and disappeared beyond it. The Wampanoags camped that night in the woods nearby, giving the anxious English cause to keep a watchful guard.

Samoset and Squanto remained with the Pilgrims. Through the negotiations, Squanto had felt a resurgence of life. He found he liked talking English again; he liked being of use to the white men. He liked the fact that his voice, even when it was the words of others, had been committed forever to a piece of paper.

Squanto stayed beside Bradford. "I will be your friend," he said.

And since Bradford was a single man, his young wife having drowned the first day *The Mayflower* was in Cape Cod Bay, he took Squanto into his home.

Bradford later wrote that Squanto was "their interpreter, and became a special instrument sent of God for their good, beyond their expectation."

He acknowledged that Squanto was the means, under God, of putting on foot and giving life to all the Pilgrims' hopes and plantations. God had indeed smiled upon their designs.

40. Squanto: "Friend of the Pilgrims"

> "He [Squanto] directed them [the Pilgrims] how to set their corne, wher to take fish, and to procure other commodities, was also a pilott to bring them to unknown places for their profit, and never left them till he dyed."—
> William Bradford, *Of Plimouth Plantation*, 1647.

The morning after the mutual protection pact, Squanto and Samoset found their translating skills used to the maximum. The Massasoit, his sixty warriors, and their families were still camped in the woods not far away, so the ordinary people of his retinue—women, boys, girls, young men who had not yet attained warrior status—took the opportunity to visit the English settlement, hoping to get a present of some sort, or a few bites of food, and at least see for themselves these yang-kaysh that all of "The People" were talking about.

All morning, they came in small groups of five to ten, smiling at the English and calling,

"Translate for me, Squanto." Or "Tell them what I want, Samoset."

The children, boys and girls alike up to puberty, were naked, and the women wore loose deerskin shifts, open at the shoulders and decorated across the bodice with black, red, and ochre designs. A few covered their shoulders with animal skins, which frequently slipped away.

The Indian women were most interested in the Pilgrim women. All those clothes! They fingered the mantles on the English women's shoulders in amazement, wanted to trade for bonnets and kerchiefs, wondered at the legs and shoes and stockings under all those skirts.

Yet, they recognized a special bond. "Neen squabs," they said, which Squanto and Samoset translated as "I am a woman."

Edward Winslow wrote the phrase in his account, which would be published as *Mourt's Relation*, in 1621, and introduced the word "squaw" to the English language.

The visits exasperated the English, for their food stores were low and, with *The Mayflower* gone two days since on its way back to England, there was no immediate way to replenish the larder. Yet they felt it would be undiplomatic and impolite to refuse hospitality to the Wampanoags.

In an effort to shift attention away from New

Plimouth and toward The Massasoit, Bradford and Carver sent word to the Indian encampment that, if Massasoit would send his own kettle, they would fill it with stewed peas, which they did. But still the Wampanoags came in a steady stream of small numbers.

"I'll swear," said Myles Standish, squaring his shoulders toward the forest, "I think they are lined up in the woods and taking turns coming into New Plimouth."

"The line had better not be much longer," said Carver, tugging his Van Dyke beard. "We'll soon be out of food and drink."

Squanto and Samoset were enjoying a short respite. Squanto slumped on a stump, while Samoset chewed on a roasted turkey leg and sipped a mug of 'strong water.'

About ten o'clock, the number of visitors began diminishing and, by eleven o'clock, had ceased. The Wampanoags were on their way home.

The Pilgrims relaxed with relief, but many picked up their tools again and set to work at building houses or sawing clapboards. "Let us thank the Lord that they are gone," said Elder Brewster, folding his hands and making a small, silent prayer.

"Let us thank the Lord that they came," said Myles Standish, standing with his hands on his hips and rocking on the balls of his feet. "We concluded a peace that must make us all feel more secure."

"Aye," agreed William Bradford, wiping his bald brow after a turn at the buck-saw. "That peace is worth several days of mild hunger."

"Our hunger is not likely to be mild, Mr. Bradford," said Governor John Carver, looking sternly at him. "Our venison and mallard are gone, and we have Indian corn for no more than a few days, perhaps a week."

"God will provide," said Elder Brewster. "Let us pray." He indicated that the Pilgrims, especially the young, should go down on their knees. Even Governor Carver, who was fifty-four years old, knelt before God while Elder Brewster clasped his hands to the sky and prayed.

***

After seeing the Wampanoags off on the trail to Nemasket and Pokánoket, Squanto and Samoset returned to New Plimouth. "I wish they had some good beer," said Samoset. "Their 'strong water' has too much water in it."

Squanto said nothing, his head down, his eyes fixed on the trail before him.

"Still, I need something to help my stomach digest," Samoset went on, rubbing his belly. "I haven't eaten so much since last thanksgiving. I'll ask for a pint."

Squanto only nodded. He was still a bit reticent about talking to anyone, much less bold enough to make a request.

When they got back to New Plimouth, the Pilgrims were holding a town meeting in Leyden Street. Squanto and Samoset stood at the side of the group, marveling at the zealous attention to business.

The Pilgrims re-elected John Carver to serve as Governor for another year, and Myles Standish Captain of their militia. Elder Brewster was chosen magistrate and given power to settle property disputes, punish infractions of morality and ordinance, and perform civil weddings.

Samoset took Squanto's arm to get his attention and shook his head in disbelief. "Don't these English know when to have fun? On such a warm sunny day!" They didn't even dance or smoke before their pow-wow, though they prayed at every turn, especially at the end.

When the Pilgrims finished their meeting, they loosened their collars and turned to work on their unfinished houses, or to saw clapboards for export to England, or till the bean fields. Samoset had to ask for a mug of 'strong water.'

"All right," said John Carver, slowly putting aside the hoe he held. "It would be ungrateful of us to deny you a draft, though our supplies are low. Without your help, we could have made scarcely any profit with the natives."

He himself went to fill a mug for both Samoset and Squanto. "We appreciate your help in talking for us with Massasoit's people," he said, handing the mugs to the Indians. He took up his hoe again.

"No slice mallard?" asked Samoset, looking at him expectantly.

"We have no mallard to slice," said Edward Winslow, who had stopped to listen. Others with tools resting on their shoulders had begun to join the group.

"Oh, well," said Samoset, lifting his mug in a toast, the way the English sea captains often did. "Let's have a little fun. Sing a little song for a little good cheer."

> *Buck up, Billy, put your belly to the bar,*
> *And we'll drink a wee pint for auld lang syne.*
> *The birds, they're asinging, ...*

He trailed off and let the song die. The Pilgrim men were standing around, their eyes as bald as birds' eggs, their brows knitted into frowns.

"What wrong?" asked Samoset, waving his

mug. "Not know song?"

"You can hardly expect decent men to know such a song," said Elder Brewster, pressing his hands into a gesture of prayer, "and, if any did, he'd dare not sing it in the sight of God, for fear he'd be stricken dead in his tracks."

"We are heartily thankful to you for your help in translating," said William Bradford, temporarily shifting the auger and saw he carried, "but, now that Massasoit and his people are departed, we have work to do. We have houses to complete."

"Why?" asked Samoset. "The sun, he ashining. The summer, she a-coming. Who need house?" He did a little rhythmic dance, his hands held up to shoulder height.

"We do not relish lying on the ground, as you natives may," said Carver, gesturing toward the woods, "with no roof over our heads. Prepare for adversity in the time of fortune, and you'll not want in the time of affliction."

Samoset had to turn to Squanto for a translation, but Squanto had trouble interpreting the concepts of adversity and affliction.

"We are in the doorway of hunger," explained Bradford, holding the auger up against his own chest. "We have too little meat to give all a bite, and scarce enough bread to last a week. God must provide for us soon, or some of us may feel the worse hurt."

Samoset was hardly convinced. His experience with Englishmen was that their stores and their power were unlimited. They only had to make a gesture to exercise either.

About noon, Squanto stripped off his leggings, went to the stream, and came back before nightfall with an arm-load of eels.

"As many as he could well lift in one hand," wrote Edward Winslow in *Mourt's Relation*, "which our people were glad of. They were fat and sweet. He trod them out with his feet, and so caught them with his hands without any other instrument."

The Pilgrims were liberal in their thanks. Myles Standish, shorter than Squanto by five inches, grasped Squanto by the upper arm in a gesture of embrace. The women laid their fingers momentarily on his sleeve, mixing their gratitude with prayer.

When Samoset went away a few days later, Squanto stayed to help the English learn how to live in New England.

***

The Pilgrims had brought no fish nets from England or Holland; so they could not take fish from the streams, though they could see plenty of them swimming in Town Brook. Nor did any of them seem to know how to knot a mesh.

They did have a supply of string; so Squanto showed them how to make a net and then how to use it. He and Edward Winslow seined up nearly a bushel of shad with the first drag, which caused the Pilgrims to break into another round of prayer and gratitude.

With Squanto as guide and interpreter, the Pilgrims made contact with some of the local Indians and managed to trade for a small supply of corn. Winslow and Standish also succeeded in shooting a few deer. So famine was temporarily held at bay.

"Time to plant fields," Squanto pointed out. But, almost immediately, he discovered that practically none of the Pilgrims had any experience with agriculture. They were tailors, cobblers, carpenters, coopers, millers, but none of them were farmers.

As he had forewarned the Pilgrims, The Massasoit and some of his people returned to the nearby fields to put in the year's crop. Every day, a few Indians came to New Plimouth to talk, trade, and beg.

John Carver, trying to be less generous and thus to discourage so many visitors, told all the Pilgrims, "Cut down on the portions you give the Indians; else we may rapidly become destitute."

The Pilgrims were reluctant to leave the building of their houses, but at last they turned to putting in their crops. Squanto took a mattock on his own shoulder and led the men to fallow fields they had not previously noticed. "Dig here, this side of clearing," he told them, indicating a marshy area. "See? Sun shine much here. Ground stay wet from old pool."

The Pilgrims wanted to lay out their fields in straight rows, but Squanto told them to dig in mounds where the sun and residual moisture in the soil worked best to their advantage.

He sank his mattock into the ground and pulled up a gob of soggy soil. "We put fish in hole with seeds," he told them. "Two, three if they small."

Why would a person do that, the Pilgrims wanted to know.

"Old field," he pointed out. "Corn need food, too. Unless you put fish in with seeds, crop come to naught."

"We set the last spring some twenty acres of Indian corn,"

E d Winslow

wrote Edward Winslow in a letter the following December, which was included the next year in *Mourt's Relation*, "and sowed some six acres of barley and peas, and according to the manner of the Indians, we manured our ground with herring or rather shads, which we have in great abundance, and rake with great ease at our doors."[1]

A "great sickness" had killed about half of the Pilgrims before July 1st, including Elizabeth Winslow, Mary Allerton, Rose Standish, William White, William Mullins and his wife, and others. John Carver, their beloved Governor, came home from the fields one day in May with a severe headache, fell comatose within a few hours, and died two or three days later.

William Bradford was elected to take his place as governor. It was thought wise to have a lieutenant governor, and they chose Isaac Allerton.

But the dying had abated as the weather improved, which had turned warm and pleasant. The Pilgrims had finished seven houses, they had made peace with the Indians nearby and, with

---

None of the Pilgrims bothered to notice that none of the New England Indians fertilized their fields with fish, in "the manner of the Indians." They practiced rotation of crops and fallowing of fields. Squanto had learned the use of fish fertilizer on Newfoundland— from English men.

Squanto's help, they had managed to trade some cloth goods for Indian corn. They had witnessed their first marriage in the colony, and all their efforts seemed well on the way to success.

The only problem was the persistent tribes across the creek: men, women, children came regularly to avail themselves of the Pilgrim's generosity. They were about to eat the English out of house and home.

41. A Coat of Red Cotton

> The Pilgrim leaders sent The Massasoit a gift of "a horseman's coat of red cotton, laced with a slight lace,"
> — William Bradford, *Of Plimouth Plantation*

About mid-June, 1621, the Pilgrims sent Squanto with a delegation to The Massasoit at his home in Sowams, partly to ask the sachem to stop Wampanoag beggars from coming indiscriminately into New Plimouth, partly to discover the way to his village in case they should need to contact him, and partly to ascertain the military strength of the Indians.

The new governor, William Bradford, appointed Stephen Hopkins and Edward Winslow for this mission, with Squanto as guide and interpreter. The Pilgrim leaders sent The Massasoit a gift of "a horseman's coat of red cotton, laced with a slight lace," and other small items.

The Englishmen wore breast-plates, but not helmets, and carried their muskets. Stephen Hopkins, a fairly sturdy man, was surprised that

Nemasket was so far away. "Quite close, I thought Nemasket must lie, since many of their people come daily to New Plimouth."

"Yes, close by," said Squanto.

"But fifteen English miles we've come already. Just how much farther can it be?"

"Close by," said Squanto. "Two more bends in the path."

After about six hours of brisk walking, the party got to Nemasket about three o'clock. The people of Nemasket received them with joy and entertained them with kindness. They gave the Englishmen Johnny-cakes of corn bread, which they called *maizium,* and shad roe in such abundance that they gave the white men wooden spoons to eat it with. Hopkins and Winslow ate both with pleasure, but the "boiled musty acorns" were unpalatable to them.

After the Englishmen had eaten, the leader of Nemasket passed by the fine-featured and delicate Winslow and asked Stephen Hopkins if he would load his musket and shoot at a crow. "They are so many," he complained, "and they eat so much of our corn. They can practically destroy a field in no time at all."

Hopkins and Winslow charged their muskets with bird-shot and killed about eighty crows in a few minutes. "Amazing!" admitted the people of

Nemasket. "Amazing, the power over the world these white men have! Even the wiry one who looked so ineffective and young had the power."

After the shooting demonstration, Squanto urged the delegation to go on. "We cannot reach Pokánoket from here in one day," he said. "But we should go on to Cohannet." Willing that the journey be hastened, Hopkins and Winslow agreed.

About sunset, they came to a Nemasket fishing camp on the Taunton River, where men were taking large numbers of bass in fishing weirs. The natives gave the white men some of their fish, and the white men gave the Indians some of their victuals, "not doubting but we should have enough where'er we came."

They slept that night on the ground in an open field, for— astonishing as it seemed to the English— the Indians had no wigwams or shelters at the fishing camp.

As always, they asked many questions of the natives. They discovered that the river headwatered not far north and west of Patuxet, ran a few miles north of Nemasket, passed this fishing camp, passed the town of Pokánoket, and emptied into Narragansett Bay, where, the Indians reported, French ships often came.

The next morning, Hopkins and Winslow continued their journey, accompanied by a half

By Charles Brashear 309

dozen of the Nemasket men. Being given bits of food and small presents, a couple of the natives "adopted" each of the white men and gave them special assistance. When they came to a small stream, the Indians carried the white men across on their shoulders and offered to carry their muskets, lest they should become weary.

Winslow noted that there were many fields unplanted, which had been planted before, and now grown up in weeds. He noted there was plenty of good water, though the Indians did not willingly drink, except at a spring. He noted the kinds of trees along the way: oak, walnut, fir, beech, chestnut in plenty, yet not so thick but a man "may well ride a horse amongst them."

At length, they came to Pokánoket and found that Sowams was a kind of suburb, but The Massasoit was not at home.

After about two hours, The Massasoit returned. Hopkins and Winslow, at Squanto's suggestion, fired their muskets in honor of his arrival. The women and children were terrified, but The Massasoit was pleased. He invited the white men to his *comaco*, and made them welcome.

The Massasoit's house was rather larger than the usual and furnished with fur-covered benches, backrests, and shelves of utensils for entertaining travelers and visitors.

The Massasoit took a liking to the fragile-looking Englishman whose face was so smooth. He could see the man had a wiry strength and endurance, even if he looked slight. The Massasoit called him "Winsnow," because the Wampanoag language had no "l" in it, and they substituted "n."

Winslow delivered Governor Bradford's message: "Inasmuch as your people come often and without fear amongst us, so we now come to the great Massasoit. The governor has sent him a red horseman's coat, desiring that the peace and amity between our two people might be continued."

He paused for Squanto to translate and for the red coat to be put across The Massasoit's shoulders. The Great Sachem was visibly pleased and much admired by the people of Pokánoket.

"Thank you, Winsnow," he said through Squanto. His primary wife fingered the coat, making a cooing sound of admiration.

Winslow went on with the governor's message: "A great many of your people come to us very often, very many at a time, and with their wives and children. As friends, they are welcome. But we are yet such strangers at Patuxet, and we do not know how our corn will prosper, nor how much food we will store for the winter. We can no longer give your people such entertainment as we have done, as we wish we still could.

By Charles Brashear 311

"Yet, if Massasoit should be pleased to come himself to visit us, or any special friend of his should wish to come, he will be most welcome. To the end that we might know when any messenger comes from Massasoit himself, our governor has sent him a copper chain; so that we might know the messenger by his bringing the chain with him.

"Then we will harken to the messenger and give credit, as if Massasoit himself had come."

The Massasoit received the chain and said, "I am glad of this. It makes a path where our words may travel. I will send one of my warriors, a special friend named Tokama-hamon. He can go back and forth with news."

"And finally, our governor requests a favor of Massasoit: that he might exchange some of his seed corn with us, so that we might try which corn best agrees with the soil where we live."

"You are welcome to Sowams," said The Massasoit. "I, too, desire to keep the peace. I will tell the people to stop pestering the English. And I will look in our baskets, soon, and find some seed corn to send to you."

Then he picked up his little scepter, this being an occasion of State, turned to his own people who were nearby and, stalking back and forth in his red greatcoat, made a speech to them.

"Am I not The Massasoit, commander of the

country all about you? Is not Sowams my town? And Pokánoket? And Wahnomoisett? And Assomet? And Kickemuit? And are not the people there my people, who follow my commands?"

"After this manner," wrote Winslow, "he named at least thirty places." Capawack, Monomet, Monamoyik, Nobsqu-osset, Matakes, Mattapoisett, Hyannis, Nauset, Cumma-quid, Mattakiesett, Scituate, Massakiesett, Cohasset, on and on. At the naming of each village, the crowd sent up a cheer, "so that it was as delightful as it was tedious unto us."

Then The Massasoit gave the Englishmen tobacco to smoke and fell to asking them about England. He complained of the French ships in Narragansett Bay and asked if they could be prohibited, for The Massasoit considered himself King James's man and this area King James's country.

"Late it grew," wrote Winslow later, "but victuals he offered none, for indeed he had not any, being he came so newly home. So we desired to go to rest. He laid us upon the bed with himself and his wife, they at the one end and we at the other, it being only planks laid a foot from the ground, and a thin mat upon them. Two more of his chief men, for want of room, pressed by and upon us, so that we were worse weary of our

By Charles Brashear 313

lodging than of our journey."

The next day, The Massasoit's people caught and stewed two large fish from Narragansett Bay that fed about forty people. The people entertained the English with gambling, singing, dancing, but little food, so that after two nights and a day, the Englishmen said they would leave, because they wished to spend their Sabbath at home.

"I am sorry that I was unable to entertain you more richly, as you deserve," said The Massasoit, on taking leave. "I will send Tisquantum to many places along your wayside, so that he may get food for you in my name. In his place, I will appoint my special friend, Tokama-hamon, who will be your friend, guide, and messenger."

On short rations, they came that night to the Nemasket fishing weir, but the Indians had all gone home; so there was no food to be had. Winslow sent Tokama-hamon forward with a note that Governor Bradford should send food to them at Nemasket. That left them with only two men, who however caught fish at the weir and roasted them for the English.

In the middle of the night, a driving thunderstorm hit, but the English went on—the Nemasket people marveling that anyone would travel in such weather—and came safely to New

Plimouth, wet, weary, and exhausted.

By Charles Brashear 315

42. A Boy Lost and Found

> "After sunset, but before dark, Aspinet came with a great train and brought the Billington boy, one bearing him on his shoulder through the water, others holding up torches. Aspinet had at least a hundred warriors: about half of them came unarmed with Aspinet and the procession through the water to the shallop; the other half stood aloof on the shore, their bows and arrows ready."
>
> —William Bradford, recording Edward Winslow's report, *Of Plimouth Plantation*

The travelers were hardly home before news broke that John Billington was lost in the woods. Bradford knew him as a mischievous boy, who had loaded a musket and fired it carelessly, albeit accidentally, on *The Mayflower* in a cabin where two kegs of powder and other combustibles were stored. It was a wonder he had not blown up the ship.

He was a troublesome boy—and recalcitrant. However, as in all cases where someone misbehaved and made trouble for the Pilgrim leaders. Bradford prayed for resignation and endurance, then set off to find the lost lamb.

The search parties discovered the pond south and west of Patuxet, where they saw signs that the boy had climbed a tree at night to be safe from wolves. They named the pond "Billington Sea." Though they stalked up and down the woods for five days, they could not find the boy.

Finally, The Massasoit sent word that some of his people had found the boy and taken him into Manomet, twenty miles down Cape Cod Bay, and that his rescuer had transported him further down the cape to Cummaquid.

Governor Bradford sent the shallop and ten men to rescue the boy. They took Squanto along as interpreter and Tokama-hamon as "special friend."

In spite of a storm, the shallop made the safety of Barnstable Harbor, where the English spent the night. The next morning, they found themselves aground, the tide having gone out. They sent Squanto and Tokama-hamon to assure the people of Cummaquid that the English meant them no hurt and to inquire about the boy.

"Oh, he's well," the people of Cummaquid replied, "but he is at Nauset. The man who rescued him in the woods is showing him in all the villages."

Iyanough, the sachem of Cummaquid, was a handsome young man, not over twenty-six years old, by Winslow's estimate, and an agreeable, hospitable person. He served the English an impromptu banquet.

A loud voice and a ruckus interrupted the meal. "Where are they? I want to see them!" It was an old woman (Winslow estimated that she was "no less than a hundred years old") who had never seen an Englishman, yet who broke into tears and screams when she got sight of them. She was breathing too deeply in great gasps and calling for a knife or lance, that she might stab one of the whites. Yet she crumpled into a heap with her sobs and weeping.

"Ask what this is all about, Squanto," commanded Winslow. He wore his breast plate, as was his habit when going among the Indians, and carried his musket charged.

One of the elders told the Pilgrims, "This old woman had three sons who were carried away seven years ago."

"They had gone on board the ship to trade with him," said another. "He shut the hatches on them and carried them away."

"She never heard of them again," added Iyanough, "and was thus deprived of the comfort of children in her old age."

She could not look at the yang-kaysh without bursting again into tears and screams.

"I remember your sons," Squanto told the old

woman. "I was captive on the same ship. Your sons did not die at sea. They came to land in a place called España, where they were getting food and the holy men of that place were teaching them the language."

Winslow tried to console the woman, through Squanto as interpreter: "We are very sorry that any Englishman should give anyone such offense. Captain Hunt is a bad man. All the Englishmen who have heard about him agree that he is an evil man."

Such an apology did not bring back the woman's sons; yet she wanted to touch Winslow's breast plate.

"As for us," he went on, "the English at Patuxet, you may be assured, we will offer you no such injury. Yea, though it might gain us all the skins and gold you have, we would not treat you so badly. For our God would surely be angry with us and come to destroy us."

Winslow gave the woman a few beads and a piece of cloth, which somewhat appeased her.

"We wish to live at peace with all our neighbors," Winslow added.

***

When the feast was finished, the Englishmen set sail for Nauset, where they hoped to locate the Billington boy. Iyanough and two of his warriors went with them. They arrived off Nauset near sunset, as the tide was ebbing, so felt they could not proceed into the harbor. Iyanough and his men went ashore anyway, and Winslow sent Squanto to tell Aspinet, the sachem of Nauset, who the English were and why they came.

Winslow and the Englishmen were apprehensive of danger, for this was the scene of their "First Encounter," where Aspinet's warriors had attacked them. They marveled all the more now, for though they had seen no houses "through snow or otherwise" on that first visit, yet they now found they were in the midst of many of them.

As soon as the tide left the shallop aground, the people came in great numbers, clamoring around the boat for attention. The English posted guards along the rails, not suffering any to come aboard, except two men— a man from Manomoyack and the man whose corn they had taken at First Encounter.

"We wish to pay you for that corn," Winslow assured the man.

Yes, he had heard that; he, too, marveled at Winslow's shiny breast plate.

"I will come to Patuxet," said the man. "Many have said the English are kind and friendly. I would like to visit them at their home."

After sunset, but before dark, Aspinet came

with a great train and brought the Billington boy, one bearing him on his shoulder through the water, others holding up torches. Aspinet had at least a hundred warriors: about half of them came unarmed with Aspinet in a procession through the water to the shallop; the other half stood aloof on the shore, their bows and arrows ready.

John Billington was being treated like a hero, borne aloft as if in honor, his neck strung with seed and bone beads and his face painted with grease-paint.

Winslow gave Aspinet a butcher knife, some cloth, and a few beads. The man who had discovered the boy in the woods was introduced and also received a present of a butcher knife.

Aspinet wanted to entertain the Pilgrims, but the Englishmen were so anxious to be gone the next morning that they invited Aspinet instead to Patuxet. "I will come soon, with all my warriors," said Aspinet.

The Nausets told a disturbing story that the Narragansetts had gone to war against some of The Massasoit's towns. Some of the Wampanoags had been hurt, and there was even a rumor that The Massasoit had been captured.

Aspinet took a bone necklace from his own neck and hung it on Winslow, saying "May our mutual enemies come to no good."

43. "The Tongue of the English"

> "We [the Pilgrims]... feared [Corbitant] had killed Squanto, for he threatened them both [Squanto and Hobamock], for no other reason than that they were friend to the English and serviceable to them."
> —William Bradford, *Of Plimouth Plantation,* 1647.

When the Pilgrims returned from Nauset, they discovered that Hobamock, a member of the Elder's Council and one of The Massasoit's chief counselors, had come to Patuxet. His wife was with him. Hobamock wore an English shirt and breech clout, but his wife was dressed in a traditional Wampanoag doeskin shift.

"Welcome, grandfather," said Squanto, for Hobamock was a close advisor of The Massasoit and a *panisee*, a man considered to have a charmed life.

"You are most welcome to New Plimouth," said Governor Bradford, heartily, although he and the other Pilgrim leaders hardly knew what to make of this development. "To what do we owe the honor of this visit?"

Squanto had some difficulty translating that question.

"My wife and I have come to live among the English," said Hobamock, simply and straightforwardly. "I want to learn the language of the English. I want to learn your ways."

A mature man, he was tall and sturdy, a superior physical specimen, who already knew enough English words to make much of his meaning clear. He planned to build a house and serve among the English as a friend and advisor to both the Pilgrims and The Massasoit.

"It is an opportunity, sent by God, to civilize and assimilate a savage," exclaimed Elder Brewster. "And is not that our mission, under God?"

Others were suspicious. "He's been sent here to spy on us," said Myles Standish in private.

"But we have nothing to hide," said Bradford, opening his hands before him. "Let our intentions be honest, and he is welcome to report them."

"All the same, I think we'd better set one of ours to learn their language equally well," said Myles. "We may not always be able to depend upon friendly interpreters."

"Aye," said Bradford. "Edward Winslow is the logical one for that service. He already knows more of their words than any of us."

The Pilgrims marked off a lot for Hobamock's house and garden at the outer edge of town, near the end of Leyden Street. Hobamock wanted to build his house in the style of the English, but the Pilgrims would not spare enough sawed boards. So Hobamock and his wife built a Wampanoag wigwam of limbs bent into a dome and covered with woven straw mats.

On further questioning through Squanto, the Pilgrims discovered more about Hobamock's purpose. The Narragansetts had indeed gone to war against The Massasoit and caused him to flee his town. No one knew at the moment where he was. Corbitant, the sachem of Pocasset, whose loyalty to The Massasoit was always suspect and whose unrelenting hostility to the whites was well known, seemed to be in league with the Narragansetts.

"This Corbitant. Isn't he one of those who swore his friendship to the English?" asked Myles Standish.

"Yes," admitted Hobamock. "He touched the white man's paper."

Standish was always concerned with the

defense of New Plimouth. "Is he a Narragansett?"

"Either he has joined the Narragansetts," said Hobamock, through Squanto, "or he is using this disturbance to cover his pursuit of his own ambitions."

"And where is this—this Corbitant now?" asked Standish.

Hobamock understood that Standish was captain of the militia, yet he was astonished that so short a man should be chosen. Still, the little man was thick and quite strong.

Squanto relayed the question and reported Hobamock's reply: "People on the path say that Corbitant is on his way to Nemasket. It is said he wishes to draw the hearts of Chief Nepeof and the Nemasket people away from The Massasoit and to himself."

"Then does he plan to bring his warriors against us?"

"He is extremely angry because of the peace you made with Aspinet at Nauset and with Iyanough at Cummaquid," Hobamock went on.

Governor Bradford was surprised that Corbitant should have such news, and that Hobamock should have received it from fifty miles away in the other direction, for Edward Winslow and the Billington rescue party had hardly returned from Cape Cod. The Indians seemed to know what was happening even before the whites.

"Those were Corbitant's towns," continued Hobamock. "He claimed their loyalty and their warriors. Now, Corbitant speaks disdainfully of the English. He says he will have vengeance on Aspinet and Iyanough, and any who helps the English. He demands that you turn Hobamock, Squanto, and Tokama-hamon over to him."

"To what purpose?" asked Bradford.

"He recently plotted to murder Tokama-hamon," reported Hobamock, "because he is a special and trusty man among The Massasoit's friends."

Tokama-hamon gathered his lance and bow and arrows. "I am not afraid of Corbitant," he said angrily. "I shall go at once to seek out Corbitant."

Squanto took the news without comment; he felt safe with the English. No Wampanoag would dare try to injure him.

"I think Corbitant would not try to harm me," Hobamock went on, "for I am a *panisee*, whom no knife, arrow, or lance can wound. Besides, I am too close to The Massasoit, who is still far more powerful than Corbitant. But Corbitant wants the death of Squanto. If Squanto were dead, he says, the English would have lost their tongue."

***

Secretly and privately, Hobamock and Squanto left Patuxet and went to Nemasket, to see if they could learn anything more of The Massasoit's predicament. Corbitant discovered where they were, set a guard, and captured them. Two of Corbitant's men restrained Hobamock, while Corbitant held a knife to Squanto's breast and acted as if he would cut his throat.

"You know he is The Massasoit's adopted son, don't you?" shouted Hobamock. "A cut to him is a cut to The Massasoit himself."

"As if I cared!" said Corbitant. "Even The Massasoit must someday awake to the truth that we would be better off, were we rid of the English and their lies."

Hobamock, described by Winslow as a "strong and stout" man, broke from his guards and ran out the door. He outran his pursuers and got back to New Plimouth, where, in a sweat and breathless, he reported as best he could what had happened. He feared Squanto had been slain. Myles Standish had learned a few dozen words of Wampanoag, which helped the Pilgrims to understand Hobamock.

The Pilgrims assembled at once and resolved to send their fourteen-man army to avenge the death of Squanto and punish Corbitant, "in defense of the great King Massasoit." They asked

Hobamock to guide Captain Myles Standish and his little militia to Corbitant. Hobamock agreed.

The next day, the Pilgrims marched to Nemasket through intermittent rain. When they calculated they were within two or three miles of the town, they moved off the path and waited for nightfall. They planned a surprise attack at midnight. Edward Winslow, Stephen Hopkins, and Hobamock gave Standish some idea of the lay-out of the town, and Standish assigned particular men to invade the houses considered most important, including the one where Corbitant was reported to be staying, and to take the inhabitants prisoner.

The pilgrims struck the little town like lightning. Armored men blitzed in at wigwam doors, their muskets loaded and pointed, yelling in pidgin Wampanoag with much English mixed in, "Towam! Friends! Friends! We are friends! Towam!"

"Fear had bereft the savages of speech," wrote Winslow in his report. They sat on their beds, naked, wide-eyed, and baffled.

"Corbitant?" shouted the Pilgrim soldiers in pidgin. "Corbitant here?"

Still, the people were unable to answer.

"Where is Corbitant?" demanded the Pilgrims, now in English, with little concern that the people could not understand them. "Bring out Corbitant, and we will not meddle with you. We come mainly for Corbitant. Bring him out, for we will be avenged upon him. He has killed our Squanto."

The Wampanoags began begging for their lives. Hobamock tried to translate their cries and pleading.

"We come only for Corbitant, and any that follow him," yelled Standish. "Do as we tell you, and we will not harm you or your women and children. Build up your fire, so we can see to search out Corbitant."

At length, Hobamock got the men of Nemasket to understand what the English wanted and that they would not harm any who obeyed their orders. "Where is Corbitant? Bring out Corbitant, for we will be avenged upon him."

"Corbitant went away," the people of Nemasket reported, shivering and wet. "He and his warriors went away. Nepeof and some of his warriors went with him, but we do not know where they went." The men in charge of the village brought forth tobacco and offered it to the English as a gesture of peace.

"What has happened to Tisquantum?" asked Captain Standish. "Did Corbitant kill Squanto?"

"Oh, no, no," said the temporary leader of Nemasket, looking apprehensively at the glint of Standish's armor. "Tisquantum is yet living. He sleeps in a wigwam near here, in the edge of our town."

Hobamock yelled for Squanto. The Pilgrims demanded the Nemasket people should build up their fires, so it would be possible to see during the search of the village.

In a moment, Squanto and Tokama-hamon came out of a remote wigwam and made their way to the town plaza, wondering what was going on.

"So, you are alive?" said Winslow to Tokama-hamon. "We feared you had joined Corbitant, or had been slain."

"You need not doubt the loyalty of Tokama-hamon to The Massasoit, nor suspect that Corbitant would dare to harm him."

"And you— you are alive?" said Standish to Squanto. "We feared you had been murdered."

Squanto hesitated before responding. At last, he understood what the ruckus was about. The Pilgrims had come to rescue him. He felt a surge of pleasure and importance at their concern. *Me? Little, insignificant Squanto? Had the English really invaded Nemasket to rescue me?*

"Corbitant not draw one drop of my blood," said Squanto, matching Tokama-hamon's cockiness. "Though he hold a knife at my throat, yet he dare not spill even one drop of my blood." He bounced slightly on the balls of his feet, for he felt stronger than he had ever felt in his life. He rolled his shoulders in a gesture of power.

Corbitant had not dared touch Tokamahamon because of The Massasoit, but he had not dared touch Squanto because Squanto could call down the wrath of the English on Squanto's enemies. He did not need shining armor on his chest. It was a heady feeling. He could feel, though he could not see, the streams of force flowing from his fingers. With a few followers, he, too, could be a sachem.

***

The Pilgrims occupied the large town-house, a wigwam in the middle of the town and facing onto the town square, glad to have a place to dry off and get warm. They set two men to watch and keep their muskets charged and their matches smoldering, while the others slept with their charged muskets in their hands. Once each hour, Standish changed the guard.

The next morning, the Pilgrim army emerged to find the Nemasket townspeople chastened and apologetic. They stood about with wooden trays and clam-shell bowls of food in their hands, offering them meekly and insisting that their hearts were upright toward the Pilgrims.

The Pilgrims accepted the breakfast thus tendered— Johnny-cakes of ground corn, roasted fish, dried quahogs, bowls of warm succotash, and fresh water to wash it down. The food made them more friendly, more ready to listen to the protestations of innocence from the Nemasket people.

Between bites of food, Squanto talked for both sides. He felt a special charge in his knowledge of both languages. Very little would happen without him. He was indispensable to both sides. He could hardly keep from giggling with his sense of his own importance.

Myles Standish had Squanto question the people of Nemasket again. "Are you certain that Corbitant and his warriors have gone away?"

"Yes. All of them, all of them" said several people at once. An elder added, "Corbitant was sorely frightened by the power of the English. He withdrew in shame and fear."

"Are you the head man of Nemasket?" Standish wanted to know.

"No. Nepeof is head man," said the elder. "Nepeof and some of his warriors retreated with Corbitant."

"So Nepeof makes war beside Corbitant?" asked Standish through Squanto.

"Oh, no," said the elder. "Nepeof waits in the woods some miles away, hoping the English will forgive him and his warriors and allow them to return to their homes. They promise to be good friends to the English."

Captain Myles Standish consulted with Edward Winslow and Stephen Hopkins. "It looks like we have accomplished our mission," said Myles. "We've rescued Squanto and chased Corbitant back to his hideout."

"Yes," agreed Edward Winslow, taking off his helmet. "It's time to become magnanimous. Make peace and renew our friendship with these people."

"You do that, Edward."

"That is the captain's privilege and duty."

"But I'm no good with the honey-tongue. I can never think of the right things to say. You do it for me, Edward, okay?"

So Edward Winslow took a position in front of the people of Nemasket, held his helmet under his arm, and made a little speech, which he later summarized in his report. He brought Squanto forward, into a place of great attention, and spoke through him. "We intend our friends no harm nor hurt. If you are our friends, you will not suffer harm nor hurt, if we can help it."

Squanto's voice rang loudly across the whole town square of Nemasket, so all could hear: "Corbitant has now escaped us. But, if he continues to threaten us, or steal our friends, or offer harm to us or any of our people, there is no place for him to hide, but we will find and punish him. There is no place that will secure him from us, however remote it may be."

Winslow paused often for Squanto to translate. As Squanto delivered the gestures of peace that were in fact veiled threats, he could see the people of Nemasket acting both relieved and newly afraid. He could bend them, the way the wind bends a tree: if he blew hard with threats, they fell away; if he soughed softly with friendship, they unfurled toward him.

"If any offers violence to Squanto, Hobamock, or any of Massasoit's subjects, we will avenge it. We will pursue him and his warriors to the backs of their houses and destroy them all."

Again, as Squanto conveyed Winslow's words, he felt the power of language to manipulate. He made it clear that he, Squanto, shared in the power of the English. Words that came from his mouth struck consternation or courage in the hearts of others. They were his servants; without a sword, he could make them follow wherever he wanted. With words— with mere words.

44. "No Need to Fear Us"

> "Before they got away, every one of them signed an acknowledgment of allegiance to King James. Probably not one of them knew what he had done, or dreamed that he had entered the town a prince, a ruler over his people, and left it a slave, for that is what the colonists tried to make of them..."
> —Alvin Weeks, *Massasoit of the Wampanoags*

In the days and weeks that followed the "voyage to Nemasket," a semblance of peace returned to the Wampanoag nation. The Narragansett threat passed, and The Massasoit returned to his home at Sowams on Narragansett Bay.

As he had promised, Aspinet of Nauset visited New Plimouth to pledge his peaceful intentions toward the Pilgrims. He was a man of average stature, no stronger nor weaker than a dozen others; yet his commanding presence told all that he was a leader. He came with his hundred warriors, sixty of whom lay down their bows and arrows and entered the town with him, while the other forty stood aloof a good way from the village, their weapons at the ready.

"Some of my people have been killed by wicked sea captains," Aspinet said in his speech of peace. "Others have been carried away into slavery, and we have never seen them again. Many white men have come only to steal or kill, but we can now see that your intentions are honest. Aspinet will not war again with you, but will war against your enemies at your side. We wish to live in peace, with our heads on our own beds at night. We are glad that your muskets are pointed away from us."

On the 13th of September, 1621, nine other chiefs came to New Plimouth to pledge their friendship. Squanto introduced each leader and translated his speech of peace and friendship."

Edward Winslow and William Bradford dutifully recorded the Indians' names, their ranks and offices, and their homes.[2] Squanto had known some of these men for years; others he was meeting for the first time.

From Narragansett Bay came Quadequina,

---

[2] But the Pilgrims did not seem to appreciate the significance of the far-flung region represented by the nine chiefs. Some had traveled as much as four days to get there.

sachem of Pokánoket and younger brother of The Massasoit, along with one of his lesser leaders, Huttamoiden. Quadequina gave Squanto a feather, a gift from The Massasoit, in recognition of Squanto's services as an interpreter. Squanto was pleased with the gesture, for a feather was a step toward becoming a sachem in his own right.

From the upper Connecticut Valley came Nattawahunt, a sachem subject to The Massasoit on the Connecticut River.

From east of Massachusetts Bay came Obbitinuat, a sachem of the Massachusetts tribe and sometimes ally to The Massasoit.

From the lower Massachusetts came Chickataubut, a sachem who had a summer home near the Taunton River, north of Nemasket.

From the outer side of Cape Cod came Ohquamehud, sachem of the lower Nausets, with representatives of Manomoyack, where Thomas Dermer had been held hostage until Squanto argued hard for his release. "So, we meet again, little diplomat," said Ohquamehud, smiling at Squanto.

"Welcome to our town," said Squanto, omitting the polite address to an elder, 'grandfather.'

With each leader, Squanto puffed up a bit more, like a turkey courting a hen. All these great

By Charles Brashear 337

sachems were friendly, dependent, and even paid homage to Squanto. Squanto felt like the most powerful leader in the Wampanoag nation. Others had now to seek his favors; no one would ever again handle him with a rope.

From the inner side of Cape Cod Bay came Cawnacomán, sachem of Manomet, who was kidnaped by Captain Edward Harlow in 1611 and returned to his home through the efforts of Epanow of Capawack.

Epanow, sachem of Capawack, was there also, though he still felt great cause to hate the English, especially Sir Ferdinando Gorges. He greeted Squanto with a handshake and a friendly grasp on the upper arm.

Squanto hesitated, in the midst of a quandary: this was the man whose attack had resulted in Thomas Dermer's death, yet he was acting with great friendliness toward Squanto. Squanto hardly knew how to respond to him. Since Epanow spoke enough English, he delivered his own speech.

From Mattapuysett on Buzzard's Bay came Corbitant, sachem of Pocasset, now meekly insisting that he was a friend of the English and promising that he would lead no more insurrections against his white friends. Sheepishly, he avoided looking directly at Squanto, at whose breast he had held a knife.

Standish asked Hobamock to verify that Squanto had translated Corbitant's speech fairly. "Yes," said Hobamock in Wampanoag. "He glows like the sun. But he dare not change their words."

Thus, the nine chiefs came from all points of the compass, at distances of three to five days travel. They came to ratify the peace and mutual protection treaty that The Massasoit had concluded with the Pilgrims.

And the Pilgrims tricked them. They inserted into the treaty an oath of allegiance to King James.[3] Now, when the Wampanoags were rebellious, the Pilgrims could claim righteously that the Indians had violated their oaths.

In Leyden Street, the one street of New Plimouth, the Pilgrims knelt to thank God for the success of their plantation and the furtherance of all their schemes. Even Elder Brewster and Governor Bradford went down on their knees. At the edge of the Pilgrims' assembly, Squanto, wanting to please his friends, followed their example and knelt also.

When the Indians, thinking they were free men, resisted being governed by the colonists, the

---

[3]Alvin Weeks, *Massasoit of the Wampanoags*

English would accuse the natives of breaking their treaty and their fealty to the English crown. Thus the English unwittingly created their abiding self-justification for their wars of extermination against the American natives.

45. A Visit to Massachusetts Bay

> "The Tarentine Federation to the north makes raids on our villages and steals our corn and furs. I dare not remain in any settled place, for the Tarentines would come and attack us." Obbitinuat, Sachem of a village on Massachusetts Bay.

Peace being restored, the Pilgrim leaders decided it was a good time to strap on their armor and visit the Indians on Massachusetts Bay, in spite of rumors that those Indians had often threatened to exterminate the English. "Bad people," said Squanto. "They bad people. Say many evil things about English."

"Nevertheless, we promised them we would come to visit and trade for their beaver furs and fortify the peace between us," said Bradford, adjusting his broad-brimmed hat.

"Besides," added Myles Standish, "it's a good opportunity to explore their country."

"And pick up what corn we can," added Edward Winslow. "It seems we're always running low on food. We've got a lot of mouths to feed."

By Charles Brashear 341

"Bad people," repeated Squanto. "Bad people."

They set out about midnight, the tide and winds being favorable, thinking they would be there by mid-morning. But it proved a much greater distance than they had thought. They finally made the lower end of Massachusetts Bay late the next night, anchored, and slept in the shallop.

When they went ashore the next morning, they discovered a basket of lobsters, which they promptly ate. Then Standish took four men with muskets and, with Squanto as guide, went in search of the people. On the path, they soon met a woman who was coming for her lobsters. They told her they had eaten them and paid her with beads and a small mirror to her satisfaction.

"But where are the people of this place," Squanto asked her, speaking for Myles Standish.

The woman pointed inland with her chin and said, "One hour's walk."

"Squanto, you go and see if you can make contact with them," said Standish. "Tell them we are peaceful. The men and I will go back to the shallop and dock it in the next inlet that offers any protection. Bring their leaders to us there."

The sachem of the place Standish chose was Obbitinuat, one of those who had signed the peace accords in New Plimouth and a man friendly to The Massasoit. He called his people to cook for the English and smoked with them. And he directed some of his people to sing and dance for the Pilgrims.

"Why were you hiding so far from the shore?" asked Standish.

"Tarentines," said Obbitinuat through Squanto. "The Tarentine Federation to the north raids our villages and steals our corn and furs. I dare not remain in any settled place, for the Tarentines would attack us. They, or the Squaw Sachem of the Massachusetts. She, too, is an enemy."

The Pilgrims explored the Bay the next day, estimating that it contained more than fifty islands. Opposite Deer Island, they anchored near the shore, looking for a village, said to be the home of the Squaw Sachem. Leaving two men with the shallop, Standish marched inland, his men under arms.

They came to a cornfield, but it had been hastily and recently harvested. A house at the edge of the field had been pulled down, and the people were gone. In the next field, they found a pile of corn, poorly covered with a mat, and no one present to guard it.

They came to the home and tomb of

Nanepashemet, "He who walks at night," the sachem of the area, who had died only last year. His house was situated on a hill and built on stilts about six feet from the ground. In a bottom a mile further away, they found his tomb: a house built inside a palisade, with moats both inside and outside the fortification.

Everywhere, they saw signs that the Indians had quickly torn down their houses and taken away what they could carry. Finally, the Pilgrims came to a clearing where the Indian women were huddled amid their small piles of corn, quaking in fear of the white men's muskets. They offered corn cakes, saying, "Please don't kill us."

"Tell them they have no need to fear us," Standish instructed Squanto. "Tell them we come in peace, to trade for their furs." He gave a few of the bolder women small presents, such as a bracelet of beads, a comb, a sewing awl.

Then the women relaxed and boiled cod to feed the Englishmen. But they were so modest and timid that it was hard to carry on a conversation with them. "Ask them where their men are," said Standish.

At length, one man came out of the woods, shaking and trembling. Standish gave him a knife, and the man began to relax.

Questioned by Squanto, he admitted, "Yes,

this is the region ruled by the Squaw Sachem, widow of Nanepashemet, but she is not at home now. She is far away, and the English can not see her." The man took the first opportunity to disappear into the woods.

"Sack these women," said Squanto.

"Sack them?" asked Standish. "You mean rob them? Pillage their goods?"

"Yes," said Squanto. "They have a little of what you want. Corn, furs, mats. All useful things. Take them and, if the women object, beat them, or shoot them. If I am sachem, I take what I want."

"I can't believe I'm hearing you right."

"Bad people. These are bad people. They have often speak bad of you and the plantation."

"I am shocked, Squanto. That's no way to be a spokesman for the English. We mean the people no harm."

"They would come and destroy you and me. They do not deserve to live. Kill them, and take their booty."

Standish pulled his shoulders up straight. "Were they ever so bad, we would not wrong them. Or give them any just reason to complain against us."

"They say many bad things," insisted Squanto. "They threaten to kill all of the English."

"Words, mere words," said Standish. "They carry no weight. They are of little consequence. Deeds are what count. Let them once attempt any thing against us, then we will deal with them in a worse way than you suggest. But as for now, we are at peace. Let us be generous to our friends."

At nightfall, the Pilgrims returned to their shallop. The Indian women followed, anxious to trade what little they had for a bit of looking glass, a shining awl, a string of beads. Some were even willing to sell the furs off their bodies, hastily and shame-facedly tying together leafy branches to cover their nakedness.

Standish thought many of them "more modest than some of our English women are."

"Plant extra fields of corn and beans," said Standish through Squanto, though he now knew almost enough Wampanoag to form such sentences, "and we promise we will come to buy the grain from you when it is ripe."

The women agreed and pledged to set extra fields.

"And save your beaver and deer skins," added Standish. "We will also come and buy your skins from you. We promise we will come again to trade."

Standish had learned a lot about Massachusetts Bay, but he came back with less than a week's supply of Indian corn.

By Charles Brashear 347

46. A Time of Thanksgiving, 1621

> "... Our corn did prove well and—God be praised!—we had a good increase of Indian corn; and our barley indifferent good. But our pease were not worth the gathering, for we feared they were too late sown. They came up very well and blossomed, but the sun parched them in the blossom."
>
> — Edward Winslow, letter of 11 Dec 1621.

The seed corn and beans were set aside, under lock and key, and the people were advised to conserve their foods and parcel them into daily quantities.

But not all of the Pilgrims were members of the Puritan sect, nor did they have the self-discipline to live at subsistence level. These dissidents also lacked the certainty of the Pilgrims that they were God's Chosen People and that somehow God would provide.

These nonconformists were not above stealing what little meal and beans there were. Though the Puritans flogged the thieves in public and locked them— head, hands, and feet— in the stocks in the public square, yet the pilfering continued.

And the situation got worse and worse. Before the harvest of 1621, the Pilgrims were drastically short of food.

"This situation requires extreme measures," Governor Bradford told the people. "We must conserve what we have, and somehow, by God's grace, find a new supply, or we will experience a general famine this winter."

"The summer is not over," said Squanto, though the weather had turned blustery and changeable— chill rain and wind one day, and clear, sunny skies another. "Plenty of nice weather yet."

"Well, we had better take advantage of it," said Bradford, pulling his blue cloak in closer, "but I don't know how we can increase our supplies."

"Harvest come soon," said Squanto.

***

In the midst of the shortage, Squanto said one day to Bradford, "The Massasoit comes to Patuxet at thanks-giving."

"Oh, no," said Bradford. "That's the last thing we need— a tribe of our friends to entertain.

Is he coming to thank us for chastising Corbitant?"

"No," said Squanto. "He give thanks for everything." Squanto held up his arms in a gesture that embraced the sky, and he turned around to all points of the compass.

"That won't feed many people," said Bradford. "We've got to find more corn. Are you sure the local Indians have no more to trade?"

"No more," said Squanto. "I get already what they have."

"Well, we'll have to go farther afield."

In October, Governor Bradford sent Edward Winslow and ten men in the shallop to visit the English fishing fleet off Monhegan Island and try to buy supplies from them. With their gray linsey greatcoats fastened tightly, they weathered wind and wave that nearly upset the little boat several times, paid high prices for small quantities of foods, and came back with a scanty supply of meal and flour, which, with rationing, lasted until the harvest began.

Bradford kept the food stored in the community house and parceled it out to families a quarter pound of bread at a time, knowing that if they had access to their full share, they would eat it all at once. Waste was punished by ridicule at church service, or by flogging non-believers in the stocks.

***

Then the harvest began. The barley was threshed and brought to storage, though some was made into mash and set aside to ferment. The beans were shelled and sacked, the squash were carried to sheds, the Indian corn was picked and stored.

"Praised be the Lord," said Bradford, satisfied with himself. "We are entering a time of plenty."

"A time of thanksgiving," said Squanto. "We celebrate. Have feast to celebrate the harvest."

About the third week in November, Governor Bradford agreed and decided to hold a harvest festival to recognize their good fortune. It was a heady time for Squanto, for this was the first time he had succeeded in manipulating Bradford.

Bradford sent four men out with fowling pieces to hunt for wild turkeys, grouse, and any other eatable fowl they could shoot.

Before they returned, The Massasoit and ninety of his people showed up with five deer on carrying poles, as well as baskets of pumpkins and other squash, beans of several sorts, and corn on the cob. In their ceremonial dress and face paint, they had come to Patuxet to observe thanksgiving with their friends and allies, the Pilgrims.

At first, the Pilgrims were dumbfounded to

see so many Wampanoags, who smoothed off places at the edge of the town. They and their families would spread their skins and camp under the open sky. The Massasoit had brought all five of his wives and his many children. The Indian women set about at once, preparing the meat and roasting it on racks over open fires. They kept their boys busy running after wood, or water, or whatever they needed in the cooking.

Most of the Wampanoags now knew a half-dozen English words, and most of the Pilgrims knew about as much Wampanoag. So there was a friendly exchange, often one holding up an item and asking what it was called.

With their baskets in their arms, the Indian women went to the Pilgrim women's houses, walked right in, set the Pilgrims' stewing pots in the fireplaces, and began cooking their mixture of corn, beans, and squash. "Succotash," they said, gleefully, pointing to the mixed vegetables in the steaming kettles. "Succotash," they repeated and would not stop until the Pilgrim women had echoed, "Succotash."

As Squanto and Bradford walked out, the smoke of many fires, pungent in their nostrils, mixed with the aroma of roasting meat. Just about every fire had a rack constructed over it: four willow limbs stuck in the ground with their forks twelve to fourteen inches from the ground, two willow branches fixed like a lintel across the two forks at either end, then twelve or fourteen peeled willow switches laid from one lintel to the other to form a grill. Everywhere, women happily used their butcher knives, slicing the venison and beaver and muskrat and wild pig and pigeons, partridges, and turkeys and putting the strips on the racks.

The men Bradford had sent fowl-hunting returned with enough wild turkeys to feed the Pilgrims almost a week, according to Bradford's estimation. They were plucked and gutted at once and set to roasting on spits over open fires, or in roasting ovens set in fireplaces.

The Massasoit had given Bradford one of the deer he had brought in, and Captain Myles Standish another. Both Pilgrims had planned to cook about half of each deer to share with the company, but both had also planned to salt or dry the other half and store it against the winter. It looked as if their harvest would be plentiful and food supplies would not be short, but it never hurt to prepare for the worst adversity.

All summer long, the Pilgrims had sawn clapboards for shipment back to England, in partial payment to the investors who had financed their way to New England. Some of these boards were now brought out and laid across saw-horses in the balmy open air.

Pilgrim and Indian women alike began bringing the cooked food to these temporary tables. Sometimes, two of them would cooperate in carrying a large platter, their commonness of purpose making language unnecessary.

And so the feast was laid. Wicker platters of steaming venison; roasting pots of wild turkey and partridges; baskets of a yam-like root which the Indian women had caked in mud and baked under their fires; kettles of succotash and roasted green corn; trays of a turnip-like root and roasted cat-tail tubers; buckets of wild apples, dried grapes and plums; wooden slabs with salad greens, wild onions, walnuts, chestnuts, filberts; earthen pots of steamed clams; stewed dried-oysters with radishes and celery stalks; Johnny-cakes stuffed with cooked pumpkin; a fruit-flavored punch the Indians made; and the first barley-malt beer of the season.

With his wives and children, The Massasoit stood at one end of the feast and made a speech, which Squanto and Hobamock translated for the Pilgrims.

"And did not Gluskabe and Great-Nephew make these deer?"

The Wampanoag crowd responded, "Yes, yes."

"And did not Gluskabe and Great-Nephew make these turkeys?"

"Yes, yes."

The chant went on to include each and every food on the table, as well as some in the forest and lakes that were not in season, and concluded with the day when Gluskabe and Great Nephew, admiring a green leafy plant, dropped a pinch of dirt between the base of a leaf and the stalk, spat on it, and waited for the sun to make First-Mother, the All-Nourisher, who later gave her body and breath that we might have corn and tobacco.

"The Spirit of Gluskabe is here in this corn, which he made."

"Yes, yes."

"The Spirit of Great-Nephew is here in this corn, to which he gave strength."

"Yes, yes."

"The Spirit of First-Mother is here in this corn, which is her body, and in this tobacco, which is her breath."

"Yes, yes."

"All-Maker, Strength-Giver, All-Nourisher gave thanks to the Great Mystery for what they gave people. Let the Spirit of All-Maker, Strength-Giver, All-Nourisher, and the Great Mystery be in this food and in us as we say thanks for the gifts of the world."

"Yes, yes."

At the other end of the table, Bradford nodded to Elder Brewster, who said at once, "Let us pray."

About half of the one hundred and two Pilgrims who had landed eleven months ago had died in the general sicknesses that had twice plagued the settlement. But there had been about ten births, and some seven houses were now finished. The Pilgrim storerooms held good supplies; they looked forward to an easier winter than the last. It was indeed, time to give thanks to the Lord for his bounty.

Elder Brewster called on God to bless the food, bless the gathering, bless the Wampanoag visitors, bless the Governor for his leadership, bless Squanto and Hobamock for their services to the two peoples, bless Plimouth plantation, its houses, its people, and the harvest. There was hardly a thing in sight that Brewster did not bless. And he asked the Lord to guide them in converting the Indians away from their mistaken ways.

Squanto stood beside him and translated for the Wampanoags, for the words behind the concepts were a bit strange to Hobamock.

At last, Bradford gave the signal to begin: "Let us eat of this bounty, and be aware of our blessings. Amen."

And The Massasoit repeated in Wampanoag: "Let us eat of this bounty, and be aware of our blessings."

Then the two tribes intermingled with food in their hands and mutual love in their hearts. Some were near-naked, some were overdressed, some were near-exhausted with the preparations, some enjoyed comfortable privileges, but all were, today, of one people.

***

With a turkey leg and a mug of beer in his hands, Squanto approached Elder Brewster and said, "One people, one God," as he made a gesture to include the feast. He rocked on the balls of his feet, the way he had seen Englishmen do.

Elder Brewster's eyes widened. "What do you mean?"

"Gluskabe and God— same thing, All-Maker. Great-Nephew and First-Man Adam— same thing, Strength-Giver. First-Mother and First-Mother-Eve— same thing, All-Nourisher."

"Blasphemy!" bellowed Brewster. "Heathen!" he huffed. "Satan," he shouted. "Defaming the holy word of God, the Gospel, God's 'spell' of magic and mystery! Open the stocks! This man hath sinned grievously! He speaks a crime against God! Throw him into the stocks and flog him until he repents!"

Governor Bradford reminded him, "Now, now, Elder Brewster, this is a time of peace and good fellowship. A time of gratitude and tolerance." But he quickly separated his friend, Squanto, from the furious old man.

***

On the second day of thanksgiving, people of both tribes went about in the autumn sun, eating left-overs at their whim, or the fresh-cooked food that was added to the table. The Pilgrim women made a sauce, flavored with drippings from their roasting pots, to pour over the cold and somewhat dry slices of meat.

The Indian women wanted at once to know how to make the sauce, and were disappointed to learn they would need skillets to cook it. But the Pilgrim women assured them they would get some for trade with the Indians, when the next ship came from England.

Captain Myles Standish took the opportunity to drill his fourteen-man army, marching them about the town square. They turned at his command, moved at a word, halted at another, worked as if the fourteen were one. The Pilgrim army paraded past both tribes, impressive and impressed with their own power and importance.

The Indian men marveled at such discipline, but did not conceive that they could do the same.

They thought the little man who led them must have some magic, to be able to lead and yet be so small.

In the afternoon, Standish arranged a shooting demonstration. The men loaded their muskets with bird-shot and fired at a clapboard target. The Wampanoags were amazed to see so many holes in the wood. These English certainly had great magic! Perhaps they would trade some English magic for Wampanoag magic? But the Pilgrim men were not about to let the Indians have muskets, or even learn how to charge and fire them.

Some of the Pilgrims offered to hold shooting matches with the Wampanoags, their muskets against the Indians' bows and arrows. But the Indians were not so simple as not to recognize a losing contest. They willingly competed with each other, often shooting at small targets pitched into the air, wagering various possessions including their weapons, their clothes, and their women's clothes, much to the amusement of the younger Pilgrims. The older Pilgrims were convinced God disapproved of any form of gambling.

Some of the non-conformists rather liked the idea, however, and soon had a great deal of fun, pitching pennies in the air, so the Indians could shoot at them with their arrows. If the Indian hit the penny, like a bird in flight, he got to keep the penny, but if he missed, he had to pay the Englishman.

"This is no time or place to gamble," said Elder Brewster, sternly, and the game had to move to the edge of the clearing.

But it was a time of tolerance and togetherness. When the Indian women joined hands in a big circle to sing and dance the Friendship Dance, the older Pilgrims reacted as if it were a scandal and a sin to dance and sing. But, when they were told it was a Friendship Dance, of no religious significance, some of the younger Pilgrim women joined in. They quickly learned the step, but only listened in bafflement to the Indian song.

The Massasoit brought his two sons by his primary wife to Bradford and asked him, through Squanto, to give them English names. "This is Wamsutta," said The Massasoit, touching the young man on the shoulder with his scepter. "He will be sachem-in-chief after me, for in our way the son follows the father, and he will rule over a great area. He therefore deserves a king's name, some great king's name."

Bradford smiled, slightly amused. Massasoit was talking as if his sons had conquered the world, or soon would. The thought gave him his first idea:

"Let us call Wamsutta, King Alexander. Alexander was a great king, who conquered and ruled over all the world that was known in his time."

The Massasoit was pleased. "So let it be. Let him be King Alexander."

"And this is Pometacom," continued The Massasoit, "though we often call him Metacomet. He, too, will rule a great area of his own and, if Wamsutta passes over, he too will rule the Wampanoag world after him. What king's name will you give him?"

But Bradford could hardly think of another great king. He could only think of Philip of Spain, with whom Queen Elizabeth had warred so long and so successfully. He stroked his beard, to give the impression he was thinking, but he could not get his first idea out of his mind.

At last, he said, "Let us call Metacomet, King Philip. Philip is King of Spain, a great country in a warm clime, where he has many subjects. That will be fitting."

"So let it be," said The Massasoit. "Let him be known as King Philip."

***

On the third day of thanksgiving, contests of strength, speed, and endurance took over the public square. The Pilgrim men stood no chance in races with the Indians, and, except for Myles

Standish, lost more often than not at wrestling; nor could they persevere as long as the Wampanoag warriors.

But they were not worried: they still had their muskets, which made one white man equal to twenty red men in a serious duel. *May it please God not to pit us in battle*, thought Myles Standish. This was a time of peace, prosperity, cooperation, tolerance, togetherness, and, above all, thanksgiving.

On the fourth morning, the Wampanoags called for one last feast, then left to return to their homes in a misting rain. Some of the Pilgrims, a glow of well-being pervading their thoughts, sensed that a tradition had begun.

47. The Snake-skin Message

> "Knowing our own weakness, notwithstanding our high words and lofty looks towards them, and still lying open to all casualty, having as yet (under God) no other defence than our arms, we thought it most needful to impale our town, which with all expedition we accomplished in the month of February...." —
>
> Edward Winslow,
> *Good News from New England,* 1622.

The messenger from Sakonnet approached Patuxet cautiously, even though Tokama-hamon, The Massasoit's special friend, had guided him through the woods. He built a fire in the snow on Watson's Hill and made sure several people of New Plimouth saw him. Then he came forward slowly, holding his palms out so the English could see he concealed nothing. The man had a message-bundle for Tisquantum from Canonicus, sachem-in-chief of the Narragansetts.

"Tisquantum is not at home, just now," said William Bradford. "He is on a hunting expedition with three of our men."

The messenger relaxed, his shoulders drooping as the tension went out of his whole body. His lips almost curled into a smile. He handed Bradford the bundle of new arrows stuffed into a rattlesnake skin so that their points were like fangs.

Bradford stepped back in astonishment.

"Tisquantum is to interpret this message to you," said the messenger, using Tokama-hamon as translator. "Will you become custodian of the message?" the man asked, shifting his feet.

"Why, yes. I'll see that he gets it," said Bradford. "Will you come in out of the cold and have some hot soup? And a mug of barley malt?"

No, the messenger did not have time to tarry, but Tokama-hamon would stay a while and drink a malt. The messenger grasped Tokama-hamon's shoulders in thanks for his service and left at once.

Bradford turned the bundle this way and that, inspecting its bindings, the arrows, the snake's head. "What is this all about?" he asked, using a mixture of English and Wampanoag.

"Canonicus, general sachem of the Narragansetts," said Tokama-hamon, nodding his head and waiting for Bradford to indicate that he understood. "Many thousand warriors."

"Yes," said Bradford. "We have heard that he has thousands of warriors. But we made a peace with the Narragansetts just this last summer. His numbers do not disquiet us."

Tokama-hamon stared at Bradford's mouth amid his dark beard, unable to understand.

"No matter," said Bradford. "What has Canonicus done now?"

"Take Aquidnick Island from The Massasoit."

"Aquidnick Island? Which one is that?"

But Tokama-hamon was unable to make Bradford understand which island was involved, whether large or small, whether near or far. Bradford just understood that it was in Narragansett Bay, and that several such islands had passed back and forth from the Wampanoags to the Narragansetts a number of times.

"Is this message"— Bradford held up the snakeskin and arrows— "Massasoit's request for assistance?"

"No. Message from Canonicus. To English."

***

In the first days of December, a ship called *The Fortune* arrived unexpectedly from England with thirty-five new colonists.

"Ye are welcome," said Bradford, holding his wide-brimmed hat in his hand and bowing to each man. "Ye are welcome. We need the added strength. We are worked nearly down to the bone."

"Welcome," echoed the other Pilgrim leaders.

"Can I help you with your supplies?" asked Myles Standish of a young man, who was wearing a ready-made suit from Birching Lane.

"No, thanks," said the man. "I can manage. I just have this one bag."

"No other?" asked Myles, astonished. "No other supplies?"

"We're lucky we got here with this much," said the young man. "Those are cramped quarters. They gave us short rations. And the waves were so bad! A little more out there, and we would have mutinied."

"Mutinied?" asked several of the Pilgrims at once.

"Terrible hardships on board," said another young man. "We were cold, and they wouldn't give us any blankets. Hungry, and they wouldn't give us any extra food. It was about time for a rebellion."

To the Pilgrims' disappointment, the same story was repeated over and over. The newcomers had brought no supplies, no tools or cooking utensils, no blankets but what they slept under on shipboard, no clothes but those they wore and a few ready-made suits from cheap haberdashers. Most of the new immigrants were very young men, fun-loving fellows, who had given little thought to what they were getting into.

"I'll tell you, it was horrible. When we saw your barren coast, we thought it about time to raise a ruckus."

With resignation and a faith that God would repay their sacrifice, the Pilgrims began sharing their supplies with the newcomers. *What else can we do?* Bradford asked himself, and was helpless to find an alternative.[4]

---

[4] Still, Edward Winslow wrote on 11 Dec 1621 of the bounty of the new land, stretching the truth to influence new settlers to come to New England: "For fish and fowl we have great abundance. Fresh cod in the summer is but coarse meat to us. Our bay is full of lobsters all the summer, and affordeth variety of other fish. In September, we can take a hogshead of eels in a night with small labour, and can dig them out of their beds. All the winter, we have mussels and othus [clams] at our doors. Oysters we have none near; but we can have them brought by the Indians when we will.

"All the springtime, the earth sendeth forth naturally very good sallet herbs [salad vegetables]. Here are grapes, white and red, and very sweet and strong also; strawberries, gooseberries, raspas [raspberries], &c; plums of three sorts, white, black and red, being almost as good as a damson; abundance of roses, red,

The Pilgrims loaded *The Fortune* with their clapboards, as many as its hold would carry, as well as two hogsheads of beaver skins which were essentially unknown in England, and the ship sailed for England on 13 Dec 1621.[5]

***

When Squanto returned from hunting, Bradford showed him the rattlesnake message-bundle, and Tokama-hamon explained how it had come to Plimouth.

Squanto could see that the message did not threaten him, personally, and it might be used to manipulate the English to his advantage. He was calm, as he and Tokama-hamon interpreted the bundle. "To send arrows in a snakeskin, in this manner, means that Canonicus considers you an enemy." Tokama-hamon nodded his agreement.

"We never wished it!" exclaimed Bradford,

---

white, and damask, single but very sweet indeed.

"Each person had about a peck of meal a week, or now, since harvest, Indian corn in that proportion; and afterwards many wrote at length about their plenty to their friends in England, not feigned but true reports."

[5] Three weeks later, this ship was captured and pillaged by a French pirate.

putting his hand on his head, where the hair was thin.

"These fangs in the snakeskin are a challenge," Squanto went on. "Canonicus signifies that he plans to war against you."

"But—but we made a peace," Bradford protested.

"That peace did not hold," said Squanto.

Bradford called the principal men of the village together—Elder Brewster, the religious leader of the plantation, though he was not ordained; Isaac Allerton, the Deputy Governor; Militia Captain Myles Standish; Edward Winslow, unofficial recorder; Stephen Hopkins; John Alden; Francis Cook; Francis Eaton, and others—and discussed what to do.

At length, they took the arrows out, stuffed the rattlesnake skin with gunpowder and lead shot, then asked Tokama-hamon to take it as a return message to Canonicus.

"And tell him this," said Bradford, rocking confidently on the balls of his feet, with his advisors standing by and nodding their agreement. "If we had a ship to travel the sea to Narragansett in this winter season, Canonicus should not have to come so far by land to us. We should meet him at his own door with more of our gunpowder and lead bullets." Bradford paused, looking to the others for their support and agreement.

"Yet, we do not wish to break the peace. If Canonicus wishes to come to us in peace, he will always be welcome. We will look for his arrival with a happy heart."

Several of those around nodded and muttered agreement.

"But, if he insists upon approaching in war, let him come. We are not afraid. Let him strike the first blow, and he will receive a thousand in return. We do not fear him. He has cause to fear us."

Nevertheless, the Pilgrims began strengthening their defenses. They built a palisade around the town, with four bulwarks extending from it, so that a few men could defend against an attack by many.

Standish divided his little army into four companies, assigned captains for each, who drilled them in marching, firing practice, and emergency procedures. Fearing that an enemy might get the advantage by getting in at the three gates and burning the Pilgrims' houses, he organized fire-fighting companies among the non-militia and instructed them in strategies for dealing with crises.

***

For the most part, the newcomers from *The Fortune* spent their time drinking, singing, and pitching horseshoes, and did all they could to get out of work. They stole eagerly from the store houses, even when they were punished in the stocks and flogged. But the Pilgrims had given so much of their harvest to the newcomers that their own supplies were short again. And, worse, the rowdies had already wasted their share.

A dispute arose about how to celebrate Christmas. Since the Puritans did not observe Christmas, Governor Bradford called everyone out to work as usual. But most of the newcomers, not sharing the Puritan belief and irritated by the Pilgrims' incessant hymn singing and praying, excused themselves on the grounds that it went against their consciences to work on the Holy Day.

"Very well," said Bradford, squaring his hat. "If you make it a matter of conscience, we will spare you from work, until you are better informed."

Returning from work at noon, Bradford found the newcomers at play in the street, "some pitching the bar, some at stool ball, and such like sports." Bradford took their games away, saying, "It goes against my conscience that some should play, while others are at work. If you feel that Christmas day should be spent in devotion, you can keep to your houses or the prayer room. If it is a Holy Day, there should be no gaming and

By Charles Brashear 371

reveling in the streets."

Bradford started scrabbling again. With Squanto's help, he succeeded in trading for some corn at Nemasket and some at Manomet. The Indian women who were carrying the corn from Nemasket to Patuxet fell suddenly ill of a high fever and bleeding at the nose and ears, and the Pilgrim men had to go out and carry the corn in.

In bitter cold weather, with a major storm coming up, Bradford sent Edward Winslow, Hobamock, and several healthy Indians to Manomet to bring home the other supply.

Cawnacamón, sachem of Manomet, entertained them in his own snug *comaco* with oysters, mussels, clams, and a bean-shaped shellfish, which his people took from the broad river that ran beside the settlement and emptied into Buzzard's Bay. Just over the ridge to the east, a creek ran down to Cape Cod Bay some eight miles away, almost in a straight line.

In the midst of the blizzard, two men from Manomoyack came in. They laid aside their bows and quivers, as was the custom when entering a friend's house. They rubbed their hands together and huddled near the fire, to get the chill out of their bodies. Silently, they took out a pipe, filled it with tobacco, and smoked, passing it to Cawnacamón and Hobamock and Winslow, but never saying a word.

At length, one of the men looked directly at Cawnacamón, made a short speech, and gave him a present of a small, closed basket of tobacco. "This is a gift from Mano-Kiehtan, sachem of Manomoyack." He added several colored beads, including drilled shells and some trade beads.

"I thank Mano-Kiehtan for his generosity," said Cawnacamón, serenely accepting the presents. He continued smoking, waiting for the real message.

Presently, the other man gave a longer speech to Cawnacamón. Hobamock interpreted it to Winslow, who had learned enough Wampanoag to understand a conversation about immediate experience, but not enough to decipher a story about remote events involving issues of justice and guilt.

A man of Manomoyack and another from Nantuckett had fallen out while gambling, and they got into a fight. The quarrel growing to great heat, the one from Manomoyack killed the other. The killer was a *Powah*, or shaman, a man of high rank among the people of Manomoyack, but the Nantuckett relatives of the slain man insisted the killer be put to death for the wrongful death of their man.

They threatened to go to war if the

Manomoyack people would not take care of this matter. Mano-Kiehtan had the *Powah* under arrest, but could not decide to give him up because he loved him so much; nor could he dispose of him himself because he was so valuable to Manomoyack. What was Cawnacamón's advice?

After a silence while all men considered the problem, Cawnacamón began asking questions of several of those present, including Hobamock.

"What do you think, my friend? You who are a *panisee* of The Massasoit's council, a man trained in the arts of gentleness and statesmanship."

After an appropriate pause, Hobamock replied: "I am but a stranger to your country, so what I say is of no consequence. Yet, I think it is better for one man to die than many, especially since he is guilty and the rest of the people of Manomoyack are innocent."

"And you, Master Winsnow. What would the English do?"

Winslow was cautious. "We do not like to meddle in other's affairs. We do not know your customs. But it seems to me that what Hobamock says has justice in it."

"So be it," said Cawnacamón. "That, too, is my answer. Let the *Powah* die."

***

When Tokama-hamon tried to give Canonicus the rattlesnake message-bundle, Canonicus backed away and refused to touch it, refused to listen to the message. Tokama-hamon, having delivered the bundle, insisted that his duty was concluded and also refused to have anything more to do with the snakeskin.

Canonicus would not permit the message to come into his house, nor remain in his village or nation; so it was taken by another messenger to another village, then by another messenger to yet another village, and, after many circuitous delays, the snakeskin returned to the Pilgrims at New Plimouth.

Bradford and Standish asked Squanto, "Does this mean the threat has ceased?"

"Yes," said Squanto. "The gunpowder and lead frightens even a brave warrior. Even The Massasoit does not know how to deal with a musket."

"We cowed them, Myles," bragged Bradford. "We cowed the craven savages."

"Yes," said Myles Standish, always the cautious one. "This time. This time. But I hate to think what would happen if three thousand Narragansett warriors decided to annihilate the hundred English men, women, and children at Patuxet. We could kill a few of them, perhaps a few dozen, but in the end we would not prevail."

"Ha!" scoffed Bradford. "They have no courage! These savages have no moral core! What strength have they against us, whom God hath given the Right?"

48. "To Serve his own Ends"

"They [the Pilgrims] began to see that Tisquantum sought his owne ends and plaid his owne game, by putting the Indians in fear, and drawing gifts from them to enrich himselfe; making them believe he could stir up war against whom he would and make peace for whom he would. Yea, he made them [the Indians] believe [that the English] kept the plague buried in the ground and could send it amongst whom they would..."
—William Bradford, *Of Plimouth Plantation*, 1647.

In March, Bradford took Squanto aside. "Hobamock says that Chickataubut of Massachusetts is in league with Canonicus of Narragansett and plans a war of annihilation against the whites. What have you heard?"

"I hear no more than you do, Master Bradford."

"But you are out among the neighboring savages so much. I just thought you might have heard something else."

"Why would I hear something else? Aren't your ears as big as mine? You suspect me of something?"

"No. No," said Bradford, acquiescing. "It's just that we promised Chickataubut that we would send the shallop to trade for his furs. This seems like a good time to do that. If there is no danger?"

"No danger that I have heard of," said Squanto.

"Well, I'll send you as guide and interpreter for Myles Standish and Edward Winslow. And bring back as much Indian corn as you can acquire."

But the winds were contrary, and Standish no sooner sailed out of Plymouth harbor and rounded Gurnet Point than the wind calmed altogether. "Nothing to do, but secure the sail and get out the oars," he told his ten men.

***

At about that moment, some Pilgrim men who were hunting in the woods nearby encountered a Wampanoag man who seemed to be fleeing from enemies. His head was freshly wounded and blood flowed down his face. The Pilgrim men tried as best they could to staunch the flow of blood from the wound on the man's forehead and cheek.

"Go home!" the man said in Wampanoag, and then in English, "Go home! Great danger." He was agitated and looked often over his shoulder.

Slowly, with their small knowledge of Wampanoag and the man's few words of English, the Pilgrim men came to understand what the man was trying to tell them.

He had been beaten in Nemasket for taking the English side, but had slipped away to warn Tisquantum and the Pilgrims. He was a relative of Tisquantum, he said. There were many Narragansetts at Nemasket, along with The Massachusetts and Corbitant. They were going to take the opportunity of the Captain and the shallop being absent to fall upon Patuxet and destroy the English.

The Pilgrim hunters returned at once to New Plimouth. Bradford fired three cannons, a pre-arranged signal for the shallop to return if it were still in range of the sound.

The shallop backtracked at once. They found the guard called out and posted on the bulwarks. They joined the defense, but after several hours nothing had happened.

Governor Bradford called Hobamock and asked him if he had heard anything about an uprising.

"I hear rumors," admitted Hobamock, always calm. "But I not repeat them. I think them false."

"What did you hear?" demanded Bradford.

"The Massachusetts and Narragansetts

together… threaten English. Some say Tisquantum join with Massachusetts. This you see when he try get men away from shallop. Get them go into far-away wigwams. There they easy to hurt. But, I think these lies."

"What of this messenger's report that Massasoit has thrown in with them?"

"Report false," Hobamock said flatly. "The Massasoit not do that, without Hobamock know it. It our way, no such happen without advice and support by men my rank. I not just any person," Hobamock went on, "but a *panisee*, one from The Massasoit's main fighters and men of heart. I not only a Wampanoag, also a Pokánoket, member of ruling clan of the Wampanoag Confederation, advisor Great Sachem's council. No such plan be, unless I help form it. There no cause your distrust. Therefore you do well continue affections for The Massasoit and Wampanoag Nation."

"I am glad to hear it," said Bradford. Yet he did not relax the guard nor the militia alert. And taking Hobamock aside, he made a request. "I want you to send your wife to Pokánoket. Let her pretend to be visiting her relatives, and yours. But let her inquire as to the truth or falsity of these reports, so that she can inform you and us of what is true and what false."

After two days of walking, Hobamock's wife

arrived at Pokánoket. When she saw all things quiet and that no rebellion was planned or had been, she told The Massasoit of the Pilgrims' suspicions.

When she returned to Patuxet, she reported through Hobamock: The Massasoit sends his thanks to Governor Bradford for thinking of him before acting in a rash way. Governor Bradford could rest assured that, if any such plot came about, The Massasoit would send word to him immediately, as the first article of their peace required.

"I am glad of it," said Bradford, relaxing his arms, which he had not realized were tense.

"The Massasoit much angry Tisquantum," she added. "If stories true, Tisquantum break Wampanoag law. Please send Tisquantum to Pokánoket, so The Massasoit question him."

But, things being calmed down, Bradford sent Standish and his ten men to Massachusetts Bay, accompanied by both Squanto and Hobamock.

"Be on guard, Myles," Bradford told Standish. "Watch both of them. Discern their intentions. There is much trouble in the air. It is best that we not be caught unaware."

***

Before the shallop returned from

Massachusetts Bay, The Massasoit came to Patuxet with ten warriors to offer his apologies in person. He was dressed in his usual way, though he had not refreshed his face-paint lately.

"Massasoit is very sorry that any person of his nation should spread such rumors. He takes the blame upon himself, and charges himself with punishing the wrong-doer. No man should go about telling such untruths." Having earned the trust of The Massasoit, Edward Winslow translated as best he could.

Bradford could not say truthfully that he had never doubted Massasoit's loyalty, but he wanted now to smooth things over. "I am glad to hear of your loyalty from your own mouth, as you hear from my mouth of my loyalty to you."

"Where is Tisquantum?" asked The Massasoit, gesturing with the little decorated wand he carried as emblem of his office. "I will take him with me to Sowams and have my council of advisors inquire into the matter. If he is guilty of spreading devilish rumors, we will punish him appropriately."

"Squanto is away on a trading expedition," said Bradford.

"When he returns, send him to me."

Bradford took off his hat and temporized. "If Tisquantum is guilty, we will willingly give him up." The execution of the *Powah* at Monomayack suggested what Massasoit had in mind for Squanto.

"He is on an expedition to Massachusetts Bay," added Winslow.

The Massasoit waited, hardly knowing how to deal with this cunning. He adjusted the wildcat skin on his shoulders.

"Tisquantum is so useful to us all," Bradford went on, replacing his hat, "Useful to the great Massasoit, equally as much as to us at Patuxet."

"That's right," added Winslow in Wampanoag. "How we understand Massasoit if we not have Tisquantum's tongue? How Massasoit understand the English?"

"Tisquantum has much abused us," said The Massasoit, clenching his fist in emphasis. "He has much abused the English. He uses a false tongue as a weapon of conquest. He tries to set himself up as a sachem. If the charges are true, he deserves to die."

Bradford hardly knew what to say. Squanto was too valuable to lose. "Yes," he said, at length, "if he hath sinned against the great Massasoit, he deserves to die. If he hath sinned against us, he deserves it. Yet, for our sake and the great love we bear toward Massasoit, we hope Massasoit will spare him."

The Massasoit hesitated, not knowing quite how to respond. Was Bradford saying that the price of continued peace was his acquiescence to the Pilgrims' private whims?

Bradford scuffed his shoe against the ground and went on. "Though Tisquantum deserve to die, yet we beg you to spare him. Without Tisquantum, I know not how we should understand the great Massasoit's words, or the words of any Indian."

Although The Massasoit was enraged against Tisquantum, he was pacified at last and went away.

***

But, within a few days, the Pilgrims and the Wampanoag both heard more evidence. Tisquantum had coerced the messenger who came to Patuxet with the wound on his head and cheek into following him, as if he, Tisquantum, were a sachem. He had threatened others, too, with his influence among the English, saying he could get them to shoot whomever he would.

He demanded gifts of furs and wampum from the Indians. In return, Tisquantum assured them that he would make the English remain peaceful. Tisquantum was trying to set up a following, trying to create a tribe at The Massasoit's expense.

The Massasoit sent a messenger who carried

the brass chain and demanded that Bradford turn Tisquantum over to him.

"The Massasoit knows you love Tisquantum. The Massasoit knows it will hurt your heart to let him go. Therefore, we have brought the Governor a present of twenty beaver skins to pad the hurt. The Massasoit, Great Sachem of the Wampanoags, will send two more warriors, laden with all the beaver pelts each can carry. For these presents, we ask the Governor's consent in taking Tisquantum to our justice."

Now Bradford could react with righteous indignation. "Tell Massasoit that it is not the manner of the English to sell a man's life at a price. When a man justly deserves to die, we give him his just reward. But we do not buy and sell men's lives. Therefore, we refuse this gift of beaver skins. Take them back to Massasoit.

"Tell Massasoit," Bradford went on, "that we love him none the less, but it is our way not to accept bribes; we cannot serve his wish and release Tisquantum."

***

Bradford ordered the Pilgrim men to watch

their Indians more closely.[6] Upon questioning some of the local Wampanoags, the Pilgrims discovered that Squanto had been trying to diminish Hobamock's influence with the English. He had bragged to the local Indians of his own power, extorted allegiance from them, put them to work at tasks for his own benefit. In fear, the local Indians felt forced to obey him and forsake Hobamock and The Massasoit.

"He says you keep the plague buried in the floor of your store-house," one Wampanoag confessed. "He showed it to me himself."

Upon being informed of this, Bradford called Hobamock and several of the Pilgrim men to the store-house. They took the man along and dug in the floor where he pointed, and, to their surprise, discovered three kegs of black gunpowder.

"Where did that come from?" asked Myles Standish.

"And how did the kegs get there?" asked John Alden.

"What, pray, can it mean?" asked Stephen Hopkins.

Soon, they observed "many secret passages between Squanto and other Indians," as Bradford expressed it in his history, *Of Plimouth Plantation*, 1647.

Hobamock, too, was totally surprised. "What it mean?" he asked.

"That's what we want to know," said Governor Bradford. "Ask this native what it means?"

The Wampanoag man readily replied, "That is the plague. Tisquantum showed several of us that this was where the plague was buried."

"Is possible?" asked Hobamock.

"It seems the culprit told them so," admitted Bradford.

"No," said Hobamock. "I mean, is possible to bury plague? And take it out again? You have the power over it?"

"Why, no," said Bradford, laughing at the man's simplicity.

Hobamock relaxed.

"No, that is purely God's Will," Bradford went on. "God has that power in his store. If He wish, He can send the plague to destroy whom He wants. At His pleasure, He can destroy whole populations of His enemies, or the enemies of His chosen people."

Hobamock shook with fear. As a *panisee*, he had been trained that no knife, hatchet, or spear could wound him. But he had no defense against the plague. And he was not immune to the whims of the God of the English.

In that moment, he decided that he would join the Pilgrims' church to protect himself. And his wife, too. They would join the English church and pray for hours, if it would protect them from such misfortune.

49. Massasoit Demands the Head of Squanto

> "...the tendency on the part of the colonists to treat the Indians as a subject race to whom they owed no duty, who were in their way, and whom they were at liberty to annoy constantly in every conceivable manner. If they had set out with a determination to arouse the natives to declare war, in order that they might use the hostilities thus begun as an excuse for exterminating them, they could not have succeeded more admirably."—
> Alvin Weeks, *Massasoit of the Wampanoags*, p.92

Massasoit came again to Plimouth Plantation to clear himself of the Pilgrims' suspicion and apprehend Tisquantum. He had refreshed his mulberry face-paint and drew a wide black bar under his eyes. He wore a single yellow feather in his long, flowing hair and a polished, etched, intricately-painted clam shell at his throat.

"You listen too trusting to the lies of Tisquantum," he said, through his interpreter, Hobamock.

Edward Winslow stood by and agreed that the translation was correct, as far as he could tell, for he was getting rather good at the Indian language.

"Tisquantum was once like a son to me," Massasoit went on. "He lost his whole family to a plague, the whole village of Patuxet where now we stand. He was alone in the world. I took him in, into my clan, and nursed him in the time when his mind did not want to live.

"But, now, his tongue has turned evil and black. He speaks untruth about the Wampanoag. He is a traitor. I am Ousa Mequin, of the village of Sowams, The Massasoit of the Wampanoag Nation. What I say is truth."

Bradford was glad of the delay in the translation, so he could invent a reply. He removed his black hat and wiped the sweat from his forehead.

"Don't say you have never doubted," Massasoit went on impatiently. "You sent Hobamock's wife to listen at my door, pretending to be involved in some other action. She found nothing, then told me of your suspicions. Tisquantum brags that he sways nations with his tongue. He stirs discontent among others for his own benefit."

"I shall inquire into this matter," said

Bradford, looking away from Massasoit. He pushed a pebble with the toe of his wide-buckled shoe. "We wish to remain friends with all our red brothers. We should be very sorry if any cause for discontent should arise with any of the savages"— he lifted his eyes to meet Massasoit's gaze directly, knowing that he had to appear resolute— "but especially sorry for any breach of peace with Massasoit. You may sleep quietly on your own pillow at Sowams, knowing that the word of the English is ever firm."

"Bring Tisquantum before us," demanded Massasoit, adjusting the thick-furred wildcat pelt he wore over his left shoulder. In his right hand, he carried the little wooden staff incised with rune-like hieroglyphics, the emblem of his office. "We will take him to Pokánoket and talk out this matter. The English need take no part in it."

"Oh, I'm sorry," Bradford dissembled, looking away toward Gurnet Point. "I think Squanto is not now among us. I think he has gone to trade for corn, perhaps with Aspinet."

Edward Winslow, seeing Bradford glance at him, added in Wampanoag, "Squanto is with Myles Standish, searching for corn among the Nausets."

Massasoit hesitated. He had never heard Edward Winslow lie, and so he, Massasoit, trusted Winslow. If he had never heard Governor Bradford lie, he had experienced occasions when Bradford

By Charles Brashear

did not tell all of the truth. Or had so slanted the truth that it told an effective lie.

"Send Tisquantum to me when he returns," ordered Massasoit. Having spoken, he turned to go. His advisors and servants turned with him, taking their appointed positions at his sides, on guard ahead or behind him, composing at once the royal party of his following.

***

At the first opportunity for a secluded meeting, Bradford sent for Squanto. "There is much trouble, my friend," said Bradford, confidentially. "Massasoit says that you have spoken false rumors about him, and that you must be taken to Sowams to answer for the crimes."

"What they saying?" asked Squanto, calmly.

Bradford looked away, examining the tree-line and the horizon. The sun beat mercilessly on the trees, threatening to wither them. They needed rain.

In mid-April, the Pilgrims had planted their first cycle of corn and, a month later, a second cycle, hoping to have two easy harvests. There had been good rain and warm weather in the spring, so that their plants came up and grew bravely, but by mid-summer a drought hit: their beans withered as if scorched by a fire; their first planting of corn put out tiny ears that had no hope of maturing.

The second planting turned yellow, and both blade and stalk bent over.

At last, Bradford continued: "They say that you are an evil person who can scorch the corn in the fields, that you have disturbed the peace by spreading rumors that Massasoit is planning war, that you have stirred malcontent among peaceful Indians, telling them lies for your own benefit."

Squanto became agitated: he rubbed his chest and arms, as if brushing sand away. "Hobamock says this. Hobamock hates me. Hobamock is jealous of my power. He only trying use words like bad weapons against me."

"Hobamock has never told us anything that is untrue," said Bradford, facing Squanto again.

"Hobamock lies," said Squanto, too quickly. "Hobamock responsible for all this trouble. Hobamock plot to bring me down from your favor."

"Hobamock says that you would be treated fairly if taken to Sowams to answer the accusations against you."

"Hobamock know," said Squanto. "Massasoit already make up his mind. You send me to Sowams to Massasoit's justice, it be my certain death. You know that, don't you?"

"Yes," admitted Bradford, aware of the execution of the *Powah* at Monomayack. "I have thought as much."

Squanto smiled, recognizing an inflexible friend and protector in Governor Bradford. A person could trust him with his own life. "I will leave the matter to your wisdom, Master Bradford," said Squanto. "Whatever you decide, I abide by your decision. Your word be my fate."

"Stay hidden," said Bradford, putting his sweaty hand on Squanto's sturdy shoulder. "Let not Massasoit's messengers nor Hobamock see you in the street of Plimouth. Let none hear your voice, until this blows over."

***

When the English did not deliver Tisquantum immediately, Massasoit sent a messenger to Bradford, "entreating him to give way to the death of Tisquantum who had so much abused him."

Governor Bradford was reluctant. "Why, Squanto does most of our interpreting," he argued to a group of Plimouth colony leaders, "and he's such a good ambassador that I don't know how we would deal with the Indians on Cape Cod if we didn't have him. He is our magic tongue."

"Edward is getting better and better at the language," John Alden pointed out to balance the discussion. "He can, at least partly, replace Squanto in our dealings. And Myles is getting good, too. Then, too, we always have Hobamock, even if it does look like Massasoit sent him to us deliberately to learn our language and be a spy."

"Spy he may be," put in Captain Myles Standish. "Still, we've not caught Hobamock in a lie yet. The man seems incapable of untruth." He folded his stubby arms and leaned back at ease.

"Squanto is more than just an interpreter," said Bradford, looking away. "He knows things about the savages' way of life that it would be hard for any of us to know in many a year. And he's taught us so many of the tricks and devices by which we survive here in Plimouth."

"But we *do* have a treaty," said Edward Winslow, looking from one of the men to another. "I just don't see how we can avoid giving Squanto over."

"An irony that would be, now, wouldn't it?" said Hopkins, smiling wryly. "After it was Squanto that did the interpreting at that treaty meeting."

"But don't you think it would mean Squanto's death?" asked Governor Bradford. "Don't you think Massasoit wants his death?"

"Perhaps it's that he deserves," said Hopkins, shuffling back a tiny step. "He's been up to a great deal of mischief in these woods, we all know. Many secret meetings between Squanto and the other Indians Hobamock reports to me, and others. Words! Words! He traffics in words."

By Charles Brashear 395

"He seems drunk with the power of his own words!" said Elder Brewster. "It has enlarged his opinion of himself."

"Aye," admitted Bradford, closing his eyes and looking heavenward, as if he could see there, inwardly, the words he would later write in his History *Of Plimouth Plantation*, 1647. "He [Squanto] seeks his own ends and plays his own game, by putting the Indians in fear and drawing gifts from them to enrich himself. Which makes them draw closer to Squanto than Massasoit for protection."

"Is it, then, but a quarrel between the two?" asked Hopkins. "Is it but a petty, personal argument? A fight over words?"

"Squanto is no angel," admitted Myles Standish. "That trick he pulled off, making the local Indians believe that we English keep the plague buried in the store-room was worthy of any devil. It terrified the Indians, as we all know, and made them envy his power."

"Such talent may garner him more than envy," said John Alden. "It's like to cost him his life, as well as his tongue."

"He's too valuable to lose," said Bradford, looking at the palms of his own hands. "Besides, I've developed a personal liking for the man. He's such a dutiful child, the way he works so hard to always please us."

"Such personal feelings must be set aside, in the face of the treaty," insisted Edward Winslow, holding both hands up in a gesture of justice. "We agreed in that treaty, hardly a year ago— we gave our solemn word that if any of the Indians did wrongdoing and sought shelter amongst us, that we would deliver the culprit. We have to give him up, or break the peace."

"Breaking the treaty isn't quite the same as breaking the peace," said Captain Myles Standish. "Our muskets and fowling pieces are stronger instruments of peace than all the paper in Plimouth. Massasoit has more cause to fear our militia than we have to fear his warriors."

"Such force is no way to solve problems, Myles," said John Alden directly to Standish, shuffling his feet in a little backward step. "Even you don't believe it is."

"Diplomacy without force is no diplomacy at all," retorted Standish. "If I had your saber tongue, I might fend and foil with it, John. But I don't. I must let other instruments talk for me."

"Well, we have to do something," said Edward Winslow. "And I'm afraid that will be our following Massasoit's wishes."

"We'll delay a bit longer," said Bradford, gazing toward Watson's Hill, as if an answer could appear there in the rolling countryside, as once

Massasoit and sixty of his retainers had. "I'll send a messenger to Massasoit and say we are still investigating the matter. Maybe if we wait, the tensions will relax of their own pulling."

But Massasoit remained firm and sent another messenger who, as Edward Winslow later wrote in *Mourt's Relation,* 1622, demanded they release Squanto as a Wampanoag subject, "whom the governor could not retain without violating the treaty."

***

In the days that followed, Governor Bradford kept Squanto out of sight and relied on Hobamock to do his interpreting with the local Indians. Without good reason, Bradford had come to distrust Hobamock, for it was clear to him that Massasoit had sent Hobamock and his wife to live in Plimouth and learn English, the way the Pilgrims had set Edward Winslow to learn the Wampanoag language.

And now the couple were attending church and asking to be admitted as members. The woman was even learning English rapidly and could recite several prayers understandably.

Impatient with the delays, Massasoit sent another messenger, who spoke through Hobamock: We do not ask the English to do our work for us. Neither do we wish the English to stand in the way of our doing our duty. We know you are hiding Tisquantum. We know you do not want to let him go. But let him go, you must!

Bradford stalled, deliberately gazing at the messengers. They all wore tight buckskin leggings and a strip of leather at the groin, which together reminded him of Irish trousers. Their upper bodies were intricately decorated in white, yellow, black, and ochre grease-paint, and they all wore neck and ear ornaments. They waited for a response. Bradford looked at the ground near their feet, saying, "We do not see that Squanto has done such grievous wrong."

"We live by Wampanoag laws, you live by English laws," said Hobamock. "Tisquantum break our law. He pay. Necessary. No matter, you not see his crimes. You honest? We have treaty? We require, you turn him over to these messengers from Massasoit."

"We will think on it further, my friend" said Bradford directly to Hobamock. Then he turned to the messengers. "Tell Massasoit that we are investigating the truth of the accusations, and, if we find them honest, we will punish Squanto ourselves."

The messenger asked for a re-translation.

"Yes," Bradford assured them. "If we find him guilty, we will punish him as he deserves."

"You are not required to do our work," said the messenger after the second translation, surprised by this turn in the talk. "But I will take your message to Massasoit."

"Yes," said Bradford, relieved. "Tell Massasoit that, in matters of decency and duty, our great love for your great leader makes his work our work. We are as one people in defending against evil."

***

Bradford then sought out Myles Standish. "We need to make ourselves into spies, Myles," he said quietly, as if he were afraid someone would overhear. "We need to know more about what is going on among our Indians. Therefore, I propose that you and I affect a great love for each of our savage wards, that we may learn by love what they would not tell us by truth."

Myles Standish waited.

"It is known that you admire Hobamock and distrust Squanto," Bradford went on. "Therefore, I want you to put on a seeming favor for Squanto. That way, your admiration for Hobamock will not deceive you, and your suspicion of Squanto will help you sift the truth. Pretend a great affection, that he may confide secrets to you."

"I will do my best," said Standish, nodding. "Squanto is a good guide. I will take him with me to map Cape Cod. That way, he will be out of town, and I will seem to be his protector."

"And I will affect a loving for Hobamock," said Bradford. "My regard for Squanto might be capable of fooling me; so it is best that I work Hobamock for information."

"These times make liars of us," said Standish. "I do not like it."

"Nor do I, Myles," said Bradford, putting his hand across Myles' shoulder as they turned to go. "But if we dissemble long enough, perhaps the problem will dissolve of itself."

***

After a few days, another messenger with the brass chain came from The Massasoit. He laid a deer-skin bundle on the ground and unrolled it, making gestures to display the various items. Inside were a number of herbs, medicines, charms, and a heavy flint knife with a rawhide handle.

Bradford waited. He recognized Massasoit's knife. Its two edges were as sharp as broken glass and the blade as thick as his thumb.

Massasoit's knife

"The

Massasoit receives your love with great joy," the messenger went on, "and accepts that your arm may become his arm. He has sent his own knife, so that his arm in Patuxet can cut off Squanto's head and hands and send them to him in Sowams."

Governor Bradford was momentarily speechless.

"Not necessary, you do with your own hand," said Hobamock for the messengers. "Treaty last year require: Wampanoag wrong-doers seek refuge among you, you deliver to us. Give Tisquantum to us, messengers be gone."

Bradford looked at the knife, but carefully avoided touching it, lest his grasping the knife be seen as a personal contract to do the work. He turned slightly aside and asked Winslow, "What can we do, Edward?"

"I don't know," admitted Edward Winslow, softly. "They've got the truth on their side. We did agree to those terms."

"Never dreaming that we would have to live up to them like this," said Bradford, sighing.

"Never dreaming," echoed Winslow.

Bradford turned again toward the messenger. "I do not think Squanto is now in Plimouth."

"We watch," said the messenger. "Some our

people see him go house three days ago. Not see him leave."

"I don't think I could find him," said Bradford.

"Call, he come," said the messenger. "Or we go that house. We bring him out."

Bradford hesitated, waiting. The one street of Plimouth, Leyden Street, ran down to the water near the rock where they had built their wharf. The weather was quiet and warm. The sun danced on its own heat waves. The view seemed a picture of peace itself.

"Well, I guess there's nothing else we can do, Edward. I guess we have to turn him over to them."

"I'm afraid so," said Winslow.

"Will you go and get him for me? I don't want to be around when we give him up."

"I understand," said Edward Winslow. "I don't relish the act, either."

"Wait, Edward," said Bradford, taking hold of his sleeve. "Isn't there something else we can do?"

"Not that I know."

From the bottom of Leyden Street came a cry of "Ship! Ship around the Gurnet!"

All eyes turned toward Gurnet Point. A ship

was indeed entering Plimouth harbor, struggling slowly on small breezes.

Bradford cupped his hands to his mouth and shouted, "To arms! To arms! All men report at once."

"Bring Tisquantum, now," said the messenger, stepping forward.

"Oh, I can't now," said Bradford, in haste to be gone. "I have to see what boat that is."

"That, nothing to do with matter," insisted Hobamock, walking rapidly beside Bradford.

"Oh, but it does," insisted Bradford, hurrying away. "It may be a French ship. They have killed some of the Dutch, we know that. It may be a pirate. They have threatened some of our people. We must know, at once, what their intentions are."

"Give us prisoner," demanded the messenger. He stepped forward, lifting his hands. As was the custom, the Wampanoag messengers had left their spears and their bows and arrows at the edge of the brook a quarter of a mile from Plimouth village. He dropped his hands, frustrated at his lack of power.

Bradford called loudly over his shoulder: "I'll know first what that Frenchman wants. He may be in league with the Indians of Gay Head. You never know. This is an emergency; you'll just have to wait." Bradford hurried down Leyden Street.

Edward Winslow followed quickly behind.

The Massasoit's messengers and Hobamock were left standing at the edge of the village. Speechless with rage, the messenger slammed The Massasoit's knife back into the deer-skin bundle and jerked the bundle shut. He glared after Bradford, then turned and "departed in great heat," as Edward Winslow wrote in his account.

The Indians were not so simple, wrote Alvin Weeks in *Massasoit of the Wampanoags*, much later, "as not to see through the subterfuge, and to read Bradford's determination to use every excuse and employ every pretended reason that presented itself for not complying with the terms of the treaty, when it was to his disadvantage to live up to its obligations."

50. In These Troubled Times

> "... the Indians began again to cast forth many insulting speeches, glorying in our weakness and giving out how easy it would be ere long to cut us off. Now also Massasoit seemed to frown on us, and neither came or sent to us as formerly."
>
> — Edward Winslow,
> *Good News from New England*, London, 1623.

The boat in the harbor was a shallop belonging to a fishing ship, *The Sparrow*, sent out by Master Thomas Weston, merchant and citizen of London. They brought seven passengers to New Plimouth, who also had no supplies with them, but were welcomed because they were wives and children of men who had come in the first settlement.

The crew of the shallop reported more than thirty English ships fishing off Monhegan; so Governor Bradford again dispatched Edward Winslow to trade for supplies. Winslow took Squanto with him, so he could practice his Wampanoag, and Squanto could practice again his sailing skills. "We'll pray for you and Squanto, Ed," said Bradford.

"You pray for Squanto, too?" asked Squanto.

"Why, yes. You're like one of us. Of course, we'll pray."

"You will pray for poor Squanto," he repeated, flattered and satisfied with himself.

The trip took several weeks, through seas that threatened to swamp their little boat at every turning. But, doggedly, Winslow pressed on, now with sail, now with oars.

Though the ships' captains were sympathetic and friendly, they had no food to spare. Winslow and Squanto returned empty-handed.

The Pilgrims also got word of a ship which had been sent out from England with supplies for their relief. The ship had been blown back twice by bad weather. It set out a third time, but nothing had been heard of it after it was three hundred leagues at sea. Debris was discovered on the Bermuda coast that could be nothing but the scraps of their hope.

On top of that, an extended drought had caused the Pilgrims' crops to wilt and their own hopes to fade.

"In these troubled times, God must be terribly angry with us, to send us so much adversity," said Elder Brewster.

Squanto and Hobamock were standing nearby. Hobamock moved close to Elder Brewster and asked quietly, "Can God do that? He change weather?"

"All things, in this world and the next, are in God's power," answered Brewster, absently. "We live or die at his pleasure. His Hand is in everything."

"That, indeed, a powerful God," admitted Hobamock.

Convinced that God was actively punishing them, for what sins they knew not, the Pilgrims agreed to set aside a day for public prayer and fasting. They assembled on a bright, clear, scorched day in the middle of the week and prayed, sang, and preached for "eight or nine hours," according to Winslow.

When they came out at the end of the meeting, the sky was overcast, and, the next day, a gentle rain began, which lasted for some two weeks. Winslow wrote: "It was hard to say whether our withered corn or drooping affections were most quickened and revived."

"Oh, the mercy of God," Elder Brewster exclaimed to the Indians. "He is as ready to hear as we are to ask."

"I thought Sunday, day you talk to your God.

But your rain dance not on Sunday," observed Hobamock. "It come middle of week."

"God never rests," said Elder Brewster. "We are appointed, every day, to do God's work on earth, and set only Sunday aside to observe God's work in heaven."

"God did nice job," admitted Hobamock. "I never see before. So much improvement in so short time. Wampanoag ask God for rain, we often get many strong storm. Our corn blow down flat on ground. Or drown in floods. We worse off than when we start. But your God make season sunny and moist. I never see the like."

***

Governor Bradford sent Myles Standish and Squanto to make a map of Cape Cod and its bay, as well as to trade for what food they could. While the shallop was anchored in a cove at Nauset, someone stole a pair of scissors and a few beads from the shallop. "Come, Squanto," said Standish, "you'll have to be my tongue. I'm too angry to try to talk."

"Only a few beads," said Squanto, smiling and shrugging his shoulders. "It means so much?"

Standish marched his men to Aspinet's *comaco*, surrounded it with musketeers with their smoldering fuses at the ready. He ordered Squanto to threaten to destroy the house and all in it, if the goods were not returned at once. "Just as we will give no offense to our friends," Standish warned, "so we will suffer no offense to be done us."

Aspinet looked at Squanto and asked in Wampanoag, "What is this all about, Tisquantum? You who know the English better than any of us, you must explain their anger to us."

"Sometimes, their anger passes my understanding, too," admitted Squanto.

Aspinet begged for time to look into the matter.

"It's a matter of simple justice, simple honesty," replied Standish through Squanto. "A wrong is a wrong, no matter its size. And it must be righted, or the fury of God may come down on us all."

Squanto translated for Aspinet, then added, "Their God is powerful. They say he commands the drought, the plague, life and death, even the fall of a sparrow. And they seem to get what they pray for."

"Well, tell him I'll look into this matter," said Aspinet. He turned to talk with some of his councilors.

Presently, Aspinet returned and asked Standish to look more closely in the shallop, for perhaps the goods had only been misplaced.

When Standish went to the shallop again,

the scissors and beads were lying openly on a seat.

"The guards have been here all time, haven't they?" asked Squanto.

"Why, yes," admitted Standish.

"How can one place goods, when guards stand here?"

"You have to be on guard at every moment," Standish said, "or these bad people will steal you blind."

Hoping to pacify Standish, Squanto agreed, "Bad people. The Nausets are bad people."

"It seems every direction we turn, the Indians are ready to cheat us again."

"They just want pretty things of the world, just like Englishmen," said Squanto. "Pretty things and enough to eat."

***

Near the end of June, two ships belonging to Thomas Weston arrived, *The Charity* and *The Swan.* They intended to establish a second colony in New England. The ships carried some fifty or sixty men, who were no better provisioned than the Pilgrims. *The Charity* departed at once for Virginia to deliver some passengers there, but was to return directly. *The Swan* and its shallop were to seek out a suitable place on the coast to plant a colony. That left a large body of strangers in

Plimouth.

"Ye are welcome to share what we have," said Governor Bradford, "though our stores are too low for us to survive. And there is much work to be done."

"Oh, we'll pitch in and work with you," said the strangers.

But their assistance was soon an plague. Though they pretended to help in the planted areas or to saw clapboards, they wasted no time in stealing what they could. Day and night, they crept into the fields and picked the young corn, which was then eatable and pleasant to taste, though still immature.

"Bad people," observed Hobamock.

"Bad people," agreed Squanto.

"We are required to view them with charity," said Elder Brewster. "One never knows when God is sending some adversity to test our resolve."

"You pray for them, too?" asked Squanto, somewhat surprised.

"Yes," sighed Brewster. "We pray that God will guide and correct the paths of all men."

When the thieves were punished or chastised, they scoffed, as well as made light of the Pilgrims: "You fellows take things too seriously. Live a little. Enjoy life while you can."

At length, their shallop returned and reported a suitable place to plant a colony on Massachusetts Bay at a place called Wessaugusett. The Indians there had been almost totally destroyed by an epidemic. Those newcomers soon took *The Swan,* removed to that place, and founded a town that some called Merry Mount.

Native messengers quickly reported that Weston's men were very abusive to the Indian people, stealing their corn, molesting their women, beating men and women for no reason other than that they were natives.

Chickataubut, sachem-in-chief of the Massachusetts people sent an urgent plea: he asked Bradford as King James's representative in New England to remove Weston and his colony.

"Bad people," said the messenger.

But Bradford could do nothing more than scold his fellow Englishmen for their rash behavior and advise them to "a better walking."

Squanto translated Chickataubut's reply: "If you can't get them to behave, we may have to spill some of their blood."

"They are bad people," said Bradford in private, "but I can do nothing."

"Pray for them," said Squanto.

"Yes. That," admitted Bradford.

Other accounts of Indian resentment drifted in. "These English are not so strong as we had thought," Aspinet of Nauset was reported to say, "and without Massasoit's protection, they would be easily destroyed."

"They are certainly weaker than they appeared," came from hostile chiefs among the Narragansetts.

"They seem unable to act when called upon," admitted Chickataubut.

Ships coming from Jamestown also brought news of the uprising of the Powhatan Indians under Ope-tsankano on the 22nd of March, 1622, which killed over four hundred of the eleven hundred in the Virginia colony.

The Virginia leaders blamed the disaster on their lax defense: many farmhouses had been built in outlying districts far from the fortifications, so the people were easy prey to the savages, who ate breakfast with their victims before falling on whole families with their own weapons.

"Let us be on guard against the same mistake," said Myles Standish.

"Aye," agreed the Pilgrim council. And they determined at once to build a fort on the hill inside their palisade. They would flatten the top, install their cannons there, and build fortified walls. In spite of the project taking men from the fields where they were badly needed, the Pilgrims began the building at once.

In August, they were pleasantly surprised when the ship, *Discovery*, under command of Master Christopher Jones, their old friend and captain of *The Mayflower*. Jones was very friendly to the Pilgrims and sold them a new supply of trade goods: beads, awls, scissors, mirrors, knives, hatchets, etc. at 100% markup.

The Pilgrims were thankful that he came along. Winslow wrote: "had not the Almighty, in his All-ordering Providence, directed him to us, it would have gone worse with us than ever it had been or after was." The Pilgrims had "no means left to help ourselves by trade…"

"That was God's work?" asked Hobamock.

"Yes," said the Pilgrims as a person, "It is an example of Divine Providence at work."

"Really? He attend such small matters?"

"No sparrow is too small for the notice of God."

51. "Pray for Poor Squanto", 1622

"Pray for poor Squanto; pray that I may be taken into your heaven. I want to go to the white man's heaven, so that I be among my friends."
     Squanto to William Bradford,
     cf *Of Plimouth Plantation,* 1647

The harvest of 1622 was meager. Many of the Pilgrims, weakened by short rations, were ill-prepared for another harsh winter.

"Maybe we go, outside Cape Cod, and see if the people south of Cape Cod have corn for trade?" suggested Squanto.

Myles Standish was sick and Edward Winslow was on an errand in Nemasket; so Bradford left the colony in charge of his assistant, Isaac Allerton, and set out on a voyage in November, with Squanto as guide and interpreter.

They rounded the Cape in choppy water and worked their way slowly down the outside. They met no one to trade with. The wind shifted so often, coming now from the north, now from the south, that Bradford furled the sail and set his men to rowing.

Bradford kept a man in the bow, casting out the sounding line over and over, for he feared running aground on the shoals. The wind kept blowing Bradford's broad-brimmed hat loose, so that he grabbed at it often, or held it in place with one hand. "Are you certain there is a passage between the shoals and the mainland, Squanto?" he asked, anxiously shifting from one foot to the other.

"Yes," said Squanto. "I have been through the passage."

"Have been through the passage?"

"Yes, twice. With both English and French captains."

"French captains? I didn't know you had ever sailed with a French captain."

Squanto hesitated, considering what his next move was. Bradford had caught him bragging. He focused on the truth. "I was with Thomas Dermer when he escaped from Mano-Kiehtan and sailed directly to Capawack. We weren't worried about the shoals. They weren't even near."

"Was that from here?" asked Bradford. "Do you recognize this place?"

"No, I don't recognize this place," admitted Squanto. "But don't worry. I know the way."

"Well, I hope so," said Bradford softly.

But as they came nearer the shoals, Bradford thought he saw the sandy bottom through the choppy water and noted the sea-birds skimming the surface for fish. "We must be almost over the shoals. We'll have to turn back."

"No, no," insisted Squanto. "We'll find the way, Master Bradford."

"Hold up, men; rest on your oars," ordered Bradford. "Let's take our bearings, and see where we are. I'd like more sunlight and less wind, if I'm to cross these shoals."

With the shallop drifting loose on the waves, the swells were soon broadside to the thirty-foot shallop and almost upset it. "Head in to the wind, men," shouted Squanto. "Head into the wind!"

"There! Off that point," said Squanto, indicating a clump of trees that came right down to the water. "There is the entrance to Manomoyack Harbor. We could ride safe there until the weather is better."

"Where?" asked Bradford, straining to see the channel. "Are you sure?"

They found the entrance to the harbor narrow and winding, and exactly where Squanto directed them. "Well, you were right, Squanto," Bradford admitted. "I would never have found this harbor."

They anchored in choppy water, gusts of wind still buffeting them on all sides. Bradford observed the tide and drift of the water and thought there must be an entrance to the harbor on the south end, but he did not move to test his theory.

At nightfall, Bradford and a guard of three men with muskets went ashore, accompanied by Squanto. They found no one, though they found their fires. The people had fled. In the trees, the wind was hardly noticeable.

Squanto cupped his hands to his mouth and yelled toward the forest in Wampanoag, "Friends. We are friends. We come in peace."

At length, a few men came out of the woods. Bradford gave each man a small present: a few beads, a needle, a bracelet, and, soon, others came back to their fires, eager also to receive a present.

Soon, the women returned to boil fish and roast venison, which they offered the English guests. The men were full of smiles, saying they were glad of the occasion to trade. When Bradford offered trade goods for corn, they said quickly, "We come tomorrow to trade with you."

Bradford sat by the fire, observing the Indians' agitation. He could understand enough of the language and their actions to construe that they were reluctant to let the English know where their houses were.

When the Indians saw that Bradford was determined to stay on shore all night, they stood up and invited the Englishmen to their houses, saying a man could hardly stay out in this season, in such a wind, and guided the party to their wigwams.

But the wigwams were practically empty. Bradford saw signs of their having been evacuated hastily. One of the guards, walking in the woods nearby to relieve himself, saw where baskets of their belongings had been taken, but by the time he told Bradford and the others, the goods and the people had disappeared once again.

The sentinels on the shallop made a crude tent of sail-cloth and rode at anchor near the shore. Bradford and his guards slept on little raised platforms in wigwams that had been deserted by their owners. The men took turns at standing watch, their muskets charged and their fuses smoldering.

The next morning, Tisquantum went into the woods and talked with the people privately. At length, the people of Manomoyack dropped, or pretended to drop, their suspicions and consented to trade with the English. For a supply of hatchets, knives, awls, beads, and scissors, they traded the English several baskets of corn and beans, amounting to ten barrels. "Hardly enough for a fortnight," muttered Bradford.

Even that much encouraged Bradford, however, and he told the people of Manomoyack of his intention to sail south along the coast and asked them if they knew of a passage between the shoals and the mainland.

"Oh, yes," the Indians replied. They had seen good-sized ships sail between Monomoy Island and the shore.

"Well, we'll try it on the morrow," said Bradford, his hopes up.

***

That night, in a Manomoyack village forsaken by its owners, Squanto fell ill. By morning, he ran a high fever and was bleeding at the nose and ears. Bradford made a sick-bed of the raised sleeping platform in the wigwam and covered Squanto with several furs. He ordered his men to stand outside, some distance away, for fear they might catch Squanto's illness. At least, the weather was nicer.

Bradford lifted Squanto's head and gave him water to drink. "Come on, Squanto. Drink lots of water. We've got to drive this out of you." And he piled on many animal furs to make Squanto sweat.

"Pray for Squanto," said Squanto.

"Of course," said Bradford, "I've been praying all morning."

"Praying not help much," said Squanto.

As the day progressed, so did the sickness: the fever burned on his brow like a coal from the fire and the bleeding at his nose and ears became profuse.

"Indian fever," said Squanto. "I dying of Indian fever."

"Nonsense," said Bradford, knowing it was true, but trying by force of will to deny it. "You can't die. God won't let you die. For our sakes, God won't let you die. You'll be better in no time."

But he was not as hopeful as he wanted to sound, for he knew there was no known cure for the fever. Once it struck, death always followed within ten to twelve hours, a day or two at most. Bradford had seen a lot of deaths, as many as six or eight in a week. Still, it was a wonder to Bradford that a person could live after so much loss of blood.

"I wish we had brought some physic with us," Bradford added, not convinced that a laxative would have done any good. He tried to get Squanto to drink more water, for he feared his friend would dehydrate.

"Pray for poor Squanto, Master Bradford."

"Of course."

"Pray for poor Squanto; pray that I may be taken into your heaven. I want to go to the white man's heaven, so that I be among my friends."

Bradford put his lean and boney hand on Squanto's brow, wondering if the boy had lost his reason in the drastic fever.

"I had thought to take a wife from among your daughters or widows, and build a clapboard house in New Plimouth, like a white man, but..."

Bradford withdrew his hand, nervously appalled.

Mano-Kiehtan, sachem of Manomoyack, arrived, saying, "I heard that Tisquantum was ill." Bradford withdrew.

"Stay back, grandfather," said Squanto. "It is the Indian fever. I have Indian fever. Stay back, or it may catch you, too."

"Ha," scoffed Mano-Kiehtan. "I am a *Paniesee*; I do not worry about such. I come to help you. I'll have my women boil some sassafras root, make some succotash. You'll be better in no time."

"Have you ever been to England, grandfather?"

"No," said Mano-Kiehtan, astonished. "No, I have never been to the white man's country."

"It is beautiful in the spring," continued Squanto. "The sun shines. The rain makes the plants grow profusely. Men and animals have no trouble finding food. I think they must have used it as the model for their heaven. It is a happy hunting ground. I never heard of Indian fever striking anyone there."

The sassafras tea and succotash arrived. Mano-Kiehtan lifted Tisquantum's head and shoulders to give him some. "Come, Tisquantum. Eat, that your body may be strong and defeat the sickness."

"The first time I went to England," Squanto continued, "I went willingly. I even participated in my own kidnaping, for I was eager to see other parts of the world. But, after that, I was always tied with a rope."

"Come. Eat your succotash," said Mano-Kiehtan. "This is the food that First Mother and Gluskabe gave the world. It will nourish your spirit. It will bring spring into your soul."

For a moment, Squanto could see Gluskabe and First Mother, like thin transparent ghosts, against the wall of the wigwam. Then, in memory, he was back in Master John Slaney's house in London, telling the guests about Corn Mother and the creation of corn and tobacco.

He wailed and tried to turn to the wall to hide his tears, for he would never again go on such an adventure. Then, remembering the resignation of Draghan, his Gypsy friend, he turned back to meet his fate, whatever it was.

"Do you remember, grandfather, you once tried to kill my best friend, Thomas Dermer? You were at each other's throats when I arrived."

"He was one of the enemy," said Mano-Kiehtan. "Better for us all, had they never come to our shores."

"Well, Epanow and the Virginia swamp destroyed him for you."

"Hardly for me!" exclaimed Mano-Kiehtan. "For all Nausets and Wampanoags. For all the Algonquin people, here and in Virginia."

"Captain Dermer was one of the few Englishmen that never tried to tie me up," said Squanto. "I loved him like a brother. When all of my clan and village died, he was my only brother. Do you think I will meet him in heaven?"

"I don't know about that," said Mano-Kiehtan. "His spirit is still here with you. It is still in your heart."

"I have been a slave all my life," said Squanto, the fever beginning to slur his words, as if he were drunk. "I have not always been in ropes or in prison, but I have always been held a slave. Sometimes, I am a slave of sorrow... Sometimes a slave of love... Sometimes a slave of hunger and ambition. But I have been a slave ... all my life.

Now I will be ... a slave of death." He drifted off to sleep.

About noon, when Squanto awoke, Mano-Kiehtan tried to give him some more of the succotash. "Come, Tisquantum. You must eat; this is the food of the gods."

"Yes," agree Bradford, who looked in. "Eating is good."

Squanto smiled and took some of the corn and beans into his mouth. "Good," he admitted. "Good with beer. You got a beer, Master Bradford?"

Bradford went out of the wigwam. In fact, he had a very small supply of beer, but he hardly wanted to waste it on a dying man.

Mano-Kiehtan gave Squanto some more of the succotash and sassafras tea. "This will make you live ten thousand years," lied Mano-Kiehtan.

Squanto smiled knowingly, and Mano-Kiehtan turned away, biting his lower lip. Abruptly, he stood up and went out of the wigwam.

Bradford brought a small jar of marmalade from his food stores, dipped up a bit on the point of his knife, and put it between Squanto's lips. Squanto let it dissolve slowly, smiling at the good taste. "Oh, you do love me, don't you, Master Bradford? I see that you love me."

"Well, yes, of course," said Bradford. "You're like a son to me."

"I would rather be your brother," said Squanto.

Bradford hesitated, disturbed by the effects of Squanto's illness. "Eat some more of this marmalade," he said, offering another clump on his knife. "We could hardly get along without you."

"I am afraid you will have to," said Squanto, turning aside from the marmalade. "God has chosen to take me away. In His wisdom and Providence, He has chosen to take me away. Tell Elder Brewster I am happy that God is taking me away. Now, I will get to see God at last. I will see God at last, and He will save my soul." He took the marmalade and let it melt on his tongue.

In the pause, Bradford was at a loss for what to say.

Squanto swooned with a wave of fever and was silent for a time. When he lifted his head again, he said, "Give my knife and scabbard to Captain Standish, he understands a good knife." He tried to remove the knife from his belt, but was too weak. "Help. Help me get it off."

Bradford hesitated again, touched by the gesture. He was reluctant to accept the knife, for that would mean he was consciously accepting the idea that Squanto was dying. He felt a tear trying to rise to his eye. He unbelted the knife and scabbard abruptly and turned his face away.

After a moment, Squanto went on. "Give my deerskin clothes to Mister Winslow; he most values and understands Wampanoag ways." He swooned, but did not faint.

Bradford could only nod.

"I want you to have my bow and arrows, for you have been like a brother to me."

Bradford was almost pleased that Squanto lost consciousness again, for he did not want Squanto to see him weep. He wiped Squanto's brow with a wet cloth, but Squanto continued bleeding profusely at the nose and ears.

In the middle of the afternoon, Squanto awoke again. Mano-Kiehtan had returned. "Take me outside to die," said Squanto, "so that they do not have to destroy this house."

"Nonsense," protested Bradford. "You're not going to die."

"I see Gluskabe and Corn-Woman coming through the shadows of the forest."

Mano-Kiehtan understood and appreciated Squanto's gesture. He picked up Squanto, bedding and all, and took him outside. The November sun was waning, though it had been a sunny day. He laid Squanto in the sand near a camp fire.

"Thank you, grandfather," said Squanto. "It won't be long now." He went to sleep again.

"He save your life many time," said Mano-Kiehtan to Bradford. "Save all English many time."

Squanto recovered once more. He could see the gossamer figures of Corn-Woman and Gluskabe at the edge of the clearing, waiting. But there was no God. No Elder Brewster, no Captain Dermer, no God. "Master Bradford? I want to see Master Bradford."

"I'm here, Squanto. I'm here."

"Bury me like a Christian?" he said. "Don't let Gluskabe drag the flesh from my bones."

Bradford nodded and waited.

"Bury me ... in a Christian grave. With Christian ... rites."

Bradford bit his lip and nodded again.

"Put up a cross... tie a piece of rope ... on the cross."

Bradford looked on, puzzled.

"In Christian grave ... I go to heaven."

Squanto died before nightfall. Bradford's men dug a grave in the sandy soil near Chatham and buried their guide, interpreter, and companion without a coffin, without a marker. Bradford sat long into the twilight, in the edge of the woods. He could not fathom God's purpose in taking away so useful a tool.

In the woods, Mano-Kiehtan and his people

wailed and howled around a camp fire all night long.

The next day, doubting his ability to successfully trade with difficult Indians without an interpreter and ambassador, and facing another tempestuous storm, Bradford decided that a trading voyage south of the Cape was doomed completely. He returned to New Plimouth with news of his failure to acquire provender and of Squanto's death.

Epilog: Pilgrims Triumphant

> "Brothers, ... you see the foe before you— that they have grown insolent and bold— that all our ancient customs are disregarded; the treaties made by our fathers and us are broken, and all of us insulted; ... Brothers, these people from the unknown world will cut down our groves, spoil our hunting and planting grounds, and drive us and our children from the graves of our fathers ... and enslave our women and children."
>
> — from a speech by Metacomet, better known as "King Philip," younger son of The Massasoit; see Keek and Sanders, eds. *Literature of the North American Indians*, p.249, 271):

The winter of 1622 was another grim and hungry time for the Pilgrims. Bradford himself sailed to Massachusetts Bay to buy the corn and beans which Standish had asked Chickataubut's people to plant. When he arrived, he discovered that an epidemic of "Indian Fever" had killed a great many of the Massachusetts people.

Chickataubut renewed his complaints against Weston's colony—Weston's men were a bad people, thieves and scoundrels, liars and tricksters, and they had to be removed.

Bradford learned that Weston's men had ruined the trade by giving as much for a quart of corn as the Pilgrims were used to giving for a basket full. He returned with an empty shallop. Shortly, he went on to Nauset, where he succeeded in buying about ten hogsheads of corn and beans from Aspinet and his people. By such small successes, he and Myles Standish managed to acquire enough food for the Pilgrim community to survive another hard winter.

Standish, understanding much of the Indian language, several times suspected plots to assassinate him and his men. Ever vigilant and suspicious, he divided his guard wherever he went, so that if one segment were attacked, the other could come to its aid with plenty of firepower.

In March, 1623, news came from Narragansett Bay that The Massasoit lay ill and was not expected to recover, and that a Dutch ship had been blown aground near The Massasoit's home. Because he had been to Pokánoket before and because he spoke some Dutch, learned during the Pilgrims' stay in Holland, Edward Winslow was selected to visit The Massasoit, pay the governor's respects, and find out as much as he could what the Dutch were up to. Hobamock went as guide, and Master John Hamden, a gentleman of London who had wintered with the Pilgrims, went along to "see the country."

At a ferry in Corbitant's territory, the people told them that The Massasoit was already dead, and buried that day, and that the Dutch would be gone before they could get there, having floated their ship again.

Hobamock wanted to turn back. "Nothing there now. Nothing there. All is lost."

"Let me think on it a moment," said Winslow. He reasoned that, if The Massasoit were in fact dead, Corbitant would be most likely to succeed him and, though Corbitant had been "a hollow-hearted friend" toward the English, this would be a good time to improve relations with him.

Winslow asked Hobamock: "Do you think Corbitant still seeks revenge against you and me for our part in the campaign to rescue Tisquantum from him at Nemasket?"

Hobamock was weeping for The Massasoit, wailing that he had never seen a more worthy man, so that Winslow had to ask a second time.

"No," said Hobamock. "Corbitant now loyal. His daughter, Weetamo, marry The Massasoit's oldest son, Wamsutta; so Corbitant now in family of The Massasoit, and his daughter will be queen. Oh, my loving sachem, my loving sachem. Many have I know, but none like thee." He beat his own chest and wailed.

By Charles Brashear 433

"If you two are willing, then," said Winslow, "we'll detour and visit Corbitant at his home in Mattapuysett."

The others agreed. Along the way, Hobamock continued complaining. "*Neen womasu sagimus, neen womasu sagimus.* There is no duplicate. While you live, Winslow, you never meet his equal among the Indians. He was no liar. He not bloody or cruel, like other Indians. If he angry or impassioned, he soon calm again and easily reconcile with those who offended him. He was ruled by reason in all his decisions, accepting even the advice of the lowest man if it the right advice."

"He was always fair and honest with me," admitted Winslow.

"His people loved him, and he loved his people," Hobamock went on. "He govern his people with kind heart and fewer strokes than many men who use greater force. You not find so faithful a friend among the Indians, Winslow. He often restrained malice against you. *Neen womasu sagimus.* His equal not come again."

At Mattapuysett, they discovered that Corbitant was at Pokánoket. Winslow sent a messenger to inquire about his plans. The messenger returned about sunset with the news that The Massasoit still lived, but there was no hope Winslow could reach Pokánoket and Sowams before he died. Still, Winslow set out at once and arrived at The Massasoit's village in the middle of the night.

The Massasoit's *comaco*, though the largest in the town, was so crowded with people that the visitors could hardly get in. Three shamans were wailing their chants at the same time, each in his own shrieking way. Six or eight women were rubbing and chafing The Massasoit's arms and legs to keep him warm. The Massasoit had lost his sight, but not his reason; so, at a break in the treatment, one of the shamans told him one of his English friends had come to see him.

"Which one?" he asked, rising on his elbows. "Which is it?"

When told, he cried out, "Winsnow! Winsnow! Come closer; let me talk with you." He held his hand in the air to touch Winslow's hand.

"*Keen Winsnow?*" asked The Massasoit.

"*Ahhe*," said Winslow, "Yes."

"*Matta neen wonckanet namen, Winsnow.*"

"Of course, you'll see me. I am here."

Winslow called Hobamock and asked him to tell The Massasoit that Governor Bradford had heard of his sickness and was very sorry, but business had kept him from coming in person. He sent his love and respects through Winslow. "He sent you something good to taste," Winslow added, and he took a bit of a marmalade on the point of his knife and pushed it between The Massasoit's teeth, which would scarcely open.

The Massasoit smiled at the sweet taste, let it dissolve in his mouth, then swallowed.

"Look! Look," said some of the onlookers, "he has swallowed. He has not swallowed anything for two days."

"Hobamock," said Winslow, "ask him to open his mouth, so I can see into it."

The Massasoit's mouth and throat were "exceedingly furred," and his tongue was swelled so badly that no food could pass. Winslow scraped his mouth with a spoon and rinsed it, getting out an abundance of corruption. Then he gave The Massasoit some more of the marmalade, which he swallowed more easily.

"Give me a drink," said The Massasoit, hoarsely.

Winslow mixed some of the confection in water and helped him to drink it.

Within a half hour, The Massasoit's condition improved. His eyesight began to come back, though still dimly, and he could sit up straighter.

Upon Winslow's inquiry, the Indians said he had not slept in two days, and his bowels had not moved in five.

"Winsnow, Winsnow my friend. Take your musket and go into the forest. Kill some fowl and make me some English pottage, like I have often eaten at Patuxet. Will you do this for me?"

"Yes, of course," promised Winslow. "And I will send to Patuxet for some medicines."

Several of The Massasoit's company who were standing by volunteered to run to Patuxet. So, at two in the morning, Winslow wrote a letter to Bradford, describing what he had found, requesting some laxative and a chicken to make soup.

Before the messengers had been gone long, The Massasoit felt hungry and asked Winslow to make a pottage without fowl. Not quite knowing what to do, but feeling he had to do something, Winslow asked an Indian woman to crack some corn and put it to soak in an earthen pot. Then as soon as dawn broke, he went out and gathered the first green leaves he could find, strawberry and sassafras leaves, which he crushed and put in the pot. Feeling he had nothing to give the concoction any taste, he went out again, dug some sassafras root, sliced it and boiled the blend for a while. Then he strained it through his handkerchief and gave The Massasoit at least a pint.

All of the onlookers were much amazed at

The Massasoit's recovery, which proceeded rapidly. He got more of his vision back and, right away, had three small bowel movements. Everyone agreed that Winslow's treatment had saved The Massasoit's life.

Instead of allowing Winslow to go fowl-hunting, The Massasoit asked him to go from house to house in the village and clean the mouths of other sick people, ("All good people," said The Massasoit), which Winslow did with willingness, but much distaste, not being accustomed to "such poisonous savours."

When the messengers returned four days later with the chicken and the laxative, Winslow did not dare give him the physic, for he was in good health again, and The Massasoit would not allow the chicken to be killed, but kept it for breeding stock.

Many people had arrived, some from as much as hundred miles away, by their own accounts; they all came to witness The Massasoit's death and pay their respects at his funeral, but were surprised to see this miracle of his recovery.

The Massasoit gave a speech to the assembly: "Now, I see that the English at Patuxet are my friends and love me, and, while I live, I shall never forget the kindness they have shown me. Whenever we meet them, let us give them our thanks. Let us give them food, and help them to survive, as they have helped me to recover."

Later, privately, The Massasoit took Hobamock and two of his closest advisors aside and, with the consent of his council, told Hobamock to reveal to Winslow the Massachusetts plot which was under way, to eradicate Weston's colony— and then Patuxet.

***

When Winslow left Sowams with the many thanks of the whole tribe, Corbitant accompanied him and earnestly invited Winslow to stay with him at Mattapuysett, which Winslow agreed to. They talked much along the way, Winslow finding Corbitant a capable politician, who loved a good joke, not less when he was the butt of it.

"Tell me, Winsnow," Corbitant asked solemnly, "if I were dangerously sick, the way The Massasoit just was, and if I should send word to Patuxet and ask for a chicken and laxative, would Governor Bradford send help?"

"Yes, of course."

"And, if he should send the help, would you come with it?"

"Yes, of course,"

"Oh, that pleases me, Winsnow! I see that you are my friend, too, as well as The Massasoit's.

By Charles Brashear 439

Thank you, thank you."

"Tell me, Winsnow," said Corbitant after a pause, "How dare you to come so far into strange territory, so far from home and help, when there are just the two of you?"

"Where there is true love, there is no fear," answered Winslow. "My heart is so upright toward all of you that I feel no fear to come among you. I am confident that I am among friends."

"But, if your love is such and produces such effects, how comes it to pass that, when we come to Patuxet, your people greet us with the mouths of their muskets?"

"Why, that is the most honorable and respecting thing we could do," said Winslow. "It is a custom among all the Europeans, to fire a salute when we meet. This is true on both land and sea, as Hobamock has seen."

Hobamock admitted he had seen the practice.

"Still, I don't like such salutation," said Corbitant.

At Corbitant's *comaco*, he served them freshly roasted goose, baked Johnny-cakes, and succotash. "You must eat as much as you can hold," he insisted.

When Winslow openly asked the Lord's blessing before he ate, Corbitant wanted to know the meaning of the gesture.

"Hereupon," Winslow wrote later, "I took occasion to tell them of God's works of Creation, and Preservation, of the Laws and Ordinances, especially the ten Commandments, all which they [the Indians] hearkened unto with great attention, and liked well of, only the seventh Commandment they excepted against, thinking there were many inconveniences in it, that a man should be tied to only one woman."

"Whatsoever we have in this world," Winslow went on, "whether good or bad, we receive from God. He is the Author and Giver of all goodness. Therefore, when we receive his Bounty, we crave blessing upon it, including our food, and when we have eaten sufficiently, it is only fitting that we give thanks to our God."

"Yes," said Corbitant thoughtfully. "That is the custom with us, too. He whom you call God, we call Kiehtan. He is the All-provider, All-nourisher. We believe almost the same things as you do, Winsnow. If you English really wanted it, Winsnow, it would be easy to convert the Wampanoags to your God and assimilate our two peoples. Then we would be one tribe, one people."

***

The next day on the trail, Hobamock told Winslow of the Massachusetts plot to destroy both the English colonies. "The Massachusetts people have decided that they will destroy Weston's colony because of their abuses to the Indians. They have about fifty warriors and think that is sufficient, for the whites there are weak and know not how to defend themselves.

But they dare not kill Weston's men without killing all at Patuxet also, for they know you English would come to avenge the death of your countrymen. So the Massachusetts have gained the assistance of the sachems and people at Nauset, Paomet, Succonet, Mattachiest, Cummaquid, Manomet, Agowaywam, and the Isle of Capawack.

They are all in league and plan to fall on all the English at the first opportunity. They asked The Massasoit to join them, but he lay ill and would neither join them nor allow any of his towns to join them. The Massasoit advises that you strike first, take away the principal leaders, and the plot will die."

"We hesitate to strike before another has struck us," said Winslow.

"The Massasoit knew you would say that. He says to tell you that, if you wait until the people at Wessaugusett are killed— and that will be easy because they are so helpless— then it will be too late to save yourselves. The Massasoit advises, and

I advise you, kill the principals, and the plot will end.

"Wituwamat, Peksuot, and those who most closely follow them, along with a few others, are the leaders. Take them away, and the others will not know what to do."

***

At the general court held on the 23rd of March, 1623, Governor Bradford revealed the plot to the assembled Pilgrims, who voted to strike first. Captain Myles Standish and eight chosen men were sent to Massachusetts Bay to pretend trade, but really to assassinate Wituwamat, Peksuot, and any other leaders they could catch. Hobamock went on the trip as interpreter.

The Pilgrims had heard much of the shame and dissipation of Weston's colony. The wastrels had used up all their food by the end of February, including their seed-corn. They had broken into the Indians' storehouses and dug up their buried caches, until the Indians became insolent and hostile.

Some of the hungry whites made themselves servants to the Indians, carrying wood and water for a meal, and living in the woods near the Indians. Some had even sold their clothes and weapons, so they now had neither food nor means to procure food. A few had become savages themselves, taking up residence with the Indians and living according to their customs. It was little wonder that the Indians wanted to rid themselves of such pests.

When Standish arrived at Wessaugusett Harbor, he found *The Swan* riding empty at anchor, neither sentry nor dog on board. When he located the people in charge, they said there was no need for a guard, that they lived without sword or musket, at peace with the Indians.

Indeed, the Indians would come into the town, take from the pots what little food the English had, and eat it before their eyes. And if any complained, they were likely to get a knife at their breasts and threats on their lives. But, other than such small things, they were all one family, one happy family at Merry Mount.

An Indian came, pretending to trade furs with Standish, but really to get information. Standish was as calm as possible, but he feared the anger in his eyes had given him away.

Shortly, Peksuot, who was a huge man over six feet tall and a *Paniesee*, approached Hobamock and said, "We understand that your captain has come here to kill me and the others. Tell him we know of it, but we fear him not. We will not hide. Let him begin when he dares, he shall not find us unaware— or easy."

Wituwamat, the principal leader of the

revolt, visited Standish and whetted his knife in front of him, which Standish took to be insulting, but bore it quietly. "See this knife?" said Wituwamat. "I took her from a white man. She is one of the best knives in the world. See how sharp the point is? And the edge is equally keen."

He showed Standish that the handle had a picture of a woman on it. "At home, I have another knife, which has a man on the handle. It has killed both English and French," Wituwamat bragged. "Some day, these two knives must marry and raise a family of good knives."

He held the knife close to Standish's face, saying "*Hinnaim namen, hinnaim michen, matta cuts*: By and by, this knife shall see, and by and by, it shall eat, but not speak."

Standish bore the humiliation with patience, biding his time.

Peksuot, too, came at another time and taunted him. He stood up close and looked down at Standish, saying, "Though you are a Captain, yet you are a very little man."

He laughed at his own joke, then added. "Though I am no sachem, yet I am a man of great strength and courage." He wore a knife on a thong around his neck and shoulder, which he flaunted before Standish.

On the next day, Peksuot, Wituwamat, and

two other of the leaders cornered Standish and four of his men in a room. "Take them," said Standish. He ducked quickly to the floor, then came up under Peksuot and lifted him off the floor, so that the big man was both surprised and lost his footing.

With much struggling, Standish wrenched loose Peksuot's knife and killed him with it.

The other Englishmen had caught the others by surprise, because they were amazed by Standish's antics, and the English managed to kill two of the other men, including Wituwamat, and captured the fourth, whom they hanged at once.

Hobamock was jubilant. "Yesterday, Peksuot bragged that he was such a big and strong man, and that, though you were a captain, yet you are a very small man; yet today, I see that you are man enough to lay him on the ground."

Then Standish and his men went on the offensive, going to what villages they had located and to the leaders' houses and killing those they caught, but many had already fled into the woods.

When things were quiet again, Standish offered the remnant of Weston's colony a haven in New Plimouth, if they wished it, or assistance in whatever alternative they chose, but he advised them they should not stay at Merry Mount.

Most of the colony took what they had on

board *The Swan* and sailed for Monhegan, where they could find other Englishmen, secure provisions, and sail for England. A few returned to Patuxet with Myles Standish.

Standish brought back to Plimouth the severed head of Wituwamat and raised it on a stake in front of the Pilgrims' newly-completed fort, where it hung for many years.

Bradford sent word to the Massachusetts people that they should not destroy or tear down the palisade or houses at Wessaugusett, or he would send another expedition against them.

But the threat was hardly needed. Driven from their homes with little provision, the Indians fell victim to an epidemic of Indian Fever, which broke out among them. The fever removed their ability to strike any blow, much less an effective one.

In the summer of 1623, Aspinet of Nauset, Iyanough of Cummaquid, and Cawnacamón of Manomet died within a week of each other. A plague had decimated the Wampanoag tribe and their neighbors again, making it easier for the English to secure their grasp on the land.

THE END

www.ingramcontent.com/pod-product-compliance
Lightning Source LLC
Chambersburg PA
CBHW060103170426
43198CB00010B/751